CHARCUTERIE AND FRENCH PORK COOKERY

Jane Grigson was brought up in the north-east of England, where there is a strong tradition of good eating, but it was not until many years later, when she spent some time in a small town in France, that she became really interested in food. She was surprised at the variety and quality of the ready-prepared food in the shops there, and felt that the *charcuteries* in particular were puzzling to an English traveller. Pâté and sausages and ham were recognizable, but what about the other things?

Originally she planned a booklet of about thirty-five recipes. Then she discovered that *charcutiers* did not mind working at their dawn trade under the curious eye of a foreigner, and that recipes were generously offered. Eventually it took four years to write this book.

After taking an English degree at Cambridge in 1949, Jane Grigson worked in art galleries and publishers' offices, and then as a translator. In 1966 she shared the John Florio prize (with Father Kenelm Foster) for her translation of Beccaria's *Of Crimes and Punishments*. Since 1968 she has been writing cookery articles for the *Observer* colour magazine; a collection of them is published under the title *Good Things* (available in Penguins), and *Fish Cookery* (to be published in Penguins).

JANE GRIGSON

CHARCUTERIE
&
FRENCH PORK COOKERY

Illustrated by M. J. Mott

PENGUIN BOOKS

Penguin Books Ltd, Harmondsworth, Middlesex, England
Penguin Books Australia Ltd, Ringwood, Victoria, Australia
Penguin Books Canada Ltd, 41 Steelcase Road West, Markham, Ontario, Canada
Penguin Books (N.Z.) Ltd, 182–190 Wairau Road, Auckland 10, New Zealand

—

First published by Michael Joseph 1967
Published in Penguin Books 1970
Reprinted 1975

—

Copyright © Jane Grigson, 1967

—

Made and printed in Great Britain
by C. Nicholls & Company Ltd
Set in Monotype Baskerville

Contents

Introduction	7
Picnic Guide to the Charcutier's Shop	13
Charcuterie Equipment	24
Herbs and Seasonings Used in Charcuterie	33
Sauces and Relishes	45
Terrines, Pâtés (Cold and Hot), and Galantines	73
Sausages and White Puddings or Boudins Blancs	114
Salt Pork and Hams	171
Fresh Pork Cookery	219
Extremities	239
The Insides	267
The Fat of the Pig	309
Blood and Black Puddings or Boudins Noirs	326
Index	337

Introduction

It could be said that European civilization – and Chinese civilization too – has been founded on the pig. Easily domesticated, omnivorous household and village scavenger, clearer of scrub and undergrowth, devourer of forest acorns, yet content with a sty – and delightful when cooked or cured, from his snout to his tail. There has been prejudice against him, but those peoples – certainly *not* including the French – who have disliked the pig and insist that he is unclean eating, are rationalizing their own descent and past history: they were once nomads, and the one thing you can't do with a pig is to drive him in herds over vast distances.

The pig as we know him is of mixed descent. An art of *charcuterie* – the *chair cuit,* cooked meat, of the pig – could hardly have been developed very far, however much people relied on pig meat, fresh or cured, as the staff of life, with the medieval pig carved on misericords, or painted in the Labours of the Months (pig-killing in November, or pig-fattening with the acorn harvest). He was a lean, ridgy and rangy beast, with bristles down his back. Two thousand years ago the Gauls in France were excellent at curing pork, and Gallic hams were sent to Rome. But what made the pig of the European sty – rather than the pig of the autumn oak forests – really succulent, was a crossing of the European and Chinese pigs in England round about 1760, by the great Leicestershire stock-breeder, Robert Bakewell.

The Chinese porker was small, plump and short-legged. The European pig was skinny and long-legged like a wild boar. The cross between the two resulted in the huge pink beast of prints by James Ward of 160 years ago. Cobbett wrote that the cottager's pig should be too fat to walk more than 100 yards. Spreading through Europe, this was the creature on which French cooks got to work when the revolution turned them out of their princely, aristocratic kitchens along the Loire and in the Île de France.

The trade of *charcutier* goes back at least as far as the time of classical Rome, where a variety of sausages could be bought, as well as the famous hams from Gaul. In such a large town slaughterhouses, butchers' and cooked meat shops were necessarily well organized to safeguard public health. This system was still being followed – after a fashion – in medieval Paris, although in the later Middle Ages a great increase in cooked meat purveyors put an intolerable strain on such control as there was. From this insalubrious chaos the *charcutiers* emerged and banded together, by edict of the king in 1476, for the sale of cooked pork only, and raw pork fat. But they did not have the right to slaughter the pigs they needed, which put them at the mercy of the general butchers until the next century. At the beginning of the seventeenth century *charcutiers* gained the right to sell all cuts of uncooked pork, not just the fat. Now the trade could develop in a logical manner. Incidentally in Lent, when meat sales declined, the *charcutier* was allowed to sell salted herrings and fish from the sea.

In the larger cities of the eighteenth century the *charcutier* developed a closer connexion with two other cooked meat sellers – the *tripier* who bought the insides of all animals from both butcher and *charcutier* and sold cooked tripe, and the *traiteur* who bought raw meat of all kinds and sold it cooked in sauces as *ragoûts*, either to be eaten at home or on his ever-increasing premises. Remember that for many people at all income levels the private kitchen was a poor affair, often nonexistent; everyone sent out to the cooked food shops for ready-made dishes. It was a big trade, jealously guarded, so that the *traiteurs* considered that their functions as *ragoût*-makers had been usurped when a soup-maker, Boulanger, who described his dishes as '*restaurant*' or restorative, began to sell sheep's feet in sauce, to be consumed on his premises. He was taken to court in 1765 by the *traiteurs*, but he won, thereby gaining enormous publicity and a fashionable trade. More important still, he had broken through the closed shop organization by which the cooked food purveyors worked.

By the end of the century the guillotine had put many great cooks out of work. They soon saw the opportunities offered by the growing restaurant trade and the old cooked food trades *vis-à-vis* the more widely distributed prosperity of a new social order. The *traiteur* began to specialize in grand set pieces which he supplied on a catering basis to nineteenth-century bourgeois homes. The *charcutier* increased the range and quality of his pork products, and began to sell cooked tripe to his middle-class clients as well. Only the *tripier* seems to have lost in prestige, supplying poor families and shabby hotels with what Henry James described as 'a horrible mixture known as *gras-double*, a light grey, glutinous nauseating mess'.

In the twentieth century all these categories have become blurred at the edges and interdependent. They have also benefited from most stringent food laws. French small-town hoteliers and restaurateurs now delight their clients with delicious preliminaries to the main course, supplied usually from the *charcuterie* near by rather than their own kitchens. This is where English hotels outside London are at such a disadvantage. There are no high-class cooked meat and bakery trades in this country. The chef with a small staff cannot send out for *saucisses en broiche*, *quiches lorraines*, or a good pâté, leaving him free, as in France, to concentrate on his meat, fish and sauces.

Towards the end of the nineteenth century, France, like every other European country, benefited from the development of refrigeration. Nobody needed the huge pig anymore. With cold storage, mild round-the-year ham and bacon curing became possible, which meant that less fat was needed to mitigate harsh-tasting lean meat. At the same time there was a big increase in machine and sedentary occupations, which lessened people's need for a high fat diet. So the pig grew smaller. Now his weight is watched as carefully as any film star's.

Probably the English pig is now being taken too far

towards leanness, at any rate for the finer points of *charcuterie*. He has become too much a factory animal: we neglect his ears, his tail, his trotters, his insides, his beautiful fat and his flavour (pig's ears by the hundred thousand are fed to mink, from one of the Wiltshire bacon factories, which is a bit like feeding caviare to canaries). But with a little care and persistence the housewife can bully out of her butcher what is known as 'over-weight pig', and for very little money she can obtain the fat parts, as well as the extremities and the offal – the basis of many of the most delicate and delightful dishes it is possible to make. The skilful and economical housewife can buy a pig's head for 3s. or 4s.; this is what she can make from it – pig's ears with a piquant sauce (page 247), brains in puff pastry (page 252), Bath chap (page 245), 1½ lb. of sausage meat for making pâté (page 115) or *crépinettes* (page 116), and some excellent *Rillons* (page 320) which are more usually made from belly of pork. There is on average 4½ lb. of boneless meat on a pig's head. And an excellent clear soup (page 264) or aspic jelly (page 265) is to be made from the bones.

So I hope that this book, in some degree, will contribute to reinstating the pig in its variety in English kitchens, as well as help the holiday maker travelling in the country where the pig is most valued.

I have naturally taken much information from French text-books of *charcuterie* and the *cuisine bourgeoise*. Nobody can produce a cookery book these days without a deep appreciation of Elizabeth David's work. I am indebted to her for suggestions, encouragement and advice most generously given; also to many French friends, particularly Madame Potier of Paris and Les Deux Sèvres, the very best of cooks; Adey Horton, of Paris, the Master of the Sunday Lunch; Maurice and the late Fernande Beaubrun of St Jacques des Guerets; Madame Champy of Trôo; Monsieur and Madame Berlu of the *boucherie* at Trôo; Monsieur and Madame Cureau of Montoire, whose *charcuterie* cannot easily be surpassed. Two Wiltshire butchers, Mr W. W. Nichols of Swindon, and Mr R. Sawyer of Wootton Bassett, have patiently supplied information and unexpected cuts of pork. Messrs Harris Ltd, of Calne, kindly allowed me to visit their factory. I should like as well to thank my family and many English friends who have been made to eat an unconscionable quantity of the diverse parts of the pig in the last four years.

Broad Town and Trôo, 1966   JANE GRIGSON

Picnic Guide
to the Charcutier's Shop

EVERY small town in France, at any rate in the more prosperous districts such as Touraine, Burgundy or the Île de France, is likely to have more than one *charcuterie*. Probably one, and one only, will be worth going to. It will be on the *place* or in the main street, its windows crowded with a variety of good things, its marble slabs and its tiled floors clean and inviting, with a brisk white-coated wife in attendance (the *charcutier* himself leads a pale, mainly nocturnal existence, at the back, transforming pork into his delicacies).

The other *charcuteries* will be mediocre, even a little grey, with fewer lines, tucked away in a side street. Only the master in each town can afford the good position, and match up to the standard which many of the townspeople demand. He is likely to have as neighbours, more or less, the one good *pâtisserie* (pastry-cook) and the best *boulangerie* (baker), with its many varieties of bread.

The *charcutier* will sell olives, anchovies, condiments, and a few proprietary goods (e.g. *saucissons secs*, salami of one kind and another). He will sell various salads of his own making, and a few confections of rabbit (e.g. *pâté de lapin*), chicken or beef. But transmutations of the pig are his mainstay.

Occasionally the butcher (*boucher*) is *charcutier* as well, particularly in smaller places, and, as you would expect, his range of *charcuterie* is fairly restricted – sausages, black puddings, a simple pâté or two, and some *rillettes*.

Many of the *charcutier's* products can be eaten cold, with salads (which are sold in cartons by weight), or bread. Below are listed his standard items, for quick use in the day's picnic shopping (with page reference to the recipes).

It must be understood that items vary according to season and province.

READY TO EAT

Rillettes. Potted belly of pork (page 320), sometimes with the addition of goose or rabbit. A major delicacy of Touraine and Anjou; but not infrequently made in factories (tins of very good *rillettes* may be bought in some grocer's shops), as well as by the *charcutier* himself.

Rillons. Small pieces of browned belly of pork (p. 320). These sometimes have an unappetizing look, altogether belied by their taste. They are among the finest products of *charcuterie*.

Petit Salé. Belly of pork and spare ribs salted and boiled (page 176), sold in larger pieces than *rillons*, delicately pink and white.

Galantine de Porc (page 243). Nearer to brawn than to galantine, made of the head-meat and scraps of the pig.

Fromage de Tête (page 239). Brawn, often bread-crumbed on the outside.

Hure (page 242). Brawn, once again, but often presented with a half-inch layer of jelly on the outside.

Pâté de Campagne (page 75). Pâté made from the lean and fat meat of the pig, veal, ham, etc. Ingredients vary locally and according to season and taste.

Pâté de Foie de Porc (page 79). Pâté made from th lean and fat meat of the pig, with the addition of pig's liver.

Pâté de Lapin (page 82). Pâté made from rabbit and pork.

Pâté de Gibier (page 97). Pâté made from pork and game,

which may be specified, e.g. *pâté de lièvre,* hare pâté. (Other pâtés are given on pages 73 to 108).

Jambon (ham), including mild cures such as *jambon de Paris, jambon de York* (i.e. ham cured in the mild York style, see page 191, but often a tinned and insipid travesty), and the delicious smoked hams, many of which are eaten raw, in very thin slices, like the famous *jambon de Bayonne.* Many regions make their own not so famous *jambons crus;* always enquire.

Jambonneau (page 191). Picnic ham, mildly cured, from the hock. Charmingly presented as small breadcrumbed cones, with a neat piece of bone sticking out of the top, like a stem. Sold by the half, or quarter, if you do not want a whole one. Much cheaper than *jambon de Paris* or *jambon cru.*

Porc Rôti (page 220). Roast pork, most usually the loin, boned and rolled, and very lightly salted.

Saucissons Secs (page 133). Salami of various kinds, regional, national and international, and other dried or smoked sausages including *saucisson à l'ail* (garlic sausage), *andouille* (large, black-skinned, tripe sausage), the slightly smaller *chorizos* or *saucisses d'Espagne* (red-pepper sausage). The *charcuterie* will usually stock frankfurters, and the very similar *saucisses de Strasbourg,* of good quality.

Museau de Bœuf en Salade. Boiled ox-muzzle, sliced thinly and dressed with plenty of parsley and chives, and vinaigrette.

CHARCUTERIE WHICH REQUIRES WARMING OR COOKING

Quiche Lorraine. Bacon, egg and cream flan – many variations, and sizes, according to region (page 181).

Oreilles de Porc (page 246). Pig's ears, cooked, in jelly. Tasty, though seldom eaten in England. In France the crisp cartilage is eaten as well as the meat, and they are usually served grilled, with a coating of egg and bread-crumbs, though you need do no more than warm them through.

Pieds de Porc (page 259). Pig's trotters, often split in half and breadcrumbed. Sold by the piece. Fry in butter, or brush with melted butter and grill.

Queues de Porc (page 263). Pigs' tails, cooked, and finished with a coating of breadcrumbs. Fry in butter, or brush with melted butter and grill.

SAUCISSES (page 114). Sausages for cooking divide into:

Saucisses de Porc. Small pork sausages, sold, as in England, in chipolata and larger sizes. By French law they are 100 per cent meat, and do *not* contain preservatives.

Andouillettes. Small tripe sausages (page 269), of bland and mild flavour, making an excellent picnic lunch. They may be contained in very knobbly lengths of gut, for which they are none the less delicious. Usually grilled when served on their own. Sometimes wrapped in stiff white paper, some-times pressed into four-sided shapes and neatly glazed with a mixture of pork and veal lard. As they are expensive, buy one or two according to the size of the family, break them up in the pan when they are cooked, and add beaten eggs, one to two per person, to make an omelette.

Boudins Blancs (page 144). White puddings, though more sausage-like and less puddingy than their counterparts in England. Of delicate flavour, containing (from the best *charcuteries*) a proportion of chicken with the pork. The most expensive of all the sausages.

Boudins Noirs (page 326). Black puddings. Spicier and tastier and with more character than the factory-made black puddings of England. Whether presented sausage-style, or in an immense coil, the cheapest of all the sausages. Delicious with fried apples.

Saucisson-Cervelas (page 143). Saveloy, or larger sausage for poaching in nearly-boiling water. Eat with potato salad, improved with some chopped raw onion, and mustard.

Saucisses de Francfort (page 132). Usually a proprietary brand, sold in plastic wrappings. Five minutes in nearly-boiling water. Eat with potato salad, etc, like the *cervelas* sausage above.

Saucisses de Strasbourg (page 132). See above entry.

Crépinettes (page 116). Small flattish cakes of sausage-meat, encased in veiny, white caul fat (*crépine*). Fry or grill.

Chair à Saucisse (page 115). All-pork sausage-meat, on a tray, in a mound. Sold, as in England, by weight, and used for stuffings and home-made pâtés.

Saucisse en Brioche (page 160). A large pork sausage, up to a pound in weight, encased in *brioche*, and sold by the slice. It has been described as an extra fine toad-in-the-hole; an extra fine sausage-roll would be a better description. Eat warm.

Friandises (page 153). Small sausages enveloped in puff-pastry, in other words, sausage-rolls. Best eaten warm.

Pâtés Chauds. Mixtures of meat cooked in short-crust pastry, pasty or turn-over style. Best eaten warm. Occasionally hot pies are baked on a large shallow plate, and sold by the slice, which will be weighed to determine the price; see *Gâteau à la Berrichonne*, page 105.

Tripes (page 279). Tripe is sold in various forms apart from tripe sausages (*andouillettes* and *andouilles,* above). Often it is sold in hunks from a jellied slab, starred with carrot rings; sometimes in pots and cartons. Needs warming through, and is intended to be improved, according to taste, by the addition of wine, hard liquor, tomatoes and parsley.

Lard is, confusingly, the French for bacon (*tranche de lard* is a rasher of bacon). *Saindoux* is the name given to what we call lard. Bacon is not much sold in France, though it is always available; housewives there use fresh pork fat cut in strips or belly of pork in cooking, where we might use fat bacon – see pâtés, page 75, and the casserole of shin of beef on page 230.

CUTS OF FRESH PORK AND OFFAL

The *charcutier* also sells uncooked fresh pork and offal, including:

échine. Spare ribs, bladebone
gorge. Neck, and part of Hand⎫
épaule. Shoulder　　　　　　　⎬ Hand of pork, shoulder
poitrine. Belly of pork
lard de poitrine. Fat belly of pork
côtes. Fore loin
carré. Fore loin in a piece
côte. Single chop
longe or *filet.* Hind loin and part of fillet
noisettes. Small round cuts from the fillet
jambon. Leg of pork
jambonneau. Hock, and hand
tête de porc. Pig's head
pieds de porc. Pig's trotters
queues de porc. Pigs' tails
abats de porc. Pig's offal
cervelle de porc. Pig's brain
rognons de porc. Pig's kidneys
foie de porc. Pig's liver

BREADS AND WINE

Since *charcuterie* and bread go together in picnic meals, here are some of the types of bread to ask for (all sold by weight, and priced by weight). The *boulanger* will always divide anything larger than a *ficelle*.

DAILY BREAD

ficelles (meaning *string*). Thin sticks of bread
baguettes (meaning *rod, wand*). Longer, thicker sticks of bread
pains (meaning *bread*). The commonest of the long loaves
pain gruau (meaning *fine-wheat bread*). Bread of the finest flour
pain au lait (meaning *milk bread*). Large and small rolls
pain de mie (meaning *crumb loaf*). Shaped like small English tin-baked loaves, but much lighter in texture. Used for *croque-monsieur* (page 212), stuffings, toast, etc.

FANCY BREAD

croissants (meaning *crescent*). Made from high-fat dough
brioches. Large and small fluted buns, made from high-fat dough, mixed with eggs
pain brioché. Brioche dough baked in a loaf-tin
pain mousseline (meaning *muslin bread*). Brioche loaf, shaped like a chef's hat

KEEPING BREAD

gros pain (meaning *large bread*). Often enormous ovals of coarser, but delicious, bread. Improves with keeping a day or two
pain complet (meaning *whole bread*). Wholemeal loaf
pain de seigle. Rye bread
couronnes. Circles (*crowns*) of bread

English cuts of pork

Spare rib

Blade bone

Hand

Belly

Chop

Loin chop

Knuckle

Fillet

Chump chop

French cuts of pork

Échine

Palette

Poitrine

Plat de côtes

Filet

Carré

Jambonneau

Jambon

Tête

Pied

WINE

Wine, *vin ordinaire, rouge, rosé* or *blanc,* is sold (like special waters, which should, incidentally, be varied every four or five days for children) by the litre. A charge above the price of wine (*ordinaire* and château-bottled) or water is made for the bottle, unless you are exchanging an empty one. Ask if there is a *bouchon plastique* (plastic cork, or rather stopper) beneath the foil cap. If there isn't, the grocer can usually provide you with one.

PICNIC STOVES

Small portable *butagaz* or *camping-gaz* stoves are obviously ideal. The cylinders are much more easily exchanged or bought in France than in this country.

Less expensively you can use small stoves (2s. or 3s. from camping stores and Woolworths), filled with solid fuel or methylated spirits (*alcool à bruler*; not coloured in France, so mark the bottle), or a primus (the French for paraffin is, confusingly, *pétrole* – not always obtainable, particularly in summer time). *The shop for paraffin and methylated spirits is the droguerie, not the ironmonger's (quincaillerie)*; the *droguerie* is usually recognizable by displays of paint and plastic household goods.

COMPARATIVE WEIGHTS AND MEASURES

Weight

Un kilo(gramme) =	1000 grammes	= 2 lb. 3 oz.	= 35 oz.
Une livre *Un demi-kilo* } =	500 grammes	= 1 lb. 1½ oz.	= 17½ oz.
Une demi-livre =	250 grammes	= 8¾ oz.	
Cent grammes =	100 grammes	= 3½ oz.	
	30 grammes	= 1 oz.	

LIQUID WEIGHTS

Un litre	=	1000 grammes	=	1¾ pints	=	35 oz.
Un demi-litre	=	500 grammes	=	17½ oz. (16 oz. = American pint)		
Un quart-litre	=	250 grammes	=	8¾ oz. (8 oz. = U.S. cup)		
Un décilitre	=	100 grammes	=	3½ oz. (5 oz. = British gill)		

or

Cent grammes	=	100 grammes	=	3½ oz. (5 oz. = British gill)	

(small amounts of liquid, e.g. cream, are sold by gramme weight).

THERE are in fact very few *charcuterie* and pork recipes that can't be carried out with normal kitchen equipment – apart from sausages. Without a sausage-making attachment to an electric blender, no one would ever attempt to make sausages more than once out of curiosity. But many butchers are perfectly willing to put your own mixture into skins for you, provided you choose a slack time, so even that difficulty can be got round.

Kenwood sausage-making attachment

On the other hand, the joy of any trade is in part due to the constant use of loved and tried tools and equipment. I wonder if I would make *rillettes* or pâté so often, if I hadn't collected an assortment of the appropriate pots in France to store them in. *Rillettes* in a jam jar, or pâté in a glass oven dish, are perfectly feasible propositions, but not nearly such appetizing ones. Junk shops in this country can usually provide old Strasbourg pâté pots, of cream to gold earthenware and a lion's head each side as lugs. For 2s. in a Newport street market I once bought a huge oval French *gratin* dish in yellow and brown ware. From Abergavenny on the same journey, a deep loaf-tin-shaped pot, in cream earthenware, for 6d., has gone into the oven a thousand times with pâté, or held brawn as it sets in the cool larder. But for brawn I really prefer pint mugs from an old pub sale, they are evenly cylindrical so that a tin of soup wrapped in silver foil acts as a weight, fitting beautifully into the mug.

Mug-shaped *rillette* pots

The brawn unmoulds in a firm roll, ready to be pushed over the warm toasted crumbs before being sliced and served.

Gratin dishes

Even without sale bargains, you will not find it expensive to buy traditional French dishes and terrines at Elizabeth David's shop at 46 Bourne Street, London S.W.1, provided you stick to stoneware. Cheaper and softer earthenware is not economical as it chips easily. If you are considering a lifetime's wear, invest in vitrified cast-iron pans produced in

Pressing brawn

splendid colours by Le Creuset; they are available at Elizabeth David's shop too, and throughout the country at good kitchenware suppliers.

But *charcuterie* does not require expensive equipment – though an electric mixer is undeniably a great help, par-

Cook's knife

ticularly if it has a sausage-making attachment. Here is a list of other things I would hate to be without in my dealings with the pig. Most of them, but not all, are strictly practical.

Sharp knives, in several sizes, the first requirement of any kitchen. Do not be tempted by stainless steel, which is more difficult to keep properly sharpened. Nowadays French carbon steel knives are cheaply available from better household stores in this country – one famous make is Sabatier. Protect the points with corks or keep knives on a magnetic holder, and use Scotchbrite to keep the blades clean.

Iron frying pan. Unless the frying process is to be concluded with the addition of wine, use a heavy inexpensive French wrought iron pan; they are cheaper than English ones even in this country. Catering supply stores often stock them, and at Elizabeth David Ltd, you will find them in many sizes (46 Bourne Street, S.W.1).

Iron frying pan

I use the lid of a black iron Dutch oven, which lives permanently in the warmth above an Esse stove, and has the additional safeguard of an inside coating of tasteless vegetable oil. This averts rusting. As iron turns a wine sauce black (harmless but unappetizing), enamelled cast-iron ware frying pans or French *Équipinox* pans are a useful, though far costlier, addition to the kitchen.

Fish kettle may sound illogical, but its strainer tray enables large quantities of *boudins blancs* and black puddings to be poached with the minimum risk of their bursting. A good, if smaller, substitute is a cheap collapsible metal chip basket or lettuce shaker, and a large saucepan into which it fits easily.

Larding needle

Larding needle, with its delicately graduated point is better for testing meat as it cooks than a metal skewer. Larding is a satisfactory by-occupation of *charcuterie* (see page 313).

Strainer trays

Strainer trays and bowls. The old-fashioned kind of meat dish provides a good flat straining surface, particularly if a galantine is to cool under a weight. Wide French shallow bowls, really for draining cheese, are practical for small things like *rillons*.

Braising pots

Casseroles and baking dishes need no suggestions from me. I prefer stoneware, or vitrified cast-iron produced by Le Creuset and many other European firms (see page 25), but glass ovenware and earthenware are quite suitable for *charcuterie* even if they are not so tough.

Chopping block, of reliable flatness and generous size.

Hachoir or Mezzaluna for chopping meat, better than mincing. Better still, if more expensive, a 'Moulinette 68' machine.

Hachoir

Parsmint, a tiny moulinex for chopping herbs.

Garlic crusher, not necessary, but a great time-saver.

Bowls of all sizes, particularly larger ones; nothing is worse than managing a large quantity of mixture in a small bowl.

A *bain-marie*

Kitchen tongs, essential for the removal of trotters, ears, etc, from simmering liquid.

Perforated spoons, *wooden spoons*, and a *ladle*.

Large sieve, and *colander*.

Bain-marie, or old roasting pan that you can use instead; there's no need to buy a special one, but do have some way of standing small saucepans and baking dishes in hot water.

Pepper mill, and *Salt mill*. Absolutely essential – see pages 39 and 41.

Silver foil, *string*, *butter muslin*, and that tubular *stockinette* sold in cycle shops and garages as well as Woolworth's and ironmongers. *Button thread* and a thick *needle* should always be to hand in the kitchen, as well.

MEASURING EQUIPMENT

Scales. Buy the new metric and pound scale made by Salters. European recipes can then be used without preliminary (and sometimes inaccurate) mathematical calculations. But here is a table of equivalents for those who, like me, have English-only scales.

1 Kilo = 1000 gr	2 lb 3 oz
750 gr	
Livre = demi-kilo = 500 gr	1 lb 1½ oz
Demi-livre = 250 gr	8¾ oz
100 gr	3½–4 oz = 1 wineglass
30 gr	1 oz

Spoons. A useful gadget for a shilling or two is a collection of little plastic spoon measures. But be careful, the spoon measurement varies internationally. The French have no dessertspoon measure, only the *cuillère à soupe,* or *à bouche,* of 15 grammes, or half an ounce, equivalent to our tablespoon, and the *cuillère à café,* of 5 grammes, or one sixth of an ounce, and about equal to our large *tea*spoon. The American tablespoon is roughly equivalent to our dessert spoon.

Luckily most recipes give more specific details for large quantities than spoonsful, and when you are down to the small quantities given in spoons there is bound to be a little give and take.

Liquid measures. As cups vary in American and English systems, I have stuck to ounces and English pints for liquid measures. You can easily find a large 2 pint aluminium jug, marked out in 2 oz. divisions, which is very useful, as a litre (35 ounces) is covered by the 2 pints (40 ounces). Here is a table of these equivalents:

40 oz = 2 pints

1000 gr = 1 litre — 35 oz

750 gr = ¾ litre — 26–27 oz

20 oz = English pint
500 gr = ½ litre — 17½ oz
16 oz = U.S. pint

10 oz = English ½ pint
8 oz = U.S. ½ pint = U.S. cup
5–6 oz = 1 glass = ¼ pint
100 gr = 1 decilitre — 3½ oz
1 oz = 1 liqueur glass

The Garlic Family between them – garlic, onion, shallot, leek and chives – provide gradation of oniony flavour from strong to mild:

Garlic. French *ail*, pl. *aulx* (*Allium sativum*). The cloves (*gousses d'ail*), i.e. the clustered bulbs of this most pungent of cooking plants, will multiply in the northern garden. But originally from Central or Western Asia, the garlic does better in the sunnier and drier climate around the Loire or in Provence, and cloves brought home from a French market stall are more powerful, as well as cheaper. English prejudice against garlic may originate in the fact that it is less easy to grow in the north than the related onion and shallot.

Onion. French *oignon* (*Allium cepa*). Onion and garlic are two of the basic culinary plants of the Indo-Europeans, and have travelled with them – like the eating of the pig – from their ancient homeland, which was probably Western Asia. No wild form of the onion is known. Onion and garlic alike were anciently applied or eaten against a multitude of ailments.

Shallot. French *échalote* (*Allium cepa* var. *ascalonium*). The familiar small cluster onions, which derive their name, according to Pliny in his *Natural History*, from Ascalon in Palestine. They are a variety of the onion anciently developed in cultivation.

Chive. French *ciboulette*, *cive*, *civette* (*Allium schoenoprasum*). Native in dry places around the northern world, chives do well in the garden, and look well. The tufts of leaves can be snipped and snipped for cooking, the small bulbs rapidly renewing the supply. See *Fines Herbes*.

Leek. French *poireau* (*Allium porrum*). Like the onion, the leek is not known in a wild form. Easily grown in northern climates, the leek, like carrot and onion, is an invaluable source of flavouring for *court-bouillon* (see page 53).

Allspice. See *Peppers*.

Anise. French *anis* (*Pimpinella anisum*). An umbelliferous herb, like coriander, parsley and chervil. The flavour in English cake-making is taken from the seeds; but this Mediterranean annual, which is easy to grow, is used fresh in pâtés, as well as salads and omelettes.

Basil. French *basilic* (*Ocimum basilicum*). From the warmth of Asia, basil can only be cultivated with us as an annual, in good summers. It does better in a greenhouse. Used fresh it is the best of all herbs, particularly with tomatoes – even dried it makes a useful addition to the seasonings of a *court-bouillon*.

Bay Leaves. French *laurier* (*Laurus nobilis*). The fact that the French for the Sweet Bay is *laurier* sometimes leads to a dangerous misidentification in cookery books, *laurier* being translated as laurel – as if it were the poisonous, broad-leaved cherry-laurel of shrubberies, so useful for asphyxiating moths and butterflies in jam jars. The Sweet Bay Tree – from the Mediterranean – is not entirely hardy with us, and may be killed or severely cut back if sharp frosts continue. The dry leaves do not keep their flavour for very long. See *Bouquet Garni*.

Bouquet Garni. The invaluable small bunch or faggot of herbs added to most meat cookery in France – tripe, stews, soups, stock, *rillettes* – and removed at the last moment before serving. The usual herbs are bay leaf, sprig of thyme, and sprig of parsley, tied together with thread. Appropriate and seasonal additions are often made.

Caraway Seeds. French *carvi.* The dried seeds of *Carum carvi,* another umbellifer grown without difficulty as an annual or a biennial. Caraway is sometimes found in England as a naturalized plant. Used in *charcuterie* in Alsace and the Franche-Comté.

Cayenne Pepper. See *Peppers.*

Celery. French *céleri* (*Apium graveoleus* var. *dulce*). Celery tops, as well as stalks, are a pleasant addition to stews, *court-bouillons* and tripe dishes. Out of season, celery seeds and celery salt (seeds powdered with salt) are a good substitute. *Un pied de céleri*=a head of celery.

Chervil. French *cerfeuil* (*Anthriscus cerefolium*). Hardy annual, as easily grown as parsley, to which it is related; does best when planted for early summer or autumn. See *Fines Herbes.* The little sprigs of leaves are known, in France, as *pluches.*

Chives. See *Garlic Family,* above.

Cinnamon. French *cannelle.* The bark of the Cinnamon Tree (*Cinnamomum Zeylanicum*), native of India and Malaysia, best bought in stick-like rolls, as the inferior bark is used for powdered cinnamon. An ingredient, together with cloves, pepper and nutmeg, of the *charcuterie* spice-blend, *quatre-épices* (see below). In Les Landes sausages and black puddings are much flavoured with cinnamon.

Cloves. French *clous de girofle.* Dried flower buds of the Clove Tree (*Eugenia aromatica*), a native of the Moluccas, now commercially grown on the east coast of tropical Africa, notably in Zanzibar and Madagascar. An onion stuck with cloves is an invariable ingredient of *court-bouillon,* and stewed meat dishes. In powder form it is used, together with cinnamon, pepper and nutmeg, in the *charcuterie* spice-blend, *quatre-épices* (see below).

Coriander. French *coriandre* (*Coriandrum sativum*). Umbelliferous annual herb from southern Europe easily grown from spring sowings, for its fragrant seeds, which impart a faintly orange flavour to meat dishes. Particularly successful with pork. Much used with sausages and black puddings.

Cumin Seeds. French *grains de cumin*. The seeds of *Cuminum cyminum*, a small umbelliferous annual from the Mediterranean, grown from spring sowing. Delicious in sausages, or in *choucroute*. It is not often used in this country, except in curry powder.

Fennel. French *fenouil* (*Foeniculum vulgare*). Has a traditional association with fish – also unfortunately with that nastiest of childhood medicines, Liquorice Powder, which is flavoured with fennel seeds. Once that distaste is overcome, if not forgotten, the finely divided leaves of fennel give a delicious flavour when sprigged into or rubbed over pork before roasting (page 223), or when fried with potatoes as an accompaniment to pork. This umbelliferous perennial is easily grown in the garden, where it likes all the sunshine available, though it is not particular about soil. The wild fennel of the seaside is identical in kind and flavour.

Fines Herbes. A mixture of fresh, chopped herbs, including chervil, watercress, chives, tarragon and parsley. Sometimes it means little more than parsley, once it included cultivated mushrooms. *Fines herbes* are used as a garnish, or in very quickly cooked dishes like omelettes; the little bunch of herbs used in prolonged cooking is known as a *bouquet garni* (q.v.).

Garlic. See *Garlic Family*, above.

Ginger. French *gingembre*. The dried rhizomes or rootstocks of the Common Ginger (*Zingiber officinale*), a native of the Pacific, now widely grown in tropical lands. Used in *charcuterie*, in powdered form, both on its own and in the blend *quatre-épices* (q.v.).

Juniper berries. French *baies de genièvre* or *de genévrier*. Bush or small tree, the Juniper (*Juniperus communis*) is not so common in Great Britain; preferring chalk or limestone, the hard little blue-black fruits, which ripen after two or three years, are more fragrant in the warmer limestone areas of France, where in half an hour one can pick enough to last (they keep their flavour well) for a long while. They impart a unique flavour to pâtés, brawn and salt pork, as they do to gin, in French, *genièvre*. Available from Elizabeth David Ltd, 46 Bourne Street, London S.W.1.

Leek. See *Garlic Family*, above.

Mace. See *Nutmeg*, below.

Marjoram. See *Sweet Marjoram*, below.

Mustard. French *moutarde*. Made chiefly from the seeds of Black Mustard (*Brassica nigra*) mixed with the seeds of White Mustard (*Brassica hirta*); mustard is grown all over Europe, Russia and North America, but chiefly and best in the United Kingdom. English mustard is usually sold in powdered form, ready to be mixed at home with water or milk. French mustard, sold in a ready-mixed paste, is blended with verjuice (the juice of unripe grapes) or unfermented wine, and spices; this is best bought by weight at French grocers and brought home in vast quantity, in bottling jars, for use in the kitchen. Small pots of some of the fine Dijon and Bordeaux blends may also be bought for table use, at a lower price than you would find them in London. Mustard is used a great deal with pork in France –

a piquant contrast to trotters, *fromage de tête*, chitterlings, pig's ears and roast loin, as well as more conventionally with ham. A successful ingredient in glazes for roast meat.

Nutmeg. French *noix de muscade*, and *mace*, French *macis*, come from the hard seed of the tree *Myristica fragrans*. The very pretty scarlet aril surrounding, like a tight skin, the seed or nutmeg itself, provides mace – usually sold in powdered form in this country; it is a useful spice with pork, with its flavour of both nutmeg and cinnamon. Never buy ground nutmeg, except as a component of the *charcuterie* spice-blend *quatre-épices*; it soon loses its flavour this way, and is little trouble to grate in the small amounts required. The tree is a native of Molucca, like the *Clove* (see above), but is now widely grown, particularly in the West Indies.

Onions. See *Garlic Family* above.

Paprika. See *Peppers* below.

Parsley. French *persil* (*Petroselinum crispum*). Biennial; and uncommonly rich in Vitamin C – though it is probably more for its flavour that French housewives place bowls of chopped parsley on the table at meal times. Pliny described it, in the first century A.D., as a plant used by everyone. The most necessary herb next to garlic, and one which needs to be grown – fortunately it is one of the easiest of plants – in quantity, spring, summer and autumn. The curly-leaved varieties (*persil frisé*) seem to have more flavour than the flat-leaved parsleys; and cannot be mistaken for useless or poisonous relatives. Dried parsley is of little use. *Persillade*, literally a garnishing of chopped parsley, is extended to mean the dish which is garnished in this way – for instance, *persillade de bœuf*. The most striking use of parsley is in *jambon persillé de Bourgogne* (recipe, page 206), where it is used by the handful to marble the pinkness of the ham with its brilliant green. Remember that parsley stalks give as much flavour as the leaves, so that they can quite well be used in a *bouquet garni* (q.v.). See also *Fines Herbes*.

PEPPERS

Pepper. French *poivre*. Long the most prized of all spices, the tropical fruits of the pepper vine *Piper nigrum* were used both by Greeks and Romans. Black pepper (*poivre noir*) is the whole fruit, shell and all, and has the most aromatic flavour; white pepper (*poivre blanc*), used in powdered form in *boudins blancs*, etc., is stronger, the fruit minus the shell – a difference already described by Pliny.

N.B. Never buy black pepper in large quantities – or ground (*en poudre*), as it loses its flavour very quickly. It is useful to have a very little white pepper, however, in the store cupboard in powder form. Peppercorns (*poivre en grains*), both black and white, are easily obtainable from good chemists – like many other spices.

Allspice. French *poivre de la Jamaique, toute-épice*. So called because it was deemed to convey in one the qualities of nutmeg, cinnamon and cloves. The dried fruit of the Allspice Tree or Pimento Tree – *Pimenta officinalis* – from Jamaica. Not to be confused with the blend of spices known as *quatre-épices* (see below), though it provides a useful substitute in this country where *quatre-épices* is not generally available.

Cayenne Pepper. French *poivre de Cayenne*. Of different origin from black pepper, being the powdered fruit of Red Peppers, various hot varieties of *Capsicum frutescens*, coming from warm countries including South America and the West Indies. Use with discretion in pâtés, *andouillettes* and sausages.

Paprika. French *paprika*. Again of different origin from black pepper, being the powdered fruits of Red Peppers from

milder varieties of *Capsicum frutescens*, cultivated extensively
in the warmer parts of Europe. An essential ingredient of
Hungarian goulash, but also a useful and decorative pepper
in *charcuterie*.

Sweet Pepper. French *piment doux*. Whole fruit of the milder
varieties of *Capsicum frutescens*, grown widely in warmer
parts of Europe. The green fruits, easily available in English
greengrocers' shops, soon ripen to red in a warm kitchen.
Use crushed in *andouilles* and sausages.

Pistachio. French *pistache*. The pale delicately-flavoured nut
of *Pistacia vera*, an oriental tree much grown around the
Mediterranean. Like the truffle, an optional extra frequently
used in *charcuterie* for the contrast of texture and colour it
provides, over and above its delicious light taste. Unlike
the truffle, it is quite cheap in this country, shelled and ready
for use in *fromage de tête*, pâtés and galantines.

Quatre-épices is a French blend of four spices, pepper, nutmeg, cloves and either cinnamon or ginger, for use princi-
pally in *charcuterie*. It is not on general sale in this country,
but if you have not brought any back from France you can
quite easily mix your own, and keep it in a well-lidded jar:

> Pepper or allspice 7 parts; nutmeg, cloves, cinnamon 1 part each.

Every big spice merchant has his own blend, so the proportions can vary – though pepper is always the main element.
Larousse Gastronomique gives this:

> White pepper 125 grams (4¼ oz.), cloves 10 grams (1½ level
> desertspoons), ginger 30 grams (1 oz.), nutmeg 35 grams (1¼ oz.;
> scant)

The disadvantage of mixing your own is that you will have
to use commercially powdered spices, if you want a very
fine powder. An electric coffee-mill does quite a good job
on cloves and white peppercorns.

Apart from its conventional use in *charcuterie* (sausages, pâtés, *rillettes*, pig's head recipes, trotters, black puddings, etc.), add it to a mustard and brown sugar glaze for baked ham, season fresh pork with it an hour or two before cooking, and sprinkle some into mashed potatoes to be served with *fromage de tête*, trotters, sausages, etc.

Saffron. French *safran*. The dried orange stamens of *Crocus sativus*, the lilac-flowered Saffron Crocus which originated in Asia Minor, formerly grown at Saffron Walden and at Stratton in Cornwall (hence the saffron cake and buns of Cornwall and Devon). Saffron is now imported, and care should be taken to buy it in the form of dried stamens (a deep-red, hairy mass – expensive at first glance, it actually goes a long way), so that you are quite sure what you are really buying. Much French saffron comes from around Boynes in the Gâtinais, the district immediately to the south and south-east of Pithiviers (Loiret).

To use the dried stamens, you mix a pinch of them with a tablespoon or two of stock, water, or white wine, according to the dish. They need crushing down, then leave them to steep and impart their brilliant colour to the liquid.

Sage. French *sauge* (*Salvia officinalis*). This small bushy native of the Mediterranean is easy to grow in England. Once established, it provides leaves for the kitchen virtually the year round, year after year. In France there is no sage and onion stuffing to accompany roast pork, though it is added to pork stuffings for pâtés and galantines occasionally. More usually it flavours wine vinegar, or a *court-bouillon*, or young peas and beans – but always very discreetly. Try it with pork sausages or *crépinettes* (page 116), but always fresh; dried sage has a much less subtle flavour.

Salt. French *sel*. The best salt to use is bay or sea salt (*sel marin*). This can be obtained at some expense at Health Food grocery stores, or direct by post from the Maldon Salt Company, Maldon, Essex, and from Tidman & Son

Ltd, 91 Old Church Road, Chingford, E.4. If you live in London, you will be able to buy more cheaply the grey *gros sel* in Soho or Scottish sea salt from Elizabeth David Ltd, 46 Bourne Street, S.W.1. Once you have used unrefined rock and sea salt, you will never return to the commercially adulterated powders on sale in every grocer's shop – the flavour has an extra fruity spiciness that improves the simplest dish of boiled potatoes. Buy a salt mill for table use, though many people like the crunchy texture of the crystals as they are. Salt for preserving and curing (see page 185) must be unadulterated. Blocks of rock salt are perfectly adequate, but sea salt makes a more interesting brine. If you go to France with a car, fill odd corners with polythene bags of Breton sea salt on sale everywhere; it works out at a fifth of the price of Maldon or Tidman salt.

Saltpetre, or Potassium Nitrate. French *salpêtre, nitrate de potassium*, is important in the making of brine because it gives meat (ham, Bath Chaps, etc.), an attractive rosy appearance, when otherwise it would be a murky greyish brown. It has no value whatsoever as a preservative, and should be used in tiny quantities as it will harden the meat, a tendency which is counteracted by the addition of sugar to the brine. Buy it in small amounts from the chemist, as it is very damp-absorbent, and keep any left over in a screw-topped glass jar.

Shallots. See *Garlic Family*, above, page 33.

Sweet Marjoram. French *marjolaine* (*Majorana hortensis*). Highly aromatic, but not the same plant as the aromatic wild marjoram of chalk countryside, though related. A tender perennial herb from Southern Europe which can be grown as an annual in northern gardens – though chancy most seasons. Use in galantines and game pâtés, sausages, stews and *court-bouillon*.

Sweet Peppers. See *Peppers* above.

Tarragon. French *estragon* (*Artemisia dracunculus*). A perennial, originating in Eastern Europe and Western Asia, which dislikes damp and is not too easy to maintain in most English gardens. Keep a branch in a bottle of wine vinegar for use in vinaigrette and piquant sauces. Chop with a *fines herbes* garnish. Best of all with chicken in a *poulet à l'estragon,* but good too in chicken galantine or with rabbit. Use fresh if possible; the dried form is very concentrated. Do not be misled into growing Russian tarragon, which has a poor flavour.

Thyme. French *thym* (*Thymus vulgaris*). Garden thyme, the fairly bushy little perennial and more or less evergreen herb, originally from Southern Europe. The cook's great standby, particularly in winter. Use in forcemeat, pâtés, sausages, and with rabbit, and in *bouquets garnis* (see above).

Wild Thyme. French *serpolet* (*Thymus serpyllum*), the wild thyme of downlands, is also used to flavour *charcuterie*. It is similar to the garden variety.

Truffles. French *truffes.* This black underground fungus rootled up by trained dogs and pigs from beneath oak trees, is the most delicate and expensive of all seasonings. At its best the truffle is bought fresh in Périgord, after the first frosts – but most of us have to be content with the tiny, luridly priced tins on sale at superior grocers' shops. There is no doubt that even when tinned, they raise good pork dishes into the exceptionally memorable class. Expensive everywhere, it is still worth buying the tiny round tins in France where they are much easier to find, and 50 per cent cheaper than in England. The white Italian truffle is delicious too, but in a defierent way, and is not suitable for use as a seasoning in prolonged cooking.

Wine Vinegar, or *Cider Vinegar.* French *vinaigre de vin*, or *de cidre*. Both are preferable to the brutishly strong English malt vinegar – especially with *charcuterie* and fresh pork recipes, and accompanying vinaigrette sauces. If the wine recommended for many of the dishes in this book is not available, a dash of good vinegar will often improve the flavour. Keep a bottle of wine vinegar flavoured with a branch of true tarragon. Stretch your vinegar by pouring in the strained dregs of a bottle of wine. Many recipes give too much vinegar – start off by using half the quantity specified, then add more to taste. Vinegar, of course, is a good preservative: if you haven't got a refrigerator, and cannot cook meat straightaway, it will keep better and improve in flavour in a marinade of oil, vinegar and spices. See *Marinade,* page 71.

COOKED SAUCES AND RELISHES

Allemande

This is a thick coating sauce, and a very useful cream sauce too, if you omit the second long cooking process.

    2 oz. butter
    2 oz. flour
    1 pint good chicken stock
    2 egg yolks
    3 oz. cream or unsalted butter
    Mace

Heat the stock in one pan, whilst you make a *roux*, by melting the butter and stirring in the flour, in another. Add the hot stock gradually and leave the sauce to bubble gently away to half quantity, giving an occasional stir with a wooden spoon.

Transfer to a basin over a pan of hot water, beat in two egg yolks carefully and add cream or unsalted butter. Keep the hot water at a simmer and go on cooking the sauce until it is very thick indeed, almost a paste.

Flavour with mace, or lemon juice as appropriate, or tomato concentrate, or onion or mushroom purée. Roll small skewers of meat (*kebabs*) in this sauce when almost cold, then in beaten egg and breadcrumbs, before deep-frying.

Albuféra

    2 oz. butter
    2 oz. flour
    1 pint good chicken stock

Up to ½ pint cream
1 tinned pimento, drained and crushed with 2 tablespoons unsalted butter
½ beef bouillon cube

Make a *roux* with the butter and flour, add the heated stock carefully and cook the sauce down gently until it is reduced by half. Add the cream. Just before serving stir in the crushed pimento and butter and half a small beef bouillon cube. Keep the sauce just under the boil until these are blended in.

A delicious sauce with a joint of salt pork.

Apple Chutney, see *Apricot Chutney*

Apple Purée, or *Sauce*

1 lb. *Reinette* apples, or Cox's Orange Pippins or Blenheims
2 tablespoons butter
Dash of powdered cloves, or grated nutmeg, or lemon

Peel and core the apples, cut them into pieces. Melt the butter in a heavy pan, add the apple, and cover. Cook very gently until the apples are soft, shaking the pan from time to time.

No water should be needed, and *no sugar.*

Finally fork the apples to a purée and season. Serve with roasted pork, or glazed salt pork, black puddings, and sausages. See *Mayonnaise Suédoise,* page 68.

Apples, Spiced

1 lb. dark brown sugar
½ pint white wine vinegar
8 cloves and half a stick of cinnamon

Bring to the boil, and simmer peeled and cored apples in it until just tender but not collapsed.

Pack the apples into a large sterilized bottling jar, pour over the spiced syrup and seal. Leave for at least one month before using. This recipe is delicious made with whole unpeeled crab apples, or Siberian crab apples, or peaches, or pears.

Apricot Chutney

　　1 lb. dried apricots or 2 lb. fresh, weighed when stoned
　　1 lb. onions sliced
　　½ lb. stoned raisins
　　1 pint white wine vinegar
　　1 lb. dark brown sugar
　　2 level tablespoons salt
　　½ lb. preserved ginger
　　½ level tablespoon mustard seed
　　1 level teaspoon cayenne pepper
　　½ level teaspoon turmeric
　　Grated rind of an orange, juice of an orange

Put all these ingredients into a pan and cook gently to a soft mash. Add 4 oz. shelled walnuts. Keep at least one month before using with cold salt pork, or ham.

(For *Apple Chutney* use 2 lb. apples, weighed when peeled and cored; substitute almonds for walnuts.)

Apricots, Spiced

Use fresh apricots, and follow the recipe for *Spiced Apples*.

Aspic Jelly

The best way to produce meat jelly is by simmering gelatinous meats and bones, plus a small amount of shin of beef – gelatinous again – which will improve the colour.

Calf's foot is the classic ingredient, but pig's trotters are more easily available and do very well. Put them into a large pot and add, for instance, a poultry carcase, a veal knuckle bone, the bones from a rolled loin of pork, as well as 4 to 8 oz. of shin of beef. For extra flavour add an onion or two, each stuck with three cloves, carrots, a *bouquet garni*, garlic, pepper, but *no salt whatever*.

Cover with water and simmer for at least four hours, or until the foot or trotters are cooked enough to eat. Remove them and serve in one of the ways suggested on pages 259–61.

Leave the broth to boil on over a high heat, without a lid. The more you reduce it, the firmer the jelly will set.

Strain off the liquid, and leave it to set.

Turn it out next day and decide whether it needs clarifying – which is perfectly simple, so don't lose heart. For two pints of jelly, beat one egg white to a light froth that just holds its shape, and crush the shell. Put the jelly into a large pan – one that holds nearly twice as much liquid as the amount of jelly being clarified, and add the crushed shell. Set the pan over a low heat, whisk in the white as the jelly liquifies, and bring slowly to the boil, whisking all the time. Reduce the heat to keep the liquid at a simmer for 10 minutes. Turn the heat off, and don't move the pan for 10 minutes. You will find that a thick, murky crust has formed including the egg and all the little nasty bits that were clouding the jelly.

Line a colander with a piece of sheeting, which should be tied in place over the handles, and suspend it over a bowl. Pour the broth gently through and leave it to drip. Don't help it along by stirring or squeezing.

Flavour with Madeira, or sherry; try a bare dessertspoon first, don't overdo it. Or lemon, or sherry, or a dash of white wine vinegar.

NOTE: Jelly does not keep well, particularly in summertime. Any aspic-covered dishes should be eaten within three days (refrigerator stored), or two days (cold larder), and preferably eaten at one sitting. A large ham, for instance, could be ruined by sour jelly. This also applies to sauces containing aspic, a coating mayonnaise, for instance, or *chaudfroid* sauce.

If you do keep jelly, boil it up every two days and keep it simmering gently for an hour.

Quick Aspic

If you really must have a quick aspic jelly, granulated gelatine can be used. The result is much more glue-like, but will do, if flavoured with discrimination.

2 beef bouillon cubes for 1¾ pints, dissolved in only ¾ pint of hot water, or good meat stock (not salty)
1 packet of gelatine (½ oz.)
1 teaspoon white wine vinegar, or lemon juice
1 dessertspoon Madeira

Dissolve the gelatine in the hot water, add the flavourings to taste, and leave to set.

When either of these jellies are still liquid, but on the point of setting and cold, they can be brushed on to a ham, or into a mould, as appropriate.

N.B. The amount of different brands of gelatine can vary: as a guiding principle use the weight required to set 1 pint for ¾ pint of stock. Aspic jelly needs to be firm, particularly for summer dishes or a winter buffet table in a hot room.

Béchamel

Sauce Béchamel is the most betrayed of all sauces. The chief culprits are the English who combine unspecified fat, too much flour and thin milk, or milk and water, then serve up the lumpy result as White Sauce. On Good Friday it may be adorned with a flicker or two of parsley, fitting companion to boiled cod.

The correct basic ingredients are butter, flour and hot rich milk – these and none other.

Various seasonings may be added; cream, egg yolks, chicken stock, mushrooms, crayfish, lemon juice may be used to build up other sauces from this simple and useful base, but butter, flour and milk are the starting trinity.

Melt 2 oz. butter in a heavy pan, but do not let it brown. Add 2 oz. of flour slowly, stirring it in with a wooden spoon. Cook very gently for 2 minutes, whilst 1 pint of good milk is heated in another saucepan until it is hot but not boiling.

Amalgamate the milk with the *roux* carefully, stirring all the time to avoid lumps. Take time to do this, removing the pan from the fire every so often to pour in more of the milk, then returning it to cook slowly together.

(Should lumps appear, beat with a rotary whisk, or in an electric blender.)

Continue to cook over a gentle heat until you obtain the desired thickness. This is best done in a double saucepan, or in a basin over a pan of simmering water. Then you can leave the sauce to reduce gently for an hour or more, which improves the flavour. Season with salt, pepper, nutmeg, etc.

If you want to keep *sauce Béchamel*, run some melted butter over the top to prevent a skin forming. A butter paper laid on the top works quite well too.

Bercy

This sauce is made in very small quantity to go with grilled pork (or other meat), liver and so on. If you have no time to produce a concentrated meat glaze (see *Espagnole* sauce), make *sauce Bercy* when you have some rich meat jelly from a roast joint. Alternatively, again, add 4 oz. butter.

Cook a tablespoon of chopped shallots or very mild onion in a tablespoon of butter until it is golden and melted. Add 4 oz. of white wine and boil down, until there is about half the quantity of liquid left. Add 4 oz. meat jelly. Season with salt and pepper if necessary, and a squeeze of lemon. Finish with a large teaspoon of finely chopped parsley.

If you feel obliged to stretch this sauce, add a cup of *velouté* sauce. But it is much better in concentrated form.

See *Butters, Bercy*; also *Sauce à l'Échalote*.

Bigarade

This is normally served with duck, but is in fact delicious with salt pork that has been finally glazed with a mixture of French mustard, orange juice, brown sugar and marmalade.

When the meat has finished glazing, transfer the juices to a small pan and add a ¼ pint of white wine to them. Boil down, then add a teaspoon of cornflour mixed to a smooth paste with ¼ of a pint of the liquid the pork simmered in. Add the juice of two oranges, and some of the peel cut into small strips. Taste, and season with a little lemon juice if necessary.

Brown Sauce. See *Espagnole*

Butters

Compound Butters, *beurres composés,* are served in small pats on grilled meat, or else used as a final enrichment and seasoning for sauces. The particular flavouring is mashed with the butter, then chilled.

Bercy, a tablespoon of chopped shallots, cooked down in 3 oz. white wine, with 2 tablespoons meat jelly added. Reduce to a strong essence, and mash into the butter whilst just warm.

Colbert, parsley, tarragon, and lemon juice, particularly tarragon.

Maître d'Hôtel, parsley and lemon juice.

Moutarde, French mustard.

Paprika, paprika pepper.

Pimento, crushed, tinned pimento, or crushed, blanched, fresh sweet pepper.

Ravigote or *Chivry.* Blanch equal quantities of chives, parsley, tarragon, and chervil, for 2 minutes in boiling salted water. Drain in a sieve, run under the cold tap and pat dry in a muslin cloth. Blanch a chopped shallot for 2 minutes – about 1 tablespoon. Pound ingredients in a mortar, adding the butter.

There are many more butters of this kind. You can invent your own, but the above are the most useful with pork.

Beurre Manié is a useful way of thickening a sauce at the last moment, but don't let the sauce boil again too hard once it is added. Knead some butter into flour, in the proportions of 3 to 4 (1½ tablespoons of flour to 2 tablespoons of butter is a useful amount). Stir pieces singly into the nearly boiling sauce.

Beurre Noir is butter cooked in a pan to a rich deep brown, *not black*. *Noisette* means cooked to a golden brown. Capers, lemon juice and parsley are often added, and a little vinegar which has been swilled round the buttery pan at the end.

Charcutière (*The Charcutier's Wife's Sauce*)

One of the delicious piquant sauces that go so well with pork. This one is distinguished by the use of sliced rounds of gherkins. See also *Piquante* and *Robert*.

    1 tablespoon butter
    4 shallots, or 1 medium mild onion, chopped
    1 tablespoon flour
    4 tablespoons white wine
    4 tablespoons white wine vinegar
    Stock to about a pint
    ½ lb. tomatoes
    Teaspoon sugar
    Gherkins, and *fines herbes* to finish
    Salt, pepper

Melt the shallots or onion to a golden hash in the butter, sprinkle with the flour and cook until it is pale coffee colour. Stir in the wine and vinegar, then the stock, until everything is smoothly amalgamated.

Leave the sauce to cook down on a low heat, until it is the desired consistency.

Meanwhile cook the tomatoes and sugar to a purée, and sieve into the onion and wine sauce towards the end of their cooking time. Taste and season. Just before serving add the gherkins, sliced, and the *fines herbes*.

Pour into a very hot sauceboat, to accompany grilled pork chops arranged around a pyramid of firm, mashed potatoes.

Chaudfroid

¾ pint *velouté* sauce, made with chicken stock
¼ pint firmly jellied stock, or aspic jelly
Appropriate flavouring (Madeira, sherry, white wine, mushroom essence)
Additional extras – 1 tablespoon cream, and 1 egg yolk

Add the jellied stock to the hot *velouté* sauce and boil down
over a good heat, until the sauce coats the back of a wooden
spoon.

Flavour appropriately, adding the cream and egg yolk if
liked. Unsalted butter can be used instead of cream.

Coat the ham or other meat with the sauce when it has
quite cooled, but before it has set.

If you are making this for the first time, and are not sure
about the consistency, cool a little of it in the ice-freezer to
test.

NOTE: You can also make this sauce with a brown stock
and *sauce espagnole*, half and half, or one third to two thirds
or
Very simply, combine thick cream with concentrated aspic
jelly.

Au Cidre

Never be tempted to use (or drink for that matter) a
beverage sold widely under various brand names suggesting
a connexion with cider. It is non-alcoholic, gassy and
oversweet, turning to a bitter nastiness when cooked. Unless
you live in Somerset or Devon, good bottled cider with an
alcoholic content can be quite expensive: wine merchants
stock it. It is worth finding out if any pub near you sells
draught cider which comes a lot cheaper than, say, Merry-
down vintage cider.

2 tablespoons chopped onion
2 tablespoons butter
2 tablespoons flour, scant
1 pint liquor from boiling the ham
¼ pint good dry cider

Simmer the chopped onion in the melted butter until golden
and soft. Sprinkle on the flour, cook until deep golden. Stir
in the cider, then the ham liquor, and simmer gently until
the sauce is reduced to the right consistency. Season with
salt and pepper.

Make this an hour before the ham is cooked, so that the
sauce can simmer to mellowness very gently.

Cornichons. See *Charcutière, Gherkins*

Court-bouillon

Ideally these ingredients should simmer for half an hour
before adding the meat – trotters, pig's head, ears, etc. –
and if you later require the stock for jelly, omit the flour.
This is added to keep the meat white rather than greyish
brown, but is obviously unnecessary if the meat has been
salted in a brine containing saltpetre, or a pinch of saltpetre
is added to the *court-bouillon* during the cooking.

> 2 pints water
> 2 medium onions, each stuck with three cloves
> 2 medium carrots, sliced
> *Bouquet garni*
> 1 clove garlic
> Celery, one stick, or celery leaves, or celery seed
> ½ pint white wine, or 2 oz. white wine vinegar
> 1 heaped tablespoon flour, or a good pinch saltpetre
> 8 peppercorns, crushed but not ground fine
> Other spices to taste

Mix the flour with a little water to a smooth paste, put with
the rest of the ingredients in a large pan. Simmer for half
an hour before meat is put in to cook. A little salt may be
added, according to the recipe, but not if you want to
reduce the stock later on for jelly or sauces.

À la Creme (*la Sauce Normande*)

There are many versions of cream sauce; if you use cider

(see *Sauce au Cidre*), as well as cream, it is known inevitably as Normandy sauce – where cider, butter and cream reach their pitch of perfection.

White wine, eggs, and changes of herbs can vary the final result. Tarragon, for instance, makes it the perfect sauce with chicken; this version with cider, or the piquant *saupiquet* version, with white wine, on page 63, goes well with ham:

2 oz. butter
1 heaped tablespoon flour
1 medium onion, chopped
¼ pint good dry cider (or dry white wine), heated
½ pint appropriate stock, ham liquor for instance, heated
4 oz. thick cream
Extra butter, up to 2 oz., cut into small pieces (or 2 egg yolks)
Powdered cinnamon, grated nutmeg, salt, pepper
A little lemon juice

Cook the onion gently in the first 2 oz. of butter until it is melted and gold. Add the flour and cook for 2 minutes slowly. Stir in the heated cider and stock. Cook down a little, until it is the thickness you require. Season, beat in the small pieces of extra butter, or egg yolks, and reheat without boiling. Just before serving add the cream and lemon juice to taste.

NOTE: Be sure to serve cream sauce in a very hot sauce-boat, with very hot plates.

Demi-Glace. See *Espagnole*

Diable

1 heaped tablespoon finely chopped onion or shallot
4 tablespoons wine vinegar
8 tablespoons white wine
8 oz. *sauce espagnole*
or 8 oz. beef or veal stock, well flavoured, and *beurre manié*, made with 1½ oz. flour and 2 oz. butter

Cook the onions, wine and vinegar until there is hardly any liquid left. Add the *sauce espagnole* or stock, and bring to the boil. Do not strain.

Add the *beurre manié* at the end, and reheat the sauce carefully for three or four minutes, without boiling too hard.

NOTE: English-style, you can add a little tomato concentrate and Harvey's or Worcester Sauce.

Serve with chops, ham, salt loin of pork.

Duxelles

This is a useful mushroom forcemeat, a dry forcemeat, which can be incorporated in pâtés, or laid inside pastry for meat cooked *en croûte* – *jambon de Reims en croûte,* page 189, or *jambon à l'anglaise,* or *cervelles de porc en chausson,* page 252.

A quantity can be made, and stored for future use. It can also be turned into a sauce by cooking it up again with some white wine and cream, or by adding a quantity of *espagnole* sauce, or some good stock and a final thickening of *beurre manié* (qq.v.).

½ lb. mushrooms, chopped fine and left on a cloth to drain
1 medium onion, and 2 shallots, chopped
2 tablespoons butter
2 tablespoons chopped parsley
Salt, pepper, mace to flavour

Melt the butter, simmer the onion and shallot gently until they turn gold. Add the mushroom, seasonings, and parsley. Cook slowly until the liquid has evaporated completely. This means you have to keep stirring towards the end, so that the mixture doesn't burn.

Leave to get cold, and pot.

NOTE: The name was given in honour of the seventeenth century Marquis d'Uxelles, by the very great chef, La Varenne, to whom we also owe the earliest really practical cookery books.

À l'Échalote

A form of *sauce Bercy*.

Chop 4 shallots, and cook them with 4 tablespoons of white wine vinegar until there is only a tiny amount of liquid left. Add some good concentrated beef stock and simmer for an hour. Thicken finally with *beurre manié*, q.v., making sure that the sauce cooks without boiling too vigorously afterwards. Finish with chopped parsley, salt and pepper to taste.

Espagnole or *Brown Sauce*

Sauce espagnole is one of the basic sauces, used as it is, like *sauce Béchamel*, or added to various ingredients to make other sauces, also like *sauce Béchamel*. In great restaurant kitchens, where large quantities of these sauces are required, their preparation is long and so is the list of ingredients.

Its beautiful flavour does need some attention in producing the stock. Using a beef bouillon cube cuts the time required – and the expense, and is not altogether to be despised, but for a really good *espagnole* sauce try the following method:

STOCK
2 lb. shin of beef, cut in large pieces, say 3 or 4
1 knuckle of veal
Bones from a poultry carcase
and/or Ham bone
and/or Pork bones
2 chopped onions
6 oz. red wine
2 chopped carrots
Garlic, *bouquet garni*, peppercorns

Fry the chopped onions and carrots in some lard, and, as they cook down and turn colour, add the shin. Brown it on both sides, pour in the red wine and add the seasonings, garlic and herbs. Bring back to the boil and then transfer

to a large pot. Pack in the other bones, and cover with water.
Put on the lid and barely simmer on the side of the stove or
in a very low oven overnight. *Do not be tempted to add any salt.*

(If you want to make some meat glaze, say for *sauce Bercy*
in a day or two, keep back half the liquid when you make
espagnole sauce next day. Reduce over a good heat, until it
is brown and treacle-thick. This is why you do not add salt
to the stock. Keep it in a pot, with a covering layer of
melted lard.)

SAUCE
2 tablespoons butter
2 tablespoons of cornflour, 1 of flour
2 pints of stock

Melt the butter, stir in the cornflour and flour. Cook for
2 minutes, then add the stock gradually to avoid lumps.
Boil this gently for 2 hours or more on the side of the stove,
or a low heat, until it is the consistency you require.

Season appropriately.

NOTE: *demi-glace sauce* is made by reducing ½ pint of
espagnole and ¾ pint of stock still further. Flavour with
Madeira.

The real excellence of these brown sauces lies in the long,
long simmering.

Aux Fines Herbes

Assemble a good handful of chopped *fines herbes* (page 36).
If you have no chives, substitute a finely chopped shallot.

Put them in a pan with 4 oz. white wine, and boil down
until there is just a little liquid left. Add 8 oz. to ½ pint of
sauce espagnole. Cook gently together, strain and serve with
a fresh sprinkling of chopped *fines herbes*.

French Dressing. See *Vinaigrette*

Madère

Sauce espagnole, flavoured with Madeira.

or

Remove the ham or salt pork from the dish in which it has been glazing. Stir three tablespoons of Madeira into the juices and bring to the boil. Add 8 oz. of *sauce espagnole*. Alternatively add 8 oz. of good beef stock (bouillon cube), and thicken finally with *beurre manié*, page 51.

or

(Elizabeth David's quick recipe) Slice an onion and a carrot thinly. Let them melt in one ounce of butter in a heavy pan. Add ½ pint of water, a chopped tomato or a tablespoon of tomato concentrate, a dessertspoon of meat glaze (page 58), or a small bouillon cube, a *bouquet garni,* and leave to cook for 20 minutes.

Mix 3 teaspoons of flour with a small glass of water. Pour through a strainer into the sauce, stirring until it thickens. Strain into a clean pan. Add a sherry glass of Madeira.

Melt 2 oz. butter in a small pan. Let it turn golden, but be careful not to let it catch. Stir into the sauce. This, as Mrs David observes, is what gives a characteristic flavour.

Meat Glaze. See *Espagnole*

Mirepoix

The name given to the dice of onions, carrots, celery, leeks, and salt belly of pork or bacon, sweated in butter and flavoured with a *bouquet garni,* that forms the basis of brown sauces, stews and braising. Or used as a garnish.

Mornay

Béchamel sauce, gently reduced in a double saucepan or a basin over boiling water, flavoured with cheese and nutmeg, mace or cayenne. Use Parmesan if you are able, or a well flavoured English Cheddar.

Moutarde

Make a *sauce Béchamel*, but substitute the liquid from boiling ham, salt pork, or trotters, for milk. Keep the sauce to the consistency of single cream.

Beat 2 egg yolks in a bowl with a heaped tablespoon of French mustard, a dash of vinegar, a tablespoon of cold water and 2 oz. of butter cut into small dice. Pour on some of the hot sauce, beating carefully, then return to the pan and cook slowly *without boiling*, stirring all the time with a wooden spoon until the sauce is the right thickness – double cream this time. Add a tablespoon of chopped parsley before serving.

Normande. See *À la Crème*

Peaches, Pickled. See *Apples, Spiced*

Pears, Pickled. See *Apples, Spiced*

Périgueux

Madeira sauce with the addition of truffles.

Any reference to Périgueux on a menu, means the inclusion of truffles in the dish. *Périgourdine* means truffles and *foie gras*; *sauce périgourdine* is Madeira sauce with truffles and *foie gras* added.

Curnonsky* gives this version of *sauce Périgueux* ade with white wine, rather than Madeira, and *sauce espagnole*.

Chop 2 or 3 shallots, and fry them to gold in a little fat – goose fat, preferably.

Add 4–5 oz. dry white wine, and set the mixture alight

Recettes des Provinces de France, 1962

with 4 tablespoons of *eau-de-vie* or brandy. Don't forget to warm the brandy first.

In another pan fry an onion, sliced, in some more fat. When it changes colour, add some flour, a tablespoon; let the mixture cook for two minutes, then stir in 1 pint warm stock. Cook for five minutes.

Add the shallot and wine mixture, and leave the sauce to simmer for 2 hours at the side of the stove, or over a low heat. Stir it frequently.

If you are using fresh truffles, peel them, and add the peelings to the sauce. With tinned truffles, chop them, and leave them to one side.

Strain the sauce, add the truffles, heat through without boiling for five minutes, and serve in a very hot sauceboat, with ham or a fine joint of salt pork.

NOTE: Also served with fillet steak, and poultry.

Au Persil

To a beautifully made *Béchamel* sauce, add plenty of chopped parsley just before serving.

Good with trotters, or with salt pork.

Piquante

Prepare like *sauce à la charcutière*, but omit tomato purée, and finish with a mixture of tarragon, parsley, chervil, paprika, capers and *only a few gherkins*.

Poivrade

Another hot, piquant sauce that goes well with pork.

1 tablespoon butter
1 tablespoon flour
3 tablespoons chopped carrot
2 tablespoons chopped onion
1 tablespoon chopped shallot

1 *bouquet garni*
3 cloves
8 crushed peppercorns
6 crushed juniper berries
8 oz. good stock, **with a** little meat glaze, if available
4 oz. red wine
1 oz. wine vinegar
Salt to be added, as necessary

Melt the butter, and fry the chopped vegetables gently until they turn golden brown. Stir in the flour, then the wine and vinegar, herbs and spices. When it is well amalgamated, stir in the stock slowly and the meat glaze. Simmer for at least an hour over a low heat – a bubble from time to time is about right.

Strain the sauce into a clean pan, and taste. Add plenty of freshly-ground black pepper and taste again. Add salt if necessary.

Au Porto

Espagnole sauce, page 57, flavoured with port, and often embellished with truffles and chopped mushrooms, sautéed in a little butter. Serve with ham.
See also *Madère*, page 59.

Robert

'It is my wish,' said the Queen ... 'to have my grand-daughter served up with Sauce Robert.'

An old sauce, with a literary history beginning with Rabelais and continuing well with Perrault's wicked queen mother-in-law.

Delicious, too, with pork.

2 tablespoons butter
1 heaped tablespoon flour
3 large onions, chopped
¾ pint good stock
Dash of wine vinegar

Dash of lemon juice
½ teaspoon granulated sugar
Tablespoon French mustard
Chopped tarragon and parsley to finish

Melt the butter, cook the onions in it until they turn golden
brown. Stir in the flour, cook for a few moments, then
gradually add the stock still stirring. Let it cook for at least
half an hour very gently, better still an hour. Flavour at the
end with the vinegar, lemon juice, sugar, mustard, and salt
if necessary. Finally add a sprinkling of tarragon, and a little
parsley.

Roux

The name given to flour cooked with melted fat, usually
butter – the start of many sauces.

Sainte-Ménéhould

As might be expected, an accompaniment to pig's trotters
and ears *à la Sainte-Ménéhould*.

2 tablespoons finely chopped onions
1 tablespoon finely chopped shallots
1 tablespoon butter
1 *bouquet garni*
2 tablespoons white wine vinegar
8 tablespoons white wine
8 oz. good beef stock
1 tablespoon flour, kneaded with 1 tablespoon butter
Good teaspoon French mustard
Chopped gherkins, parsley, tarragon, chervil
Freshly-ground black pepper, salt

Melt the onion and shallots in the butter. Add the wine and
vinegar and cook until no liquid remains. Add the beef
stock and the *bouquet garni*. Simmer for half an hour at
least. Finally thicken with the *beurre manié*, being careful
to let the sauce cook gently afterwards.

Finish with the mustard, gherkins, chopped herbs, pepper
and salt.

Saupiquet

Here is a beautiful piquant cream and wine sauce, superb with ham in this version, from *French Provincial Cooking*, by Elizabeth David:

    2 tablespoons butter
    2 tablespoons flour
    4 shallots
    8 oz. good beef stock
    6 tablespoons wine vinegar
    6 tablespoons white wine
    3 crushed juniper berries
    up to 7 oz. thick cream
    Extra butter to finish

Chop the shallots very finely, and put them in a small thick pan with the vinegar. Boil until there is no liquid left, but don't burn the shallots.

Meanwhile in another pan melt the butter and make a *roux* with the flour. Cook until it is pale coffee colour. Pour in the heated stock slowly, stirring until the mixture thickens. Add the wine, then the shallots. Cook gently for half an hour, removing any scum which rises to the surface.

Sieve the sauce into a basin over a pan of simmering water, add the bubbling cream which you have heated to boiling point, then the extra butter.

The sauce will now keep hot until you want it. 'It will be a beautiful pale coffee-cream colour, smooth, but not very thick.'

Soubise

A beautiful golden bland onion sauce, delicious with pork.

    1 lb. mild onion, chopped small
    2 oz. butter
    1½ oz. flour
    4 oz. water

Dash of white wine vinegar
Salt, pepper, nutmeg or mace
A little stock may be necessary, or juice from the pork

Make a *roux* with the butter and flour, cooking until it is very pale coffee colour, no more. Add the cold water, and then the chopped onions, vinegar, pepper and a little salt.

Cover closely and cook on a low heat for a good half hour. Stir from time to time, but the onions should provide enough juice to keep the sauce from burning. If extra moisture is required use stock or the juice from roast pork.

Go on cooking until the onions have melted into a thick cream of a sauce. They won't need to be sieved. Flavour with nutmeg or mace.

A lighter, but not so delicious Soubise sauce can be obtained by stewing 3 large chopped onions in 2 oz. of butter, sprinkling on a tablespoon of flour, and then adding $\frac{3}{4}$ pint hot milk. Flavour finally with salt, pepper and nutmeg or mace.

This is in effect an onion-flavoured *sauce Béchamel*.

Spiced Fruit. See *Apples, Spiced*

Suprême

Take equal quantities of the simplified *velouté* sauce on page 66, and chicken stock, and boil them down in a heavy pan until they are reduced by half. Add cream towards the end of this process. Finish the sauce with unsalted butter.

Use, say, 8 oz. *velouté*, 8 oz. stock, 4 oz. cream, and a final 2 oz. butter.

Taste and adjust the seasoning if necessary.

Serve with brains, kidney and so on, as well as with the conventional chicken breasts.

Tomate

One of the most useful sauces of all, particularly delicious if you can flavour it with fresh, chopped sweet basil.

1 oz. butter or 2 tablespoons olive oil
2 tablespoons chopped onion
2 cloves garlic, chopped
1 heaped tablespoon flour
1 lb. tomatoes (or use a large tin)
4 oz. red or white wine
1 level tablespoon sugar
Salt, plenty of freshly-ground black pepper
Bouquet garni
1 tablespoon tomato concentrate
1 tablespoon wine vinegar
Freshly-chopped basil, or tarragon, or parsley

Cook the chopped onion and garlic gently in the butter or oil. Sprinkle on the flour, and when it has cooked in, add the wine. This will make a small amount of thick sauce.

Add the tomatoes cut in half (no need to peel), the *bouquet* and sugar. Put the lid on the pan and cook for an hour slowly. Longer, if you like.

Strain through a sieve, rubbing the tomato pulp through as well, into a clean pan. Flavour with tomato concentrate, vinegar and extra salt, pepper and sugar as required. English tomatoes need a great deal of additional seasoning.

Serve with a sprinkling of chopped herbs, a good sprinkling. This sauce should be very rich and spicy, with the fresh contrast of herbs.

Velouté

Velvety sauce. One of the basic sauces; forming with *sauce espagnole*, or Brown Sauce, and *sauce Béchamel*, or White Sauce, the trio of the *grandes sauces* from which so many other sauces derive. *Velouté* sauce is a *Béchamel* sauce made with hot veal or chicken stock, instead of milk. Mushrooms are a characteristic additional flavouring. Like the other two *grandes sauces*, *velouté* gets better in flavour and smoother in texture with long, long gentle cooking.

UNCOOKED AND OIL-BASED SAUCES

Mayonnaise

Do not be frightened at the thought of making mayonnaise. Provided eggs, oil and bowl are at warm-room temperature, and you do not try to rush the early stages, you are bound to succeed. Large quantities of mayonnaise are usefully made in an electric blender, or with an electric mixer. But for small family amounts, many people prefer a bowl and wooden spoon as the flavour really does seem to be better when mayonnaise is made this way. A heavy mortar is sensible; a pudding basin or mixing bowl needs a tea-towel twisted round the base to keep it steady, otherwise you will be following the bowl round the kitchen as you beat. A French friend uses a fork and a shallow soup plate with great success.

    1 egg yolk
    ¼ pint oil, olive, walnut or vegetable oil
    1 teaspoon French mustard, heaped (optional)
    Good pinch of salt
    1 tablespoon wine vinegar or lemon juice

Beat the egg yolk well with the mustard and a bare teaspoon of the vinegar. It will thicken a little.

Add the oil slowly, drop by drop, beating all the time. It is useful to have a mayonnaise-boy at hand to drip in the oil – a favourite job with children, who are fascinated by the magic transformation. As the mayonnaise thickens, the oil can be added in slightly larger quantities. But be cautious.

(If the mayonnaise becomes too thick, add a little more of the vinegar, or a bare teaspoon of hot water at a time, until the consistency is more manageable.)

(If by sad chance the mayonnaise curdles, add a tablespoon of boiling water and beat. If this doesn't succeed, put a fresh egg yolk into a clean basin and start again, pouring the curdled mayonnaise onto the second yolk drop by drop.)

Finally taste the mayonnaise and adjust the seasonings. You may or may not require the rest of the vinegar.

Lemon juice is often used instead of vinegar. In Denmark a very little curry powder is added at the beginning, half a teaspoon to one yolk of egg; this is occasionally pleasant with cold pork as a change. Children particularly enjoy mayonnaise flavoured with tomato concentrate and chopped parsley.

Coating Mayonnaise

Although mayonnaise spreads quite well as it is, the addition of cold but unset aspic jelly (page 47), makes it a great deal easier to manipulate smoothly. Add 5 tablespoons of jelly to quarter of a pint of mayonnaise (5 oz.), and use the mayonnaise before the jelly has time to set firmly. See *Chaudfroid*, page 53.

Mayonnaise Suédoise

As far as cold pork (and duck) is concerned, this is the best variant of mayonnaise:

Add an equal quantity of cold apple purée to the mayonnaise. If the purée has been made with cooking apples, be careful not to oversweeten.

Flavour carefully with horse-radish, grated or in cream (see *Raifort*, page 69), and *vin rosé*.

Rémoulade

This is a type of mayonnaise, but 2 hard-boiled egg yolks are added.

Pound the hard-boiled yolks in a mortar and mix them to a stiff paste with one raw egg yolk, a teaspoon French mustard, salt, pepper, $\frac{1}{2}$ a teaspoon sugar, $\frac{1}{2}$ a teaspoon wine vinegar and, if you like, $\frac{1}{2}$ a teaspoon of curry powder.

Add $\frac{1}{4}$ of a pint of oil drop by drop, being careful that it is at room-temperature, as if you were making Mayonnaise.

Season with a *ravigote* (bundle) of green herbs, chopped, and extra vinegar to taste.

Delicious with cold ham, salt pork and pork.

Tartare

Sauce tartare is either a *vinaigrette* or mayonnaise sauce, seasoned with finely chopped shallots, *fines herbes*, capers and gherkins.

A *vinaigrette* basis is best when the sauce is served with hot gelatinous meat like trotters, pig's ears and pig's head.

Use mayonnaise basis if serving with cold meat or fish.

Verte

Sauce verte is a pretty accompaniment to cold ham or salt pork. It is a mayonnaise (page 67), coloured and flavoured with blanched green herbs, which are then drained and pounded.

A mixture of parsley, chives, tarragon, chervil, sorrel and spinach, according to what is available, is tied together and plunged for two minutes into boiling water.

Drain well, pound in a mortar, and add to the mayonnaise. If you are using an electric blender for the mayonnaise, you do not need to pound the herbs; just drain them well and let them cool a little.

If you grow sorrel, the blanching process can be eliminated. Put three or four leaves into the electric blender, set it going and add the mayonnaise. The result will be a very fresh green, with a clear taste. No other herbs are needed.

Raifort

Horse-radish sauce is delicious with sausages, particularly when they are being served with a hot potato salad. Most English recipes include a quantity of vinegar, malt vinegar at that. Lemon juice is a much better idea.

1 rounded teaspoon or more grated horse-radish
4 oz. carton of thick cream
Teaspoon granulated sugar
Salt, pepper and lemon juice to taste

Whip the cream so that it is evenly thickened, but not stiff. Fold in the horse-radish, then the sugar and a dash of lemon juice. Taste and season.

NOTE: A good hot horse-radish sauce (for salt pork or hot ham) can be made by adding the cream to half a pint of *sauce Béchamel* in a double saucepan. Make very hot, but do not boil. Add horse-radish to taste at the last moment and season with lemon juice, sugar, salt and pepper.

Vinaigrette

Universal French dressing for salads of all kinds, usually made in this country with far too much malt vinegar, which is stronger and harsher than wine or cider vinegars, and to be avoided. Many cookery books give the proportions of 1 part vinegar to 3 parts oil, without warning about the different strengths of various vinegars, but this is too strong. I find 1 part wine or cider vinegar (or lemon juice), to 5 or 6 parts of oil is more satisfactory.

Seasonings vary according to the salad, the time of year, and individual preferences. Here is a guide:

1 tablespoon wine vinegar
5–6 tablespoons oil
1 good teaspoon French mustard
1 teaspoon granulated sugar
Plenty of pepper freshly ground
Plenty of parsley, chopped
1 crushed clove of garlic
1 tablespoon chopped shallot or mild onion

Mix vinegar, sugar, and mustard till it thickens together. This happens quickly. Stir in the oil and add the seasonings to taste – don't be afraid of the raw shallot or onion.

To this *vinaigrette* basis, you can add many things:

À la grecque. Add a tablespoon tomato concentrate.

Ravigote. Add a bundle or *ravigote* of green herbs, chopped fine – parsley, tarragon, chervil, chives, watercress, can be included for instance.

Next, stir in some capers and a small chopped gherkin or pickled cucumber.

The result should be thick and piquant, to contrast with the gelatinous meats (trotters, pig's ears, pig's head) it usually accompanies.

Two chopped anchovy fillets are often added as well.

See *Tartare.*

Marinade

To marinade a piece of meat, is to leave it for some hours, even days, in a mixture of wine or vinegar and oil, heavily seasoned with spices and herbs.

The process has three effects – it gives added flavour, it tenderizes the meat, and it keeps the meat in good condition, a poor man's refrigerator.

Apart from cheaper cuts of meat for stewing or cooking as kebabs, legs of mutton and pork are often marinaded to give them the flavour of venison and wild boar respectively. In this case the marinade is cooked first, then the meat rests in it for two to four days.

But first the simple uncooked marinade:

2 oz. chopped carrot
4 oz. chopped onion
2 sticks of celery, chopped
2 cloves garlic, crushed
3 sprigs thyme
3 sprigs parsley
1 bay leaf
6 black peppercorns crushed, and any other spices you like –
  e.g. juniper berries, coriander seeds, *quatre-épices*
½ pint dry white wine
¼ pint of oil

Use a deep dish that only just holds the meat; mix all the ingredients given above and pour over the meat in the dish. Cover and leave for at least four hours, better still twelve – or according to the recipe. The marinade can be strained and used as basting liquor when the meat is cooking, or to make a sauce. Turn the meat in its dish from time to time, so that it becomes impregnated by the flavours of the marinade.

Provided you keep a fair amount of wine, vinegar or cider, the other ingredients can be varied a great deal both in kind and proportion.

The cooked marinade:

> 5 oz. chopped onion
> 5 oz. chopped carrot
> 2 stalks celery, 2 oz. celeriac, or teaspoon celery seeds
> 3 cloves garlic
> *Bouquet garni*
> Extra parsley
> 2 sprigs rosemary
> 8 crushed juniper berries
> 8 coriander seeds
> 10 crushed peppercorns
> 3 teaspoons salt
> 1 pint white wine, cider or red wine
> ¼ pint wine vinegar

Brown the vegetables in oil or lard, including the chopped garlic. Add all the other ingredients and bring to the boil. Let it get cold. Skin the leg of pork (or mutton), score the fat lightly, and turn it over in the marinade twice a day, for two to four days according to the weather. Watch the humidity – a coolish muggy day or a damp cool larder do as much harm to meat, from the keeping point of view, as higher but dry temperatures.

The meat should be braised on a bed of vegetables, browned lightly in butter first (see *Mirepoix*), with the marinade poured over, plus 2 pints of stock. Cover and cook in a slow oven for about four hours.

TERRINES AND PÂTÉS

WHAT is a terrine, what is a pâté?

A meat loaf is a terrine, a pork pie is a pâté. But only from an academic point of view. Nowadays the words pâté and terrine are used interchangeably by French and English alike.

Terrine, with the same origin as our English *tureen*, means something made of earth, of *terra*; we use the word to describe a deep, straight-sided oval or oblong dish, and stretch it to include the contents.

Pâté shares a common Romance origin with English words such as patty, pastry, and paste, and with Italian and Spanish words like *pasta*. Even though derived from the Greek verb, Πασσω to sprinkle, it early acquired cereal connotations. Sometimes pâtés are hot, sometimes cold. Pastry is kept mainly for hot pâtés (what we call pies), and for the finest cold pork-based pâtés, or game terrines. Flat strips of pork fat are used to preserve moisture and flavour in more humble mixtures.

Many modern English cookery books give excellent recipes for making pâtés. *Pâté maison* is on the menu in many English restaurants. It is the first thing that travellers in France think of buying for a lunchtime picnic. In the midday shade of a walnut tree, or poplars bordering a canal, two or three pâtés are laid out on the cloth, with new crusted bread, good butter, fruit, cheese and wine – not always very good wine perhaps, but very good pâté, and each day's choice differing in flavour from the one before.

I am not thinking of exotics – the Pithivier lark pâté, for instance, the truffled foie gras pâtés of Perigord, or the

superb range of Battendier's game pâtés in Paris – but of
the simple pâtés produced in unique variety in every
village in France, above the size of a hamlet.

Our small market town, Montoire, with its 2708 inhabitants, has four *charcuteries*. There are three pâtés on sale
daily (the number increases dramatically at the great Feasts
and on Sundays) in each shop, *pâté de foie*, *pâté de campagne*
and *pâté de lapin*. But none of them are quite the same,
although the four *charcutiers* are using roughly similar
recipes. So there is an immediate choice of twelve. Our own
village of 549 inhabitants produces two pâtés – not counting
rillettes, and *fromage de tête* and *hure* (pages 320, 239 242)
which further extend the picnicker's choice.

When you go into a strange *charcuterie*, be brave. Take your
time and buy small amounts of all the pâtés. There will
not be sulks and sighs *à l'anglaise* – nor murmurings from
the other customers behind. An enterprising greed is the
quickest way to any French person's generosity and kind-
ness. Often persistence is rewarded by kindly hand-outs of
saucisson and black olives to small daughters and sons.

All pâtés have a basis in the pig (though with the mousse-
like ones it is a tenuous connexion, rather than a solid
basis). Hare and game pâtés, for instance, often consist of
small pieces or strips of the name creature layered with a
pork forcemeat. As they cook slowly, pâtés have a permanent basting from the bards of pork fat which line the dish.

Variety, as I have said, is infinite. By the addition of
different alcohols, different combinations of spices and
herbs, orange juice and rind, an egg, a little flour, some
truffle parings, one recipe can be stretched interestingly
over months. You can chop the meat larger or smaller, or
mince it. You can layer large pieces with a virtual mousse.
You can pour off the fat after cooking and substitute a
jelly made from game-bones, or flavoured with Madeira,
or Port, or lemon-juice. You can alter the flavour by keeping the pâté for a couple of days (indeed you should do
this), or for weeks (run a good layer of lard or butter over
the top) not in the deep freeze but just in the cool.

This sounds expensive, and the very best pâtés are; on the other hand I make a cheap pâté, which is always appreciated:

2 lb. meat, equally fat and lean, cut from ½ a pig's head
2 oz. lean bacon
Extra pieces of fat cut from the head, to put on top
1 large egg
2 oz. Madeira, sherry, or a little brandy plus wine
½ lb. onions, or shallots softened in butter
1 tablespoon of flour, herbs, pepper and salt, plus a teaspoon of lard for greasing the pot or terrine.

Mince the meat twice, stir in flour, onion, alcohol, egg and seasonings. Grease the terrine, pack in the meat, set in a pan of hot water coming half way up the side of the terrine, and bake in a moderate oven for an hour and a half with strips of fat on top, and a lid of silver foil. Keep for two days in a cool place, under a light weight.

What could be simpler or cheaper? As in all *charcuterie*, the performance is not difficult, but care and judgement are at a premium. The most amateur cook can turn out a good pâté, once these four points are understood:

1. As much fat meat as lean, including the lining strips of fat.

2. Avoid bacon in large quantities.

3. Counteract crumbling when cold by the use of egg, a little flour, and jelly, and by cooling under a weight.

4. Avoid overcooking. The pâté is done when it appears to be floating in its own fat, or when a knitting or larding needle is stuck in the middle and comes out clean.

PORK TERRINES

BASIC METHOD

Pâté de Campagne

1½ lb. lean, boned shoulder of pork (*épaule*)
3 oz. veal, ham, or lean beef

½ lb. flair (leaf, flead, body) fat (*panne*)
½ lb. back fat (*gras dur*), cut into strips, or streaky bacon
½ lb. belly of pork (*lard de poitrine*)
½ lb. onions, chopped
3 oz. butter or lard
¼ pint dry white wine
2–3 oz. brandy, calvados, marc or eau-de-vie
1 level tablespoon flour
1 large egg, beaten
Seasonings – salt, pepper, *quatre-épices*, nutmeg, mace, crushed
   juniper berries, thyme, parsley, garlic, etc.

Terrine

If the butcher won't cut the back fat into thin slices, and
you can't do it without slicing yourself, cut it as thin as you
can safely manage, then beat it out with a wooden mallet.
Salt and pepper lightly, leave in the cool. Caul fat, softened
in tepid water, is a good substitute.

Chop all the other meat finely. Put it through the mincer
if you must, but the 'Moulinette 68' is better. Mix in the
seasonings you have chosen, and the alcohol, and leave to
marinade overnight.

Next day cook the onions gently in the butter or lard until
they are a golden hash. Do not brown them.

Beat the flour and egg together to a smooth paste, and add
with the onions to the meat mixture.

Grease a terrine with lard. Any oven-proof dish will in
fact do – there is no need to buy one of those dramatic
dishes with dead hare lids, and simulated pastry sides.
Provided it holds two liquid pints, it doesn't matter what

shape it is. If you like, you can divide the mixture between several smaller dishes.

Some people line the terrine next with shortcrust pastry, and cover the meat with a decorated pastry lid. But unless you want that kind of a showpiece (which adds considerably to your labour), a lining of pork fat strips is quite enough. (See *Raised Pies*, page 101).

line terrine with fat strips of bacon

put in tin half full of water, cover with foil

cooked pâté weighted with tins

Finished pâté

The seasoning of pâtés is a personal affair, but allow for the fact that foods to be eaten cold need more seasoning than foods to be eaten hot. It's prudent to try out a small rissole (fried or baked), before irrevocably committing the pâté to the oven. Should you have overdone the seasoning, add more chopped meat, or – in desperate situations – some breadcrumbs.

Fill the terrine absolutely full, and mound over the top – it will shrink in the cooking. Lay a lattice of fat pork strips on top and cover with foil.

Stand the terrine in a larger pan of hot water, which should come about halfway up the side, and bake in a slow oven for $1\frac{1}{2}$–3 hours, according to the depth of the dish: small but deep dishes of pâté take longer than wide shallow ones. Oven temperature should be about 340°F., Mark 3 or 4. The pâté is done when it appears to swim in fat, quite free of the sides of the terrine; you can also test it with a metal knitting or larding needle – if it comes out clean the pâté's cooked.

You can also cook pâtés like steamed puddings, on top of the stove. If you want an addition to the store cupboard, try bottling the pâté in preserving jars like fruit. It needs two hours' cooking. This is widely done in France.

Pâté can be served straight from the cooking dish. If you do this, remove the foil 20 minutes before the end of cooking time so that the top can brown appetizingly. Cool for an hour, then weight it gently.

Remember that it will taste better the next day.

For very elegant meals, the pâté is finished with meat jelly. If there is much fat, pour it off, add the jelly in a liquid state, and don't weight the pâté until the jelly is beginning to set. Be careful to eat the pâté within three days if you have a refrigerator, within two days at most if you haven't, for jelly sours quickly. Turn to page 47, *Aspic Jelly*, for the recipe – flavour finally with Madeira or port.

If the pâté is to be the main dish of a meal, serve a green salad with it, and some small pickled gherkins. In France crusty bread is always served too, but English factory bread is flabby and needs toasting, or, better still, baking in thin slices to a golden brown crispness.

Although bottling is the best way of keeping pâté, it also keeps well under a half inch layer of lard, in a cool dry larder. A month is a safe length of time. To do this, allow the pâté to cool for an hour, then weight it not too heavily (a dish with a couple of tins on top, or a foil-covered board). Next day melt plenty of good quality lard and pour it over the pâté, so that it is completely covered to the depth of half an inch. When the lard has set cover it with silver foil, smoothing it on right close to the fat. Then put another piece of foil over the top, as if you were finally covering a jam pot. Store in the fridge if possible.

Pâté de Foie de Porc

1½ lb. pig's liver, weighed when hard bits are removed
1½ lb. belly of pork, salted in mild brine for 12 hours (page 185)
  or 1 lb. fresh belly, ½ lb. green streaky bacon
½ lb. flair fat
Strips of hard back fat to line terrine and cover
  or a large piece of caul fat
1 large egg
2 tablespoons flour blended with ¼ pint dry white wine
Seasonings to taste

Follow the recipe above.

Pâté de Foie Fine

1 lb. pig's liver
½ lb. lean veal (fillet) weighed without bone (*rouelle de veau*)
½ lb. cooked ham fat, or very fatty ham
6 oz. fresh white breadcrumbs soaked in a little milk
2 large eggs
½ gill brandy, or other hard liquor
2 heaped tablespoons of parsley
Salt and spices according to taste, including a bay leaf
4 heaped tablespoons onion melted in some lard (*do not brown it*)
Plenty of fat *bardes* to line the terrine and cover

Mince the meat finely – mix everything together, except bards and bay leaf.

Whirl in the Moulinette or electric blender, if you have one, or put through the mincer again.

Finish according to the Basic Method, laying the bay leaf on top of the final cover of fat.

Pâté de Foie

(Very simple, suitable for children's sandwiches.)
 ¾ lb. pig's liver
 2 lb. belly of pork
 3 heaped tablespoons onion, chopped and melted in butter
 1 large egg beaten with 1 heaped tablespoon flour
 Salt, parsley, spices
 Strips of pork fat to line and cover, or caul fat

Mince or chop the meat. Mix everything together except the strips of pork fat to line the terrine.

Finish according to the Basic Method.

Fromage de Foie d'Italie

 ½ lb. pig's liver
 1½ lb. fat belly of pork
 ½ lb. flair fat
 Strips of pork fat to line terrine and cover, or caul fat
 1 large egg
 3 tablespoons flour mixed with ½ gill dry white wine
 2 tablespoons brandy, or hard liquor
 Salt, spices, parsley

Mince the meat, except for the fat strips, then mix it in the electric blender with the other ingredients. If you cannot do this, mince the meat several times as finely as you can.

Finish according to the Basic Method.

Pâté for Picnics

James Beard gives this recipe of his mother's in *Delights and Prejudices*. I have reduced the quantities, and do not restrict its consumption to picnics.

FORCEMEAT

½ lb. chicken livers, stiffened in 2 tablespoons butter
1 lb. fillet of veal, weighed without bone
1 lb. lean belly of pork
½ an onion
1 large egg
3 cloves of garlic
1 tablespoon salt
½ teaspoon ground black pepper
5 oz. brandy
½ teaspoon thyme, ¼ teaspoon savory, pinch nutmeg and ground clove

FILLING

1 lb. cold tongue
½ lb. flair fat
plus
Bacon strips to line and cover

Make the forcemeat first. Whirl the livers in the blender with the egg, garlic cloves, the half-onion cut up, and 2 oz. of the brandy. If you don't have a blender, you will have to chop it all finely.

Mince the veal and lean belly, and mix all the ingredients for the forcemeat together by hand.

Cut the filling into long strips (⅜ inch thick for the tongue, ¼ inch thick for the pork fat).

Line the terrine with the bacon strips (or fat pork bards). Lay in a layer of forcemeat, then a layer of tongue-and-pork-fat strips. Repeat, then cover with a layer of forcemeat. Cover with more bacon or bards. Bake (in a *bain-marie* – in other words a pan quarter filled with hot water) for 2½ to 3 hours at 325°F., just under Mark 3.

Cool and serve in thin slices. It will keep in a refrigerator for a week, but wrap it in foil to keep it moist.

NOTE: This demonstrates the method used for many game pâtés – layers of a fine forcemeat alternating with strips of solid meat. Here is an even grander recipe, from the Restaurant Cazalis at Chartres:

Le Pâté de Viande de Chartres

FORCEMEAT

1 lb. lean shoulder of pork
1 lb. lean fillet of veal
½ lb. chicken livers
1½ lb. hard back fat
1½ oz. spices
1 small liqueur glass cognac or other brandy
2 small liqueur glasses port
5 egg yolks
8 oz cream

FILLING

½ lb. tongue ⎫
½ lb. ham ⎪ All cut in strips and marinaded for two
¼ lb. fillet veal ⎬ hours in some brandy
¼ lb. hard back fat ⎭
Also
1½ lb. puff pastry

Line the terrine with pastry, keeping back enough for the lid. (See also *Raised Pies*, page 101). Layer forcemeat, filling, forcemeat, filling, and finally forcemeat, as in the recipe above. Put on the pastry lid and decorate. Do not stand in a pan of water, but bake in a slow oven for two to two and a half hours, protecting the top when necessary with grease-proof paper.

When the pâté is quite cold, pour in meat jelly (page 47) flavoured with port. Do this through a funnel by way of vents in the pastry lid. Or remove the lid carefully with a sharp, pointed knife, so that it can be replaced tidily when the jelly has been poured over the filling.

RABBIT, POULTRY AND GAME PÂTÉS (PÂTÉ DE LAPIN, DE POULE, DE DINDE, D'OIE, DE CANARD, DE GIBIER)

Rabbit Pâtés

In early October, we are honoured – and appalled – by an invitation to inspect the finest rabbits in the *vigneron's* hutches, so that a proper choice may be made for the wine-harvest lunch pâté. The ritual victim is then fed, and fed. Ten days later, feeling squeamish, the women in the family sit in the Beaubrun's cool, pale green kitchen, chopping and mixing the ingredients for the pâté, while Fernande Beaubrun prepares the *poule au riz* which will be eaten afterwards. In the vineyard beyond the village, Maurice Beaubrun works hard with preparations for the next day's work, cursing cheerfully – and filthily – under his breath. There is much excitement, particularly if the summer has been hot and the grapes are sweet and full. Because of these associations perhaps, this is, to me, the best of all pâtés:

Pâté de Vendange

2½ lb. rabbit meat, weighed without bones
2 lb. fat belly of pork
½ lb. lean veal or ham, uncooked
Extra back fat, cut in strips, to line the terrine
1 lb. onions, chopped
Plenty of garlic and thyme
Salt and pepper
2 eggs
2 tablespoons plain flour
About ½ pint *rosé* or white wine
2 oz *marc*, or brandy

Chop or mince the rabbit, belly of pork and veal. Mix in the chopped onions and seasonings, and pour on the wine and brandy.

Leave, if you can, to marinade for four hours.

Line the terrines with the strips of fat pork.

Make the flour into a cream with some of the marinading liquor, beat in the eggs, and add to the meat and onions.

Pack into the lined terrines, cover with a layer of strips of fat. Seal on the lids with a flour-and-water paste, stand them in pans of hot water and cook in a slow oven for three hours. Let the pâtés cool for five hours with the lids still in place.

Pâté de Lapin, a second method

> 2½ lb. rabbit, weighed after boning
> ½ lb. veal, weighed after boning ('pie veal' does well)
> 4 oz. ham
> 4 oz. lean belly of pork
> 4 oz. hard back fat
> Strips of back fat to line pot
> 1 glass brandy, liqueur size
> Herbs, spices, salt

> THE STOCK
> The rabbit bones, skin from the belly and the ham
> Veal bone, or beef bone
> 2 carrots
> 3 large onions
> 1 leek
> 8 oz. water
> 8 oz. dry white wine (or *rosé*)
> Pepper and *bouquet garni* and spices
> NO SALT to start with

Ask the butcher to chop the veal bone. Put all the ingredients for the stock into a pan, simmer for an hour, then boil hard to reduce by half – which is why you do not add salt until the very end.

Of course this stock can be made in advance and simmered for longer.

All the meat – except for the lining strips – can be minced. Alternatively you can lay aside some nice pieces of rabbit and veal, and mince the rest. If you follow the latter method, you will layer forecemeat and pieces in the terrine, starting and ending with forecemeat.

Mix the brandy and seasonings with the forecemeat. Leave in a cool larder for an hour or two (preferably two), whilst the stock is finishing.

Line the terrine with fat, put in the meat, cover with a layer of fat and pour in the stock. Cover with silver foil, and bake for two hours standing in a pan of water in a slow to moderate oven.

For poultry and game pâtés, many French recipes insist that the final flavour is better if you do not remove the lid of the terrine until the pâté is quite cold. Baking pâté in a pastry case is said to conserve the flavour too: you will often notice in French restaurants and *charcuteries* that it is the finest pâtés, and the most expensive, that have received this treatment. Lark pâtés from Pithiviers, duck pâtés from Amiens, for instance.

However I think that a double layer of silver foil, pressed and tied firmly onto the terrine, is the simplest and most efficient way to seal in the flavours. And in the matter of game and poultry pâtés, I leave the foil lid completely undisturbed until the pâté has cooled for several hours. This differs from the finishing of pork pâtés, which have their foil lids removed 20 minutes before the end of cooking time so that the tops brown nicely.

Pâté de Lapin, a third method

   1 lb. rabbit, weighed when boned
   1 lb. veal, weighed when boned
   1 lb. belly of pork, weighed when boned
   ½ lb. hard back fat
   6 oz. scraps of meat, left from the weighing of rabbit, veal and pork, made up with ham
   Onions melted in lard, parsley, thyme, garlic to taste
   Salt and pepper

Chop and spice the first three ingredients.

Make a good reduced stock with the bones, and wine, as in the previous recipe.

Cut the hard back fat into small dice – *do not mince.* Mince the onions and meat scraps, if you have any, together; mix in with back fat, add herbs and seasonings.

Grease a terrine thoroughly – no lining strips of fat, this time – with either butter or lard. Lay in a layer of rabbit-veal-pork, then a layer of the onion-fat mixture. Do this once again, then cover with a final layer of the rabbit, etc. Pour over the reduced stock, and fix the lid onto the terrine with a flour-and-water dough. Cook as for the previous recipe.

NOTE: This recipe can be adapted to suit goose, duck, game, instead of rabbit. There should be equal quantities of whatever creature you choose, veal and belly of pork. Vary the other ingredients accordingly.

Terrine de Lapin

I find that this is the most successful hot rabbit recipe, as well as one of the simplest. It is, in effect, a hot pâté or pie – which I have put here as it does not require pastry, as most hot pâtés do.

1 rabbit
Plenty of strips of hard back fat
Plenty of chopped onions – about half a pound to three-
    quarters
2 medium carrots, chopped
Plenty of thyme
Garlic, spices, salt and pepper, according to taste

Joint the rabbit, then cut the joints into suitable serving pieces. Do not bone.

Line the terrine with strips of fat, as if you were going to make an ordinary pâté.

Put in a layer of rabbit, then a good layer of chopped vegetables, thyme, spices and so on, then a few strips of fat – no need to cover the layer completely. Then another layer of rabbit, the rest of the vegetables and spices, then a complete cover of strips of fat. Pour in enough dry white wine or rosé to come about half way up the meat, and 2 liqueur glasses (2 oz.) brandy or eau-de-vie de marc.

Fix the lid on with flour-and-water paste, or use a double-layer of foil as a lid, stand the terrine in a shallow pan of hot water and cook in a slow oven for two hours.

Serve with boiled potatoes, and a plain green salad to follow.

This recipe sounds disgustingly fatty – but it isn't. The

best flavour is obtained by using a wild rabbit (*lapin de la garenne*).

Chicken and Turkey Pâtés

It is not worth making a chicken pâté with a battery hen. Try and choose a hen you know – or that the poulterer knew – had once run around in a yard, scratching in the grass and weeds, pecking up good corn and generally improving its *post mortem* flavour. In other words an honest boiling fowl. If you are using a turkey, or part of a turkey, round about Christmas, it should be quite easy to get a well-flavoured bird; the kind that hang up plucked, except for a few throat and head feathers, rather than the kind in a polythene bag in the deep freeze. Battery turkey is slightly more worth using than battery chicken – but only marginally so, and considering the expense of such a large bird I would not bother with it.

½ lb. nice pieces of chicken or turkey breast
2 lb. boned chicken or turkey, taken from the rest of the bird
½ lb. shoulder of pork
½ lb. veal
½ lb. hard back fat
½ lb. ham (if you can't get veal, use 12 oz. each pork and ham)
Strips of hard back fat to line and cover the terrine, or caul fat
1 oz. salt
Pepper, *quatre-épices* or other spices to taste
2 oz. brandy
2 large eggs

Put aside the pieces of breast and the strips of fat, whilst you mince the rest of the meat and mix it together with the seasonings, egg and brandy.

Line the terrine with strips of fat, layer in the forcemeat and pieces of breast, starting and ending with forcemeat. Cover with a layer of strips of fat, and a double foil lid. Set the terrine in a shallow pan of hot water, and cook in a slow oven (Mark 2–3, 320°F.) for two to three hours according to the age of the chicken. If you are worried about its antiquity, try the pâté after two hours with a knitting needle (metal). It will come out clean if the pâté is cooked. Turkey should be ready after two hours. Cool under a light weight.

Pâté de Poule, or de Dinde, a second recipe

Breast of chicken cut in nice pieces, about ½ lb. (or turkey)
2 lb. boned chicken (or turkey)
1½ lb. lean pork
1½ lb. salted fat belly of pork (or 1 lb. salted lean belly, plus ½ lb. hard back fat – or ¾ lb. green streaky rashers, plus ¾ lb. hard back fat)
Strips of hard back fat to line and cover, or caul fat
Pepper, salt (be discreet, in view of salt pork)
3 heaped tablespoons parsley, chopped
Quatre-épices, or spices preferred
10 juniper berries, crushed
2 oz. *eau-de-vie de marc*, vodka, or brandy

Follow the method of the previous recipe.

The following three pâtés are delicious, but I doubt I would make them unless I had an electric blender. If you are a patient siever, or Mouliner, you might like to try them but it is certainly hard and heating work.

Chicken Liver Pâté

Elizabeth David's version, quoted from *A Book of Mediterranean Food*, is the most popular with our visitors. I do it in the blender, however, putting the liquid from the pan in first then tipping the lightly cooked livers onto the fast whirling blades. Half quantities and a little more butter do very well – however the quantity can be divided amongst several small pots, covered with ½ inch of melted butter, and a foil lid, for eating on different occasions.

'Take about 1 lb. of chicken livers or mixed chicken, duck, pigeon or any game liver. Clean well and sauté in butter for 3 or 4 minutes. Remove the livers and to the butter in the pan add a small

glass of sherry and a small glass of brandy. Mash the livers to a
fine paste (they should be pink inside) with plenty of salt, black
pepper, a clove of garlic, 2 oz. of butter, a pinch of mixed spice
and a pinch of powdered herbs – thyme, basil and marjoram.
Add the liquid from the pan, put the mixture into a small earthenware terrine and place on the ice.
'Serve with hot toast.'

Le Gâteau de Foie Blond de Poularde de Bresse au Coulis de Queues d'Écrevisses

This famous but, as Elizabeth David says, 'virtually un-
cookable' dish, was originally described in *La Cuisine au
pays du Brillat Savarin,* by Lucien Tendret, published in
1892. The combination of chicken liver and shell fish may
sound odd – but it works.

½ lb. chicken livers
2 oz. beef marrow
1 oz. concentrated jelly or juice from roast beef
3 oz. milk
2 whole eggs,
2 egg yolks
½ clove garlic, pepper, salt

Whirl the ingredients in an electric blender; otherwise
pound the livers, mix in the other ingredients, and put
through a sieve. You should end up with a thick cream.
Pour it into a well-oiled soufflé dish or pudding basin,
leaving plenty of room for the mixture to rise without
spilling over. Cover with foil, tied on with string, and stand
on a rack in a pan of cold water, coming halfway up the
side of the dish. Bring slowly to just below the boil – a
shudder should be heard from time to time, that's all; leave
to simmer for an hour and a half.

Meanwhile make the sauce:

20 freshwater crawfish tails
3 oz. softened butter
4 oz. thick cream
2 egg yolks
4 oz. mushrooms, chopped small, cooked in a little butter

Whirl the first four ingredients, cook them slowly in a basin over a pan of hot not boiling water. Stir from time to time, but provided you keep the temperature of the hot water below boiling point you will not need to hang over it. At the very last moment, when the *gâteau de foie* is turned out onto a hot serving plate, add the mushrooms to the sauce and pour over the *gâteau*.

Pâté de Dinde et Foie de Porc

If you are roasting a large turkey, catch it before the legs are quite cooked and save them until you can make this pâté. Use butter to roast the turkey, and keep its liver to one side.

Cut the meat off the turkey legs and weigh it.

ADD

⅔ of the weight in pig's liver
⅔ of the weight in fat belly of pork (salted or fresh)
⅔ of the weight in the fat from roasting the turkey
Turkey liver
Strips of fat pork to line and cover the terrine
Parsley, spices, garlic, salt and pepper to taste
1 bay leaf
2 oz. *eau-de-vie*, brandy, vodka, or *marc*

Because the turkey is half-cooked, this pâté does not spend so much time in the oven, and the oven should not be quite so warm. Mince both livers and belly of pork, cut turkey into ¼ inch dice. Put the alcohol and half of the turkey fat, melted, into the electric blender and spoon the minced meat in. Whirl everything as smooth as possible, adding a little more turkey fat and seasonings to taste. If you don't care for the thought of tasting, bake a little in the oven and try that. Add diced turkey.

Line the terrine with the strips of fat pork, pour in the mixture, cover with more strips, and a double layer of foil as a lid. Set the dish in a shallow pan of hot water and bake for ¾ to 1 hour at Mark 2, 310°F.

Like the chicken liver pâté, this one improves with a day or two's keeping. If you want to keep it longer run melted butter over the top to a depth of ½ inch.

Serve with hot toast, or bread baked in the oven in crisp slices.

Pâté de Foie Gras, and Goose Pâté

I suspect that some of the emotion turned against factory-farming in this country is stimulated by the tastelessness of the result. Were battery chicken as delectable as *foie gras*, what then?

Consider the French and *foie gras* – 'Les oies sont des animaux rustiques par excellence quit coutent peu à nourrir' (and they also like to overeat, so they are easily fattened) 'et permettent de preparer de succulentes charcuteries dont la finesse et la délicatesse sont d'une renommée mondiale.' In other words the goose supplies a comfortable combination of gastronomic excellence, thrift and *la gloire*.

Professor Zeuner considered that there is no evidence for or against the statement that the goose was the earliest bird to be domesticated. The word for goose in all Indo-European languages is the same, but it is the Romans who seem to have been the first to attempt a *foie gras* on modern lines, and they liked to buy a special breed of geese from Germania and Belgian Gaul, which were driven in slow herds over the Alps to Rome. Recent estimates and experiments suggest that this was a six months' walk.

The *foie gras* goose is much larger than our common grey farmyard goose, and provides far more fat, in which the famous *confits d'oie* are preserved (page 123), as well. The names of the two related breeds, Toulouse and Strasbourg, give an indication of the best areas in which to find good *foie gras*. Geese are fed intensively on a diet of hard-boiled eggs, soaked breadcrumbs, potato mash, skimmed milk, oats and barley mash – in other words the antique diet of cereal mushes fed to Penelope's geese in Homeric times. But the process of *gavage* is a modern one, comparatively speaking, whereby the enlargement of the goose's liver is completed by funnelling a mash of maize into the creature's throat. The funnel is thoughtfully provided with a rounded rim, so that no injury occurs. The fattening geese are also kept in a confined space at a steady temperature. Sometimes with their feet nailed down.

Foie gras is enormously expensive, whether you buy it in Strasbourg or Fortnum and Mason's. Supported by its essential ally, the truffle, you may see it for sale in Périgueux in January or February, in its unprepared state.

Pâté de Foie Gras aux Truffes

Soak a fine *foie gras* (they can weigh up to 3½ lb.) in cold water overnight, after you have carefully removed any dark greenish parts stained by contact with the gall. Next day dry it very carefully with a cloth, slice in half and trim to a good shape. Make little slashes with the point of a sharp knife, so that small pieces of truffle can be inserted. Season with salt and pepper, and marinade for an hour at least in some brandy or good *eau-de-vie* or Madeira.

Meanwhile make the forcemeat. The proportions of belly of pork, liver trimmings and truffles vary a great deal in different recipes – they can be 6:1½:1, or 1½:6:½. The mixture should be bound with an egg and seasoned.

Line a terrine with thin strips of pork fat. Lay in one third of the forcemeat, then half the liver; then another third of the forcemeat, the second half of the liver, and finally the last of the forcemeat. Pour over the marinade juices, cover with foil, and cook in a slow oven in a shallow pan of hot water for two to three hours according to the depth of the terrine.

Foie Gras en Brioche

Truffle and marinade the *foie gras* as in the above recipe.

Meanwhile make a brioche dough and as it rises bake the *foie gras* for 15–25 minutes, according to size, in a low oven, wrapped in a piece of caul fat. Let it cool down until it is warm, then line the mould you intend to use with the brioche dough, put in the *foie gras*, and make a lid of dough. Leave it to prove and bake at 400°F. Before you put it in

the oven brush over with beaten egg and water for a good
glaze. This is a good recipe for stretching *foie gras,* if you
have individual popover tins or the fluted French brioche
tins. Of course they will not take so long to cook – 20
minutes for the small ones, and 40 minutes for the large.

See *Saucisse en Brioche,* page 160, for dough recipe.

Pâté d'Oie

Supposing you have the whole goose, you could make a
goose-neck sausage (page 122), an *halicot* of the wings, feet,
and carcase, some *confits* (page 319) and this terrine:

> 2 lb. goose meat (include the heart and lungs)
> Goose liver (*foie gras*)
> 1 lb. veal, weighed without bones
> 1 lb. belly of pork, weighed without bones
> Truffle parings
> 2 large eggs
> 1 glass of brandy, *eau-de-vie* or Madeira (2–4 oz.)
> Salt, pepper

Make a forcemeat from all the ingredients except the liver,
though the trimmings from the liver may be included. Line
the terrine with strips of pork fat, arrange the forcemeat and
liver, and cook as in the first recipe for *pâté de foie gras.*

I have made this terrine successfully, though less exotic-
ally, with a common goose, and an ordinary goose liver.

Foie Gras aux Raisins

Marinade the *foie gras* in Madeira, after seasoning it well,
for at least an hour. Wrap it up well in some caul fat and put
it into an ovenproof casserole. Pour over the marinade
juices, put the lid on and cook in a moderate oven for half
an hour to forty minutes, pouring on a little more Madeira
after fifteen minutes. Prepare some grapes by peeling and
pipping them, and add them to the *foie gras* after you have
poured off the juice and removed the fat. Pour back the
juice, and cook the *foie gras* in a slow oven for a further 20
minutes.

Alternatively you can fry slices of *foie gras* in butter, and serve them on slices of fried bread, decorated with peeled and pipped grapes. Keep them hot in the oven while you dilute the pan juices with a Frontignan or muscatel wine. Pour over the slices of *foie gras*.

If you are lucky, you may find these dishes on a menu in the Languedoc, made with either goose or duck liver.

Duck Pâtés

Duck pâtés vary from the usual layered forcemeat and meat style of game and poultry pâtés, to a virtual galantine (page 109) in which the skin is stuffed with fine forcemeat and liver or *foie gras*. In France ducks are fed, like Toulouse and Strasbourg geese, with a maize mash until they reach 9 or even 11 lb. The liver weighs up to a pound and a half in the largest birds, and its flavour is said to be even more delicate than that of *foie gras d'oie*. However it has the great disadvantage of dissolving into fat when cooked, far more than goose liver does. Any *foie gras d'oie* recipe can be used.

Good-sized deep-freeze ducklings can quite well serve for the following recipes. But don't expect the full flavour of the best duck pâtés made in France, at Amiens for instance, or in Normandy at Duclair or Rouen, or in Languedoc.

Terrine de Canard

    2 lb. boned duck, including the heart
    The duck liver
    ½ lb. boned veal
    ½ lb. belly of pork
    Strips of pork fat to line terrine
    2 oz. truffles (optional)
    2–3 oz. Madeira, or brandy, or both
    1 large egg
    Salt, pepper, thyme, parsley
    (2 oz. orange juice, and some grated orange rind can be used)

Cut some of the duck flesh into nice strips or dice, and leave them overnight in the alcohol, and orange juice if used, together with seasoning.

Next day prepare the forcemeat with the rest of the duck, the veal and the belly of pork, minced or chopped finely. Bind with the egg, season with salt and pepper, and herbs.

Line the terrine with strips of pork back fat. Lay in a layer of the forcemeat, then a layer of the marinaded duck, the liver cut into pieces and the truffles. Repeat this, and cover finally with a layer of the forcemeat. Cover with strips of pork fat, and a foil lid, and cook for two hours in a slow oven in a shallow pan of hot water.

EITHER

Cool for at least five hours, without removing the lid; cover with half an inch of lard and the pâté will keep for weeks in a cool, dry place.

OR

If you want to serve the pâté almost immediately, pour off the fat as soon as it is cooked and replace with a well-flavoured jelly made from the duck bones. Add some Madeira or brandy to it, and some gelatine if it doesn't set well – test this by preparing the jelly the previous day and leaving it to set overnight. Take no chances.

Pâté de Canard

    1 duck, with its liver, and extra livers or *foie gras*
    2 lb. lean pork
    ½ lb. fat belly of pork
    Truffles (optional)
    2–3 oz. brandy or Madeira
    1 large egg
    Salt, pepper, and *quatre-épices,* or mixed spices

Bone the duck (or persuade the butcher to do this for you), and remove as much of the flesh as possible without tearing the skin. Leave the legs alone.

Chop or mince the duck meat and the pork, leaving it for

two hours to marinade with the brandy or Madeira and seasonings. Bind with the egg.

Lay the skin of the duck out flat, inside up, and put half the forcemeat in the middle flattening it out. Next put a layer of the duck liver and *foie gras* and truffles. Then the rest of the forcemeat. Pat this into a nice shape, so that the livers etc. are completely enclosed in the forcemeat, then wrap the skin round and sew it into shape. Grease a terrine and press the duck gently into it, easing in the legs, so that the whole thing lies tidily. Cover with strips of fat pork, then a foil lid. Bake in a moderate oven for an hour and a half.

Serve quite cold.

Pâté de Canard d'Amiens

Enough short-crust pastry to line and cover the dish, made with half as much butter as flour, and cold water to mix, plus a pinch of salt for flavour.

    1 duck, with its liver
    2–3 oz. *foie gras* (or 4 oz. chicken livers)
    1 lb. belly of pork
    ½ lb. rabbit
    ½ lb. lean pork
    4 oz. meat jelly or good stock
    4 oz. Madeira
    4 oz. brandy or *eau-de-vie*
    2 medium eggs
    Salt, pepper, thyme, bay
    ¼ lb. mushrooms
    Enough strips of pork fat to cover the bottom of the dish

Ask the butcher to bone the duck; or do so yourself by cutting it along the back, and easing the flesh carefully off the bones without breaking the skin. You need a small sharp knife with a good point.

Make the short-crust pastry.

Make the forcemeat. Chop the mushrooms small and cook them down in a tablespoon or two of butter. Chop the livers, truffles, pork, rabbit, and mix them all together. Heat the *eau-de-vie* or brandy in a small pan, set alight to it and pour it over the chopped meat, etc. Add the mushrooms, eggs, meat jelly, Madeira, seasonings and herbs. Whirl it in the Moulinette 68, or put it twice through the finest blade of the mincer to get it as smooth as possible.

Stuff the duck with a third of this forcemeat, or a little less, and fold it over into shape.

Line the terrine with pastry, lay on it a layer of strips of pork fat, then some of the forcemeat and the duck. Pack the rest of the forcemeat round and over the duck, covering finally with a few fat strips of pork and a pastry lid. Make a hole in the middle, and decorate suitably. Brush with egg. Bake in a moderate oven for an hour and a half, placing greaseproof paper over the crust if it colours too quickly.

Make a good jelly from the duck carcase and pork bones, flavouring it with Madeira. Pour this into the pâté through a funnel next day and leave to set.

NOTE: You can make a very attractive-looking pâté by not using the terrine. Cut two pastry ovals larger than the duck, which should be completely covered with the forcemeat before being laid on one oval, and covered by the other; press the pastry edges firmly together, decorate the top and make a hole in the middle. Brush with egg and bake.

It should need about an hour and a half, and will have to be protected by a double layer of greaseproof paper. Pour in the jelly next day.

This is the old way of making the Amiens duck pâté; though the duck was not boned, but three-quarters cooked before the pâté was put together. Nowadays boning the duck makes the whole thing much easier to deal with, both from a cooking and from an eating point of view.

Game Pâtés

The great area for game pâtés in France is the Orléanais, covering much of the departments of Loir-et-Cher, Eure-et-Loir, and Loiret.

Partridge (*perdreau*), lapwing (*vanneau*), larks (*alouettes* or *mauviettes*), thrushes (*grives*), and hares (*lièvres*) with 'golden coats, the colour of ripe corn', fatten on the wide cornfields of the Beauce which stretch from Blois to Chartres, and on the abundant vineyards of the Loire. So if you are by good fortune in these golden, blue-skied districts after the corn and wine harvests, in October, look for the game pâtés of Chartres, the very famous lark pâtés of Pithiviers and the thrush pâtés of Gien, because you will not be able legally to make them for yourself when you return home.

A little further south the Sologne shelters the finest game in all France, in the meres and woods which replace now its ancient, ague-ridden marshes. There you might find woodcock (*bécasse*) on the restaurant menu, the finest of game birds.

At Christmas-time, you will find a magnificent choice of game pâtés in Paris and other large towns, at the leading *charcuteries*. But for most of us in England, Scotland, Wales and Ireland, it comes down to the pigeon (*pigeonneau*, U.S. squab), or hare, with an occasional grouse (*tétras*) or capercaillie, pheasant (*faisan*) or patridge (*perdreau*). Pâté is an excellent way of serving an elderly bird – particularly if you have a number of guests, who would otherwise not get more than a mouthful. Very small amounts of game can be neatly diced and mixed into a very smooth forcemeat of equal quantities of lean and fat pork, but here is a slightly more elaborate and traditional method:

Game Pâté

Bone your animal, setting aside the nicest pieces to make a layer or two later on in the terrine. Weigh the rest, making it up to $1\frac{1}{2}$ lb. with boned veal. Add $1\frac{1}{2}$ lb. hard back pork fat (*not bacon*) and mince finely.

Bind the mixture with 3 eggs, and as much brandy as you can muster up to 5 oz. ($\frac{1}{4}$ pint). If you're short on spirits, make up the volume with dry white wine, or stock made from the bones of the game. Season with salt, pepper, spices, thyme, parsley and crushed juniper berries. Leave in a

cool place for several hours or overnight. Line the terrine
(2½ pint capacity) with strips of pork fat, layer forcement
and game pieces, beginning and ending with forcemeat.
Put a few fat strips on top, and a foil lid. Stand in a pan of
hot water and bake for 2 to 2¾ hours. Cool under a light
weight. Keep for 24 hours.

Gâteau de Lièvre

Here is an old recipe for a hare pâté. Try it if you are having
a large party, but it is prudent to bake the mixture in
several terrines rather in the one large stewpan recommended, then you can run a layer of lard over any you do
not use at the time, and keep them for several weeks.

'Chop all the meat of a hare, and of a rabbit, half a leg
of mutton, two pounds of fillet of veal or fresh pork, and
two pounds of beef suet; season these with pepper and salt,
fine spices pounded, chopped parsley, shallots, a quarter of
a pound of pistachio nuts peeled, about a pound of raw
ham' – use uncooked gammon – 'cut into dice, half a
pound of truffles or mushrooms also cut into dice, six yolks
of eggs, and one glass of good brandy; garnish a stew-pan
all round with slices of lard, put all your preparation close
into it, and cover it over with slices of lard' – i.e. hard back
fat, not the modern lard but the French *lard* – 'also, rather
thick; stop the pan all round with a coarse paste, and bake it
about four hours; let it cool in the same pan, then turn it
over gently; scrape the lard quite off, or leave a little of it,
and garnish it with any sorts of colours; or to make it more
even, and to give it a better form, cover it over with hog's
lard or butter, in order to garnish it with different colours
according as your taste shall direct.'

Game pâtés can be tackled quite a different way, as these
two recipes from *French Provincial Cooking*, by Elizabeth
David, show:

Terrine de Gibier (Game Pâté)

A wild duck (mallard), 1½ lb. of fat pork, ¼ lb. fat, mild bacon, seasonings and white wine as above (coffee cupful).

The orthodox way to make a game pâté is to strip all the flesh off the bird in its raw state. It is a tedious, wasteful process until you have done it many times, so it is permissible to half roast the bird, let it cool, and then remove and mince or chop the meat.

Put your duck, therefore, to roast for 20 minutes or so in a medium hot oven. When cool remove all the meat and discard the skin, but be careful to preserve as much as possible of the juices which run out during the process. Chop or mince the meat coarsely. Blend it throughly with the minced pork and 2 oz. of the fat bacon, cut into little cubes, and which supply the squares of fat characteristic in these home-made pâtés. Add the seasonings and the wine . . .' and cook in a pan of water in the usual way for 1½ hours, at 310°F. or Mark 2.

Any game birds can be turned into pâté in this way, allowing approximately the equivalent weight in pork of the uncooked weight of the bird. So instead of one mallard you would need three teal, or two stewing partridges, or two large pigeons, which make a cheap and excellent pâté. A domestic duck, being so fat, needs only a small proportion of pork, or a mixture of pork and veal.

For a *terrine de lièvre* or hare pâté, also allow equal proportions of fat pork, or even a little more, for hare is very dry, and the flavour too needs softening to make a successful terrine.

Terrine de Porc et de Gibier (Pork and Game Pâté)

Here is a pâté on a somewhat larger scale, suitable for a party or for a buffet supper. It will be sufficient for twenty to twenty-five people, and is all the better for being made three or four days in advance.

Quantities are 2 lb. each of belly of pork and leg of veal (the pieces sold by some butchers as pie veal will do, as these are usually oddments of good quality trimmed from escalopes and so on), ½ lb. of back pork fat, and 1 wild duck or pheasant. For the seasoning you need 2 teacups of dry white wine, 1 tablespoon of salt, 8 to 10 juniper berries, 1 large clove of garlic, 10 peppercorns, 2 tablespoons of stock made from the duck carcase with a little extra white wine or Madeira.

Mince the pork and the veal together, or to save time get the butcher to do this for you. Partly roast the duck or pheasant, take all the flesh from the bones, chop fairly small, and mix with the pork and veal. Add 5 oz. of the fat cut into little pieces, the garlic, juniper berries, and peppercorns all chopped together, the salt. Pour in the white wine, amalgamate thoroughly, and leave in a cold place while you cook the duck carcase and the trimmings in a little water and wine with seasonings to make the stock. Strain it, reduce to 2 good tablespoons, and add to the mixture (if it is necessary to expedite matters, this part of the preparation can be dispensed with altogether; it is to add a little extra gamey flavour to the pâté).

Turn into a 3-pint terrine; cover the top with a criss-cross pattern of the rest of the pork fat cut into little strips. Cover with foil. Stand in a baking tin containing water, and cook in a low oven, Gas No. 3, 330°F., for two hours. During the last 15 minutes remove the paper, and the top of the pâté will cook to a beautiful golden brown.

One wild duck or pheasant to 4 lb. of meat sounds a very small proportion for a game pâté, but will give sufficiently strong flavour for most tastes. Also the seasonings of garlic, pepper, and juniper berries are kept in very moderate proportions when the pâté is for people who may not be accustomed to these rather strong flavours, and with whose tastes one may not be familiar.

RAISED PIES

If you would like to make a set-piece of a pâté, line the terrine with shortcrust, puff or hot-water raised pie pastry, and decorate the lid with crescents and diamonds in the French style, or roses and leaves. If you want to do this, a hinged mould makes the job easier and the final result prettier. They are used in France for pâtés to be bought in the autumn in Pithiviers, just as they are for the traditional English pork and raised game pies. Grandmothers can sometimes supply them, or good, old-fashioned kitchen equipment firms. Some hinged moulds are provided with a base, others have to be used on a baking tray. A cheap alternative is a cake tin with a removable base – but then the pie will lack its flamboyant moulding.

Finer pâté recipes provide ideas for the filling, or the sweetbread recipe on page 107. The mixture must justify the presentation. Think of most commercial pies on general sale in this country: hopes raised by a golden exterior are sadly disappointed at the first mouthful. For this reason it is worth making your own pies at home with a straight-forward, well-seasoned pork mixture of good honest excellence:

Raised Pork Pie

For an oval mould, 4 ins. deep, $8\frac{1}{2}$ ins. long by $5\frac{1}{2}$ ins. across.

JELLY

2 lb. pork bones, plus a veal knuckle bone or a pig's trotter. Medium-sized carrot. Medium-sized onion stuck with four cloves. *Bouquet garni*. Peppercorns.

FILLING

$2\frac{1}{2}$ lb. boned shoulder pork, or neck, with nearly as much fat as lean meat

$\frac{1}{2}$ lb. piece of lean bacon

Sage, or other fresh herbs

Salt, pepper, spices

$\frac{1}{2}$ lb. thinly cut back rashers

PASTRY

$1\frac{1}{4}$ lb. plain flour, 7 oz. water, 9 oz. lard, $\frac{1}{4}$ oz. salt, 2 level table-spoons icing sugar

Deal with the jelly first – it can be made the night before, if you like, or else fit in the preparation of the filling, and pastry making, while it simmers. Put the bones and vegetables into a large pan, cover with water and bring to the boil. Fix on the lid and leave to bubble gently for three hours. Be sure to add no salt. After three hours, strain off the liquid into a clean pan and boil it down hard to a pint. Season with salt, pepper and a little lemon juice, and put it in a cool place to set.

For the filling, mince $\frac{1}{2}$ lb. of the pork and 2 oz. of the lean bacon finely together. Cut the rest of the pork into half-inch cubes, and brown gently in their own fat for 15 to

20 minutes. Cut the rest of the lean bacon into slightly smaller pieces than the pork, put them into a pan, barely cover with cold water and bring to the boil; drain, mix with the browned cubes of pork, season and leave in a cool place.

Traditionally the pastry is made on a marble slab. I find a big bowl, or the electric mixer, less messy. First the dry ingredients are sieved together into a mound, in which a well is made. Bring the water and lard to the boil in a saucepan and pour it slowly into the well, mixing everything together with a wooden spoon (or the electric beater). Knead this hot dough until smooth. It needs to be malleable, but not so hot and soft that it slips down the mould when you try to pat it into place.

To assemble the pie, grease the hinged mould and put the lump of pastry into it, keeping aside enough for the lid. Now gently but firmly smooth it up the sides of the mould, paying attention to the crevices and shapings so that they are evenly covered. Cracks must be avoided. Line the pastry with the thinly-cut back bacon rashers. Put half the minced pork and bacon as a bottom layer and fit in the seasoned cubes. Don't thrust them in or they'll dent the pastry walls.

Hinged pie mould

Cover with the other half of the minced meat, doming it gently above the rim of the mould – this gives a pleasantly rounded form to the pastry lid, before the meat shrinks inevitably in the cooking.

Brush the pastry rim with beaten egg. Roll out the pastry

lid and fix into place, with a knocked-up edge. Make a central hole, just large enough to take a small kitchen funnel, through which the jelly will be poured in later on. Keep the hole open during baking with a roll of paper, or a pastry rose with a stem, which can be gently removed when the pie is baked. Brush the top with beaten egg, put on the other decorations and brush them with egg too. Lay three thicknesses of greaseproof or brown paper on top of the pie, and bake at 300° to 320°F., Mark 2, for 1½ hours. The paper stops the lid of the pie browning too vigorously.

Let the pie cool in a larder for ¾ of an hour before removing the hinged mould. If you do this too soon, the sides sink outwards in a spare tyre, and crack. Brush the sides with beaten egg and return to the oven for them to glaze (protect the top again with paper).

The pie should cool for two hours before adding the jelly; it will still be warm enough to absorb it evenly. If you've made the jelly well in advance, reduce it to a semi-liquid state by standing the bowl in some hot water for a few seconds, stirring all the time to keep it smooth. Remove the paper roll or rose from the pie, and pour in the jelly through a funnel or in careful spoonsful. Serve the pie cold. You will find that the meat has taken a pinkish tinge from the saltpetre used in curing the bacon, and is appetizingly marbled with firm jelly.

HOT PÂTÉS OR PIES

Any pâté mixture can be baked in pastry, and served hot as a pie. If you do this, omit the usual lining of pork fat in strips. The sausage-meat recipes on pages 115–16 provide ideas for simpler mixtures. The secret of a good pie is the seasoning, this needs courage and judgement; the rest of the process is easy enough.

Gâteau à la Berrichonne

Once in Paris, near the Palais Royal, we bought a solid-looking but delicious wedge of an enormous wheel of a pie. It was made quite simply of a pork forcemeat or sausage-meat baked in flaky pastry, resembling our English Figet Pies (sausage-meat, layered with grated apple, grated onion and grated potato in various combinations, which I can thoroughly recommend), but altogether lighter. This is understandable as no rusks or cereal are used in the manufacture of French sausage-meat, and more attention is paid to the seasonings. The pork had also spent a few hours in brine (page 185), which give it a pinkish saltpetre glow.

Use a deep pie plate, so that you are able to have a good inch of filling.

If you use a 9 inch pie-plate, you need 1 lb. puff pastry, and 1½ lb. meat (boneless) for filling. The simplest way in England is to buy ½ lb. fat pork, ¾ lb. lean pork, and a generous 4 oz. of lean bacon (the bacon cure will impart a pinkish appearance to the uncured meat). Alternatively, buy neck or shoulder pork which has a high proportion of fat to lean (about 40 per cent fat to 60 per cent lean), and ask the butcher to put it in brine for a few hours – or brine it yourself. This very mild curing improves the flavour. (*If the butcher has salted the pork for you,* try out an experimental rissole first, before mincing the bulk of the meat. If it's too salty, put the rest of the meat into a pan of cold water, bring gradually to the boil and simmer for two minutes. *If you use the mild brine* on page 185 you don't need to do this.)

Mince the meat. Season with parsley and thyme, salt and freshly ground pepper. Add some *quatre-épices*, or mace, but the predominant seasoning should be herbs, and two to four tablespoons of fine breadcrumbs. If you are making an enormous cartwheel of a pie for a party, you will need proportionately more breadcrumbs – one ounce to every half pound of meat is about right.

Line the pie plate with just over half the pastry and brush

it with white of egg. This keeps it from becoming too soggy.
Pack in the filling, cover with the rest of the pastry, decorate,
knock up the edges and brush with an egg yolk-and-water
glaze.

Bake in a hot oven for 15 minutes, Mark 7, 425°F., then
reduce the heat to Mark 4, 355°F. for a further half an
hour. If your pie is enormous, give it an hour at the reduced
temperature, covering the pastry after the first fifteen
minutes with greaseproof paper.

NOTE: You can layer the meat with grated apple, onion,
and potato as they do in the North of England. Some people
add defrozen uncooked peas, so that a whole meal is eaten
in a convenient form – ideal for picnics, and it tastes nicer
warm than very hot. Good solid open-air food, though I
always omit the potato as that makes it too solid for most
people these days.

Game and Poultry Pies

If you want a more elaborate hot pie, you should layer the
forcemeat with strips or small dice of meat (rabbit, hare,
chicken, goose, game); or else make small *ballotines* of birds
or a larger one of a duck and encircle with forcemeat inside
the pastry, like the Amiens duck pâté on page 96. The thing
to remember is that for a dry-fleshed animal, a hare for
instance, the proportion of fat to lean meat in the forcemeat
must be 50/50. For goose or duck, it can be 2/3. Anything
extra you can afford to add in the way of truffles or *foie
gras* will turn a good game or chicken pie into an experience
long remembered. Everybody has their own preferences for
different seasonings. Elizabeth David is a devotee of
juniper berries; several cooks I know swear by grated orange
rind and juice; at the sight of a rabbit I think of thyme, and
when March comes hares require spices and port and hard
liquor and red currant jelly or chocolate.

Pâté Chaud de Ris de Veau, or d'Agneau

Here is a hot pâté of delicate flavour, whose ingredients are within the range of nearly every supermarket-goer. The result, though, does not betray its origins.

    1 lb. sweetbreads (calves' or lambs')
    ¾ lb. lean pork, weighed without bone, or veal and pork
    ¾ lb. hard back pork fat
    2 large eggs
    1 tablespoon of flour, heaped
    4 oz. double cream
    4 oz. mushrooms
    2 oz. butter
    Seasoning, salt, pepper and thyme
    Enough pastry to line and cover, made of:
    8 oz. flour
    5 oz. butter and lard, or butter
    1 level tablespoon icing sugar, pinch salt, cold water

Stand the sweetbreads in cold, salted water for an hour. Then simmer them for 20 minutes in chicken stock, sharpened with a little lemon juice. Drain and take off the gristly hard bits and divide them into smallish pieces.

The forcemeat can be made whilst the sweetbreads are cooking. Mince the pork and fat as finely as you can. Add beaten eggs, flour, and cream. If you have an electric blender whirl the mixture in this. Season with salt and pepper, and thyme.

Slice the mushrooms (more than 4 oz. does not hurt, and if you can use field mushrooms, or even better *Trompettes des Morts* (*Craterellus Cornucopioides*) the flavour will be greatly improved). Fry them lightly in butter. If you have plenty, mix half into the forcemeat after it has been whirled in the blender.

Now assemble the pie. Line a pie dish with pastry, then line the pastry with a thick layer of forcemeat, keeping aside enough to cover. Next put in the sweetbreads and mushrooms, and cover with the last of the forcemeat. Put on a pastry lid, decorate, knock up the edges and brush with egg yolk-and-water glaze. Bake in a moderate oven for an hour, protecting the pastry lid with greaseproof paper if necessary.

GALANTINES

The derivation of the word Galantine is obscure. Snowdrops, rushes with aromatic roots, Chinese galangale (a mild spice of the ginger family), gelatine and the popular fish galantines of the Middle Ages, have all assisted, incongruously, in the speculations. But from a *charcuterie* point of view, the word takes on interest in the mid-eighteenth century, meaning then 'a particular way of dressing a pig', along the lines of the recipes given on pages 113 and 244. By the turn of the century Galantine was used in France in its modern sense to describe a cold dish of chicken, turkey, etc., and veal, boned, stuffed, simmered in a cloth and pressed, making an elegant appearance swathed in and surrounded by its own jelly. Although talking of fish, Chaucer nicely described the emotions a galantine in its jelly might arouse:

> Was never pyk walwed in galauntyne
> As I in love am walwed and y-wounde.

Such enthusiasm is particularly delightful to the cook, because a galantine is not at all a difficult dish; its preparation is lengthy, but the result is never in question. Like pâtés, it should be prepared at least a day in advance for all the ingredients to settle down together and mature.

In the *charcuterie*, the galantines look like pale-coloured pâtés, with a geometric patterning of fat, truffles, pistachio nuts, tongue, *foie gras*, and jelly. From a commercial point of view it is necessary to prepare them in long metal loaf-tins, rather than with boned birds, so that every customer's slice has its exact share of all the good things. I find these galantines disappointing, very often. Their almost classical intarsia prepares one for a supreme experience, and of course one is let down. Galantine of rabbit or pig's head is inevitably prepared in this way, but for attractiveness and flavour, poultry, veal and game galantines should be tackled like this:

BASIC METHOD

Chicken, weighing about 4 lb. when dressed.

FORCEMEAT
1¼ lb. lean meat (pork, pork and veal, or veal and ham)
1 lb. hard back pork fat
¼ lb. streaky bacon
2 eggs
Herbs, spices, salt and pepper

OPTIONAL SALPICON
Pistachio nuts, blanched
4 oz. cold pickled tongue
4 oz. ham fat or pork fat
Truffles
Foie gras
Liver from the chicken
Brandy, Madeira, sherry or *eau-de-vie*

STOCK
Calf's foot, or pig's trotters
Veal, ham or pork bones
Onion stuck with four cloves
Carrot
½ bottle dry white wine
Stock made from chicken bouillon cubes
Bouquet garni

Choose a mature bird. Battery chicken is useless, as flavour is needed.

Cut the flesh from neck to tail down the back, and by using a very sharp knife to scrape the flesh off the bone, you will not find it difficult to achieve a flat, if locally lumpy, oblong of bird. Do not pierce the skin, though this can be remedied by removing a piece of flesh from, say the leg, and lying it over the small tear. The worst part is the legs. Take your time, and gradually pull the muscles and skin off inside out, as your knife loosens them from the bone. Lay the final result, skin side down, on a clean cloth and distribute extra bits of flesh over the thinly covered parts. But don't get fussy and niggly with it. Sprinkle on some salt and pepper, leave in the cool.

Put the carcase on to boil in a large pan, together with a calf's foot or pig's trotters, a ham bone if you have one, an onion stuck with four cloves, a carrot, *bouquet garni*, and a mixture of wine and stock. Any other scraps of pork skin, or pork, veal or poultry bones, would not come amiss. You need as good a stock as you can make.

Assemble any attractive bits and pieces that you can manage – the liver of the bird, *foie gras*, truffles, pistachio nuts, cold tongue, cold ham, ham fat or pork fat – and decide whether you are going to make a formal arrangement, or whether you are going to dice these and mix them right in with a fine forcemeat. This collection of larger pieces is known as a *salpicon*. Leave them to marinade in some brandy or Madeira or sherry.

Make the forcemeat – as fine as you can – of *equal parts of lean and fat meats*. Pork entirely, with a little bacon, if you like; or lean veal and lean ham and fat pork; or the lean flesh from an extra bird and veal or pork or both, and an equal quantity of fat pork. You need about 2 lb. for a 4 lb. chicken, correspondingly more for a turkey, less for a partridge or pheasant. Bind with 2 eggs; season with salt, pepper, herbs, spices, according to your preference and the creature concerned.

I don't advise the use of shop-bought sausage meat, ever. It's too stodgy. If you can't face the tough mincing required, ask the butcher to do it for you.

If you want to include the *salpicon*,
either add it to the forcemeat, stirring it in well, so that you have an evenly marbled mass to lay on the boned chicken, *or* put two layers of it, attractively arranged, between three layers of forcemeat, on the boned chicken.

If you are omitting the *salpicon*, lay the forcemeat by itself on the chicken.

The next step is to wrap the back edges up and over the forcemeat, etc., and sew it into a rough chicken-shape.

Wrap this tightly in cheesecloth and tie the ends securely.

Meanwhile the stock ingredients have been bubbling away. Let them have two hours before adding the bird, which also requires two hours once the liquid has returned to the boil. Keep it simmering gently, not galloping.

Take the pan off the heat, but don't remove the chicken for another hour. You have to squeeze a good deal of liquid out of it, so you don't want it too hot. On the other hand, don't squeeze it dry either, and don't put too heavy a board and weight on it – you want a succulent galantine. Forget about it overnight.

For the jelly, you use the simmering liquid. Strain it and taste. Reduce if necessary, or zip it up with extra seasonings, lemon juice, Madeira, port, sherry. Leave it in a bowl to cool – it will be much easier to remove fat from jelly than from liquid.

If the liquid doesn't gel, or doesn't gel firmly enough, add gelatine crystals ($\frac{1}{2}$ oz. to 1 pint).

If the jelly is murky, clarify it (page 48).

Next day unwrap the chicken, very carefully, remove the button thread, and put it onto a wire rack over a dish. Melt a little of the jelly until it just runs and brush it over the bird. You can then put some decorations on, once the jelly has reset. Brush on another layer to hold the decorations. When that has set, transfer the chicken to the final serving dish. Arrange round it chopped jelly, holding back some to whip into mayonnaise (page 67).

Everyone has their own ideas on decoration. But I would recommend the abstract and simple – tomato flowers and cucumber leaves raise suspicions that the cook has got something to hide. Picot-edged oranges and daisied eggs are for spoiling the fun at nursery teaparties, where chocolate biscuits and sardine sandwiches would be much more welcome, and at wedding receptions, where one begins truly to understand how England acquired her unenviable gastronomic reputation.

Galantine de Veau

Breast of veal, large flat piece, bones removed.

FORCEMEAT
½ lb. lean pork, minced well (or pork and veal, or veal and ham)
½ lb. fat pork, minced well
2 eggs
Pistachio nuts ⎫
Truffles   ⎬ optional
Plenty of herbs, but don't muddle them – either parsley, or
    basil, or marjoram
Salt, pepper

STOCK
Veal bones, pork bones
Onion stuck with four cloves
Carrot, chopped roughly
Salt, pepper

You can follow the Ligurian style with advantage, by
folding the breast of veal in half, and sewing up two of the
sides. The forcemeat is put into this pocket, or *cima,* and
then the third side is sewn up.

Let the stock simmer for a good hour before you put the
veal, wrapped in a cloth, in to cook. It will need two hours
very gentle simmering.

Follow the method for galantine of chicken, but let it
cool completely in the liquid. Glaze with jelly only: this
dish is not usually decorated.

Galantine de Faisan (*de Dinde, de Pigeonneau, de Pintadeau*)

Follow the Basic Method, but adjust the quantity of forcemeat to the size of the bird. Ideally there should be an
extra bird to hand so that the forcemeat can be made of
half pheasant, half fat pork. With a turkey this is easy, as
there is plenty of meat on the one bird for you to remove
some for the stuffing. But an all-pork forcemeat will be
delicious enough, if the extra game can't be managed.

Galantine de Cochon de Lait.

1 sucking pig (boned, except for head, trotters and tail).

FORCEMEAT
1 lb. meat from the sucking pig
1 lb. lean veal
1 lb. hard back fat
1 whole egg, 2 egg yolks
Truffles, if possible
4 oz. breadcrumbs, soaked in a little milk, then squeezed
Salt, pepper, spices, parsley

SALPICON
The liver of the sucking pig
¾ lb. hard back fat, cut in finger strips
½ lb. ham cut in strips

STOCK
1 pint dry white wine
2 pints water
3 large carrots, sliced
2 large onions stuck with 4 cloves each
2 bay leaves, sprig thyme, parsley
2 pig's trotters, or calf's foot
Veal bones, pork bones
Pig's skin

Follow the Basic Method.

Simmer for four hours, turning the pig over at half time. Do not glaze, but serve surrounded with chopped jelly, made from the stock.

Galantine de Porc

See page 244, but use a hand of pork, boned, rolled and tied. Finish with plenty of parsley mixed in with the chopped meat.

Sausages and White Puddings or
Boudins Blancs

SAUSAGE, *saucisse*, *saucisson*, derive ultimately from the Latin *salsus*, salted, probably by way of a Late Latin word *salsicia*, something prepared by salting. The Romans are, in fact, the first recorded sausage-makers, their intention being – as the derivation suggests – to preserve the smaller parts and scraps of the pig for winter eating. Though unwise to say so in a Frenchman's hearing, the Italians are still the supreme producers of dried and smoked sausages. They use beef, as well as pork, but not usually donkey as some Frenchmen firmly believe.

For the fresh sausage, France is the country. It is still an honourable form of nourishment and pleasure there, protected by law from the addition of cereals and preservatives, produced in ebullient variety – both regional and individual – by thousands of *charcutiers*. In other words, the French sausage is freshly made, well-flavoured, and, apart from seasonings, 100 per cent meat. Inevitably you pay more than in England, but the money is better spent. For picnickers the sausage is an ideal alternative to pâtés; cook it in foil in hot wood ashes, or unwrapped on a metal grill. At the weekends, look out for the light puff-pastry sausage rolls, *friandises*, and on Sundays for the luxurious *saucisse en broiche* (recipe, page 160), which can be bought by the piece – though if you want to be sure of it, order on Thursdays, no later.

Although the meat is basically pork, from neck and shoulders and fat belly, a resourceful use of seasonings (spices, onions, sweet peppers, chestnuts, pistachio nuts, spinach, quite large amounts of sage or parsley, champagne, truffles) produces a variety of sausages that an English traveller, going through France for the first time, may find bewildering.

Making a good sausage is a simple affair, though you mightn't think so from the nasty pink packages sold in grocers' and butchers' shops in this country. Even if you haven't an electric mixer with a sausage-making attachment, you have two alternatives: prepare the mixture and take it in a bowl to your butcher for him to put into skins; or else buy a good sized piece of caul-fat as well as the pork and make *crépinettes* – little parcels of sausage-meat wrapped in beautiful veined white fat and either fried or grilled, or *gayettes*, or faggots which closely resemble *gayettes*. Some cookery books suggest frying the meat in a rissole shape, with perhaps an egg and breadcrumb coating, but *crépinettes* are a more succulent solution.

First of all, though, sausage-meat. It is so simple to buy the necessary lean and fat pork and put it through the mincer that I cannot see why butchers find it worth their while to sell sausage-meat, with its high proportion of cereal and its poor seasoning:

Sausage-Meat (*Chair à Saucisse*)

Either
1 lb. lean pork from neck or shoulder
½ lb. hard back fat
1 level tablespoon salt
½ teaspoon *quatre-épices*, or spices to taste
Freshly ground black pepper
Plenty of parsley, or sage, or thyme

Put the lean and fat pork through the mincer once, or twice, according to the texture desired. Season.

Or
1 lb. lean pork from neck or shoulder
1 lb. hard back fat
1 rounded tablespoon salt
Teaspoon spices or *quatre-épices* or cinnamon alone
Freshly ground black pepper
Plenty of parsley or sage or thyme

Prepare as above.

Or

½ lb. lean pork from neck or shoulder
½ lb. veal
½ lb. hard back fat, or green bacon fat
Seasonings to taste

Or

½ lb. poultry, game
¼ lb. pork, lean
¼ lb. veal
½ lb. hard back fat
Seasonings to taste

NOTE: If you want to bind these sausage-meats or force-meats (*farces*), say for stuffing a bird, or making a pâté, remember these proportions:

To one pound of meat (lean and fat)

1 whole egg
1 level tablespoon salt
1 level teaspoon spices

Optional extras:

2 oz. brandy
1–2 oz. breadcrumbs

SAUSAGES WITHOUT SKINS

Crépinettes

BASIC METHOD

Ingredients for one of the sausage-meats above, plus a piece of caul fat.

You will find that the caul fat is stiff, and easily torn if you try to pull it out. Soak it in a little tepid water with a tablespoon of vinegar, when the mixture is prepared, and it becomes pliable and easily cut into rough 4 or 5 inch squares with a pair of kitchen scissors. Lay one of the squares over your hand, put a lump of sausage-meat in the middle and wrap it up. The conventional shape is a flattish, rather round-angled triangle or oval, about half an inch thick. See that the edges overlap each other nicely. Continue until you've used all the mixture.

The *crépinettes* are now ready to be fried, or else brushed with melted butter or beaten egg, rolled in white bread-crumbs and grilled.

Crépinettes aux Pistaches

To 1 lb. of sausage-meat, add 2–3 oz. of blanched pistachio nuts. Follow the Basic Method.

Crépinettes aux Marrons

To 1 lb. of sausage-meat, add 4 oz. of roughly chopped chestnuts – not too fine, or you lose the mealy chestnut texture. (Slash half a pound of chestnuts, put them on a baking tray and leave in a hot oven for ten minutes before shelling them.) Follow the Basic Method.

Crépinettes au Cumin

To 1 lb. of sausage-meat, add the flesh of one red pepper, which has been well seeded, then blanched for five minutes in boiling water and roughly chopped – and 2 crushed cloves of garlic, 2 oz. caraway seeds. Follow the Basic Method.

Crépinettes

Crépinettes de Foie

Beautiful *crépinettes de foie* can be made from the livers of
chicken and other poultry, game and so on. The heart
could be added too. Weigh the liver and heart.

To each 2 oz. add:

3 oz. fresh hard back fat, or ham fat
4 oz. finest fresh pork tenderloin, or mild ham
1 small egg
1 tablespoon thick white sauce
Salt and fine white pepper
Parsley, or a dash of Madeira, or brandy

Mince the meats well. Beat the egg and add not quite all of
it to the meat, with the white sauce. Season with salt,
pepper, parsley or alcohol, and wrap in squares of caul-fat.
If you have some truffle parings, or truffles to spare, add
them to the mixture when you make the actual *crépinettes*,
in a central sandwiched layer surrounded by the forcemeat.

These *crépinettes* should be brushed with the remaining
beaten egg, rolled in white breadcrumbs and gently fried
in butter or fat from the bird.

(If you want to put this mixture into sausage skins, don't
fry the result. Leave them for two days in a cool, dry larder,
then simmer them for 45 minutes in stock or water – prick
with a needle as they rise to the surface. Eat them cold.)

Gayettes or *boulettes*

Gayettes de Provence

Gayettes, a French equivalent to our West Country faggots, are often to be found in *charcuteries* and homely restaurants in Provence and the Ardèche, where they make a speciality of *gayettes aux épinards* (below). They look like faggots, very appetizing in their brown hummocky rows. Strictly for hungry picnickers on chilly days, when they taste delicious if you wrap them in a double layer of silver foil and reheat in wood ashes on the edge of the fire. The non-spinach *gayettes* are often eaten cold, in slices, as an hors d'œuvre. I recommend black olives with them, and plenty of bread and unsalted butter.

    1 lb. pig's liver
    ¼ lb. hard back fat
    ¼ lb. lean pork (neck or shoulder)
    Piece of caul fat
    2 cloves of garlic, crushed
    Salt, pepper and spices to taste
    Plenty of parsley, or other herb, chopped

Mince the meat, season and wrap in pieces of caul fat – as for *crépinettes*, but *gayettes* are more the shape of small round dumplings. Lay them close together in a lard-greased baking dish. The oval, yellow and brown French gratin dishes are ideal.

Melt a little lard and pour over. Bake for 40 minutes in a medium oven. The top will brown nicely, and you can turn them over half time though this is not the conventional thing to do. Like faggots, *gayettes* are good tempered – you can stretch the cooking time with a slower oven and raise the heat to brown them at the end. Eat cold, sliced, as an hors d'œuvre.

Gayettes: economical recipe

From the *charcutier's* point of view, *gayettes* are a way of using up the pig's lungs and spleen. If you want to be really economical, you can do the same and ask the butcher for a mixture of liver, lights and spleen, with more liver than anything else. Cut off all the gristly bits when you get home, weigh the result, and add one third of the weight in sausage-meat (half fat, half lean pork).

Then follow the above recipe.

Gayettes aux Épinards

½ lb. sausage-meat (half lean pork, half back fat)
½ lb. Swiss Chard leaves, or Spinach or Perpetual Beet (*poirée*)
½ lb. spinach (*épinard*)
Few leaves of garden sorrel (*oseille*)
2 oz. plain flour
A dash of hard liquor
Caul fat
Salt and pepper and spices

Wash the beet greens and spinach, shake off as much water as possible, and put in a pan over a low heat with a knob of butter or lard. No extra water should be needed, if you keep the pan covered and shake well from time to time to prevent sticking. Drain well, and chop with the *uncooked* sorrel. Stir in the flour, then the sausage-meat and seasonings. Finish like *gayettes de provence*, but eat them hot.

NOTE: Frozen spinach does quite well, follow instructions on the packet and dry thoroughly. Allow for different quantity.

If you can't get beet leaves, use all spinach and a stalk of celery chopped finely but not to a mush.

If you can't get sorrel, use a squeeze or two of lemon juice. Though I should say, go out and buy a packet of sorrel seed immediately. Once sown, it's there for ever, welcoming the spring with its clear sharp taste and lasting until the first severe frosts. Invaluable for soups, spinach purées and sauces for veal or fish.

Boulettes de Bretagne

Boulettes are sold in Breton *charcuteries*, and, as their name suggests, they are round like large bullets, resembling the southern *gayettes* or English faggots in appearance, though the meat mixture is a little different. They are eaten cold, sliced, with crusty bread or toast, like a pâté:

Piece of caul fat
1 lb. lean pork, boned } or 1¾ lb. interlarded pork
¾ lb. fat pork
¼ lb. lean bacon, smoked or green
Pepper, herbs, a little salt

Mince the lean pork, fat pork and bacon together coarsely, or chop them by hand. Season the mixture, but don't use too much salt owing to the inclusion of the bacon.

Follow the *gayette* recipe for forming the *boulettes*, and baking them.

Faggots

Whilst I am making *gayettes* (which keep well in a refrigerator, or under a half-inch layer of lard), I often make a dish of faggots to be eaten hot from the oven at a hungry family lunch. Peas are the traditional accompaniment to this favourite Wiltshire dish; preferably *petits pois* cooked with a sage leaf or two, and finished with a sprinkling of chopped sage. And potatoes, boiled in their skins, then peeled and quartered. Homely perhaps, but most satisfactory, like the *gayettes aux épinards*.

The big Oxford Dictionary gives the meaning of faggot as bundle – in this case a somewhat derogatory description of the ingredients – deriving from the Old French *fagot*. And what about *gayette*? Do both words come from *fegato*, the Italian for liver? But *fegato, fagotto, fagot* or *faggot*, here's the recipe:

1 lb. pig's liver (or liver and kidney)
10 oz. fat belly of pork, fresh or salted
  or 6 oz. hard back fat and 4 oz. lean pork
Large piece of caul fat
2 medium onions, chopped
Sage leaves
½ teaspoon mace (or nutmeg and cinnamon)

 2 medium eggs
 4 oz. fresh breadcrumbs
 A little well-flavoured stock, or gravy left from a roast
 Salt, black pepper
 1 clove of garlic crushed

Put the meat, minced, in a heavy pan with the onion, sage leaves, chopped, garlic, salt and pepper. Give it half an hour on a low heat, stirring occasionally to prevent it browning.

Drain off the juice into a small basin, mix the meat with the mace, beaten eggs and enough breadcrumbs to make a stiffish, easy to handle mixture. Taste and adjust seasoning. Put the caul fat into a bowl of tepid water with a tablespoon of vinegar, and cut, when pliable, into 5 inch squares, wrapping each one round a dumpling-sized piece of the meat mixture. Choose a shallow, attractive baking dish that can be put on the table, grease it with lard and lay in the faggots, side by side, touching. Add the stock, or gravy. They will need 40 minutes to an hour in a moderate oven. Half way through pour off all the juice into the basin containing the juice from the first cooking. Stand in cold water, or put in the fridge, so that the fat rises and can be skimmed off; add the fat-free gravy to the dish five minutes before serving.

Faggots are very good-tempered too, provided you cook them slowly. The heat can always be raised at the end if they need further browning. You can eat them cold, sliced like the Provençal *gayettes*; or reheat them under a lid of silver foil.

Like *crépinettes* or sausages, you can keep them for weeks, without a refrigerator, by putting them in a clean dish after they are cooked, and covering them with melted lard to a depth of half an inch. A sort of *confits*, in other words, like:

Goose, Duck, or Turkey Neck Sausage (Cou d'Oie, de Canard, or de Dinde Farci)

Buy your bird with the head on, or get the butcher to cut off the head just under the beak. Feel where the neck ends in the breast, and cut it off there. With the aid of a sharp knife, you will find it quite easy to strip the skin carefully off the flesh and vertebrae so that you end up with a tube. Alternatively you can slit the skin from top to bottom, so that you end up with a rough rectangle of skin.

Make a sausage-meat to fit the occasion – either very simple, or with pistachio nuts, or truffles and *foie-gras* – and stuff the neck. Tie it at both ends. Any scraps of meat from the neck can go in the sausage-meat, scraps of ham and so on. If you have a rectangle, not a tube of skin, you lay the sausage-meat on it, and perhaps put the creature's liver in the middle, completely enclosed by sausage-meat. Sew the skin back into sausage shape with needle and button thread.

In France, on farms in the south-west, this stuffed neck would be cooked in goose fat with the rest of the bird, to go into the pot of *confits d'oie*, but for most people, it is more convenient to poach the sausage in stock, very gently, for 40 minutes. Let it cool in the stock, dry and slice for an hors d'œuvre. A very successful Christmas Eve or Boxing Night supper dish, but don't forget to remove the thread just before you slice it.

SMALL FRESH SAUSAGES
(Saucisses de Porc)

Assuming that you have an electric mixer with a sausage-making attachment (or else a cooperative butcher, who will fill the skins for you with your own mixture), it is the easiest thing in the world to make good sausages. Three things to remember – try to get meat from what is called 'overweight pig', most pork on sale nowadays is from very young pigs bred for tender, lean, and rather tasteless meat, so tell the butcher that you want something a little older and with more flavour; keep a high proportion of fat in the mixture, at least a quarter of the total weight of meat, and in some cases a half; and don't add cereals, rusk, or breadcrumbs if you can help it, anyway never more than one tenth of the total weight of lean and fat meat together.

Skins, prepared from sheep and beef guts, are to be obtained from any butcher who makes his own sausages. They are preserved in salt, and will keep that way indefinitely. When you want to make some sausages, take a length or two and soak them overnight. Next day push one end of the length over the tap and run cold water through, wrinkle them on to the sausage-making attachment and there you are. Don't fill the skins too tightly or they'll burst, even if you prick them with a fork, when they are fried. Hanging them up in a cool, dry place for two days is also a good idea – this gives them a chance to mature, as you will see if you try eating some immediately and some two days later.

All-meat sausages are naturally much less stodgy to eat, and make a great difference to dishes like *cassoulet,* home-baked beans and pork sausages, sausage rolls or toad-in-the-hole, where the accompaniments are on the hefty side. *Saucisse en brioche* would be impossibly doughy with an English-style sausage, which habitually contains one-third of its weight in cereals. If you have some sausage-meat over, prepare a *chou farci,* page 148.

Even if you aren't provided with a refrigerator or a deep freeze, you can keep sausages in lard, like the *confits* described further on from page 318. Sauté them gently in a little lard until they are a good golden colour, pack them into sterilized stoneware pots or large bottling jars and cover them with melted lard to a depth of at least half an inch above the highest sausage. When the lard has solidified, cover with silver foil or seal. *Crépinettes* can be kept in the same way, for weeks, even months, in a cool dry place. When you want to use them, stand the pots or jars in a very slow oven until the lard is melted. In theory you can remove the few sausages you require, push down the rest, and leave the lard to solidify again. But in practice, I prefer to use a whole pot at once – which means more pots and more lard. Incidentally the flavour of sausages kept in this way will be much better than the flavour of sausages kept in a deep-freeze. As the preserved sausages are already cooked, they will need only the briefest frying to make sure that they are thoroughly heated inside and crisped up on the outside.

SAUSAGE RECIPES

Any of the mixtures given under *Sausage-Meat* (page 115) and *Sausages Without Skins* (page 116) can be used.

Saucisses de Campagne

These country sausages are very good in *cassoulets*, or in thick cabbage soups (*potées*, or *garbures*) which are very popular in the French countryside in winter, being a complete meals in themselves (recipes, pages 168–70).

Ideally you need beef intestines for the skins, but most of us have to make do with the usual sheep guts. Anyway, ask for the widest sausage skins possible, not chipolata ones.

1 lb. lean pork, neck or shoulder
½ lb. hard back fat
½ gill red wine (2–3 oz.)
1 level tablespoon salt
¼ teaspoon granulated sugar
¼ teaspoon each pepper and spices (*quatre-épices*)
A good pinch saltpetre

Mince the meat, not too finely, and add the wine, saltpetre and seasonings. Fill the skins, twisting them every six to eight inches. Hang them in a dry, airy place (60°F.) for 5 days in cold weather, 3 days in cool but mild weather, and only 2 days in hot or very damp weather. (They will, in fact, keep in a really cool place, once dried, for several weeks.)

If you want to vary the seasonings, you could use savory, tarragon, garlic, thyme, wild thyme, chives, bay leaf, coriander, sweet marjoram, shallots, crushed juniper berries, parsley, pimento, sage. Anything, in fact, that appeals to you.

Poach these sausages or stock in simmering water for quarter of an hour. If you are making a hearty vegetable soup, add them 20 minutes before the end. Remember to prick the sausages well before you put them in the hot liquid.

Saucisses de Toulouse

This is the famous sausage cooked in with *cassoulet* (page 163); it is also good with a hot potato salad, after brushing with melted butter and grilling, or simmering in water for ten minutes.

> 1½ lb. lean pork (neck or shoulder)
> ½ lb. hard back fat
> Level tablespoon salt
> Level tablespoon granulated sugar (scant)
> 1 pinch white pepper
> 1 pinch saltpetre

The distinguishing characteristic of this sausage is its coarsely chopped meat – mincing is too fine. Mix in the seasonings, and leave overnight in a dish with a lid, a pyrex casserole is ideal. Next day stir the ingredients up well and fill the skins, using the very large-holed plate of an electric mincer with the sausage-making attachment. They are ready for use, but to my mind improve with keeping a day or two.

Elizabeth David suggests stiffening them by dipping into boiling water for a few moments, before frying or grilling. This is a good idea.

Saucisses au Foie de Porc

This is a heavier sausage, more like a black pudding. It goes well, too, with apple purée, or apple rings lightly fried in butter.

> 1 lb. leg of pork, salted in brine for 3 days
> 1 lb. pig's liver
> 1 lb. hard back fat
> ½ lb. onions, chopped and melted in butter

Heaped tablespoon of salt
Teaspoon each of black pepper and *quatre-épices*
2 oz. kirsch (Alsatian or German-Swiss kirschwasser)

Mince the liver two or three times, until you get a virtual
purée. Put the lean and fat pork twice through the mincer.
Mix in the cooked onions, which should have been reduced
to a mash, and the other seasonings and kirsch. Hang in a
cool, airy place for two whole days, then poach in very hot,
but not boiling water, for an hour. Prick them with a needle
as they rise to the surface. Drain well, leave to cool, then
fry lightly in butter, or grill.

Saucisses d'Alsace-Lorraine

    2 lb. lean pork (shoulder)
    1 lb. hard back fat
    1 heaped tablespoon salt (1 oz.)
    A pinch of ground ginger
    ½ teaspoon each pepper, sugar, *quatre-épices* (cinnamon, nutmeg,
       cloves, pepper)
    Good pinch saltpetre

Mince the meat and fat, season, and fill the skins. These are
Christmas-time sausages, and the chains are tied together
at each end to form a circle, once you have twisted the
sausages into 4-inch lengths. Dry them in an airy place
(60°F.), hanging from a hook, for twenty-four hours. If
you want to continue the festive tradition, brush a third of
them with caramelized sugar or edible red colouring, and
wrap the rest in silver and gold foil. Hang them on the
Christmas tree, on Christmas Eve. Eat them for Christmas
night supper, simmered in stock or lightly fried, with a hot
potato salad, or potato purée.

Saucisses de Périgord

A more elegant festival sausage.

    1 lb. lean pork
    ¾ lb. hard back fat

Level tablespoon salt
½ teaspoon each pepper, mixed spices or *quatre-épices*, sugar
2 oz. dry white wine
Up to 2 oz. truffles

Mince the meat, mix in the rest of the ingredients and stir
well. Leave a day in a covered dish for the ingredients to
blend their flavours well together, then fill the skins.

Saucisses au Champagne

The *charcuterie* textbooks say that this sausage, the finest of
them all, should be made from the still-warm, freshly-killed
pig, so that the champagne can be really well absorbed.
You must scald the mincer and basin, too, so that the meat
won't lose temperature before you amalgamate it with the
champagne.

It is excellent made with butcher's meat, for a special
occasion.

    1½ lb. lean meat from the shoulder or leg
    1½ lb. hard back fat
    1 heaped tablespoon salt (1 oz.)
    1 level teaspoon *quatre-épices*
    5 oz. truffles
    ½ bottle champagne
    3 new-laid eggs
    1 level teaspoon white pepper

Mince the meat finely, two or three times. Mix in all the
seasonings, except the truffles, and stir in the champagne
gradually. Finally add the truffles. Put into chipolata skins,
twisting every six inches. Leave in a cool place, not a
refrigerator, for two days to mature.

Melt some butter in a heavy pan, and fry the sausages
gently to a golden brown.

SMOKED SAUSAGES
(*Saucisses Fumées*)

Unlike the *saucissons secs*, page 135 the first four recipes require only a slight smoking, for flavour rather than preservation, so it would be all right to use the Abu Smoking Box which gives no more – be warned – than a smoky taste and appearance. Alternatively if you want to experiment with proper smoking, say in an old farmhouse fireplace, or by means of a trench and crate (William Heptinstall's method, described in *Hors d'œuvre and Cold Table*, Faber & Faber, though not altogether adequately from a complete novice's point of view), sausages are a good way of starting as they are reasonable to make. See page 194.

And of course you can always eat the sausages without smoking them. If you have an Aga, leave them hanging nearby to dry out, provided the temperature never rises above 70°F.; 60°F. is the ideal. This is quite successful with *chorizos*, a red peppery sausage of Spanish origin, but very popular in France, particularly in the south-west, as you would expect, where it is added to thick vegetable soups (*garbures*) and *cassoulet*, or served, after 15 minutes simmering, with a purée of chick peas. The peppery seasonings can be varied to taste:

Chorizos

    1 lb. lean pork, neck or shoulder
    ½ lb. hard back fat
    ½ gill red wine (2–3 oz.)
    1 level tablespoon salt
    ¼ teaspoon granulated sugar
    A good pinch saltpetre
    1 whole red sweet pepper, on the small side, and 1 small chili
    ¼ teaspoon spices
    ¼ teaspoon Cayenne pepper
    1 large clove of garlic, crushed

Cut the pepper and chili in half, remove all the seeds carefully as well as the stalk and put through the mincer (coarse plate) with the lean and fat pork. Add the rest of the ingredients, and fill wide sausage skins (1 inch diameter), twisting every five to six inches. Smoke lightly, or dry above the stove, at a temperature between 60° and 70°F., overnight.

Saucisses Espagnoles

- 1 lb. lean pork
- 1 lb. hard back fat
- 1 level tablespoon salt
- 1 teaspoon *quatre-épices*
- ½ small sweet red pepper, crushed, or ½ teaspoon Cayenne pepper
- 1½ oz. raisins, chopped

Mince the meat, add the crushed pepper, seasonings, and chopped raisins. Fill the skins, twisting at four to five inch lengths, and smoke lightly. Use in the same ways as *chorizos*.

Saucisses Viennoises (from Vienne, Isère, not Vienna, Austria)

- ½ lb. lean pork
- ½ lb. veal
- ½ lb. fillet steak
- 1 level tablespoon salt
- ½ teaspoon each Cayenne pepper, saltpetre, and coriander
- ¾ pint warm water

Mince the meat as finely as possible – twice through the machine at least. Add the seasonings and the warm water, stirring it in bit by bit. Fill wide, 1 inch diameter, sausage skins (beef skins are the ideal), smoke quickly and simmer for ten minutes in water just on the boil. Prick with a fine needle as the sausages rise to the surface. Eat with a hot potato salad, dressed with a horse-radish flavoured vinaigrette.

Saucisses Allemandes (Saucisses d'Augsbourg)

> 2 lb. lean pork, from the neck
> ½ lb. hard back fat, or green back bacon fat
> Good pinch of saltpetre
> ½ teaspoon black pepper
> 1 teaspoon *quatre-épices*, or mixed cinnamon, nutmeg, cloves
> 1 rounded tablespoon salt

Mince the pork coarsely, season it, and finally add the back fat or green bacon fat cut in very small dice – about ⅛ to ¼ inch, chopped rather than diced perhaps, but as regularly as possible. Fill the skins, and dry at a temperature of about 60°F. for four days, in an airy place. Smoke them lightly and quickly, then simmer for 15–30 minutes (according to the thickness of the sausage – beef skins, 1 inch diameter, are the best, but you may have to make do with the smaller sheep-gut skins).

If you are experienced in smoking meat, you might like to try these two sausages which are so popular in north-eastern France. Frankfurters are well-known in this country, but not the cumin-flavoured *saucisses croquantes,* though some delicatessens sell them under their German name *Knackwurst*:

Saucisses au Cumin, or *Croquantes*

> 1½ lb. lean pork from shoulder or neck
> 1 lb. lean beef
> ½ lb. hard back fat
> 2 slightly rounded tablespoons salt
> 2 large cloves of garlic, crushed to pulp with a little salt
> 1 teaspoon black pepper
> 2 teaspoons chopped red pepper
> Scant teaspoon saltpetre
> 2 oz. cumin seeds, crushed in the mortar

The beef has to be minced very finely indeed, and seasoned with a little salt and the saltpetre; then the pork (lean and fat) has to be minced not quite so finely. Mix everything together very thoroughly, with an electric beater if possible, so that you can add 8 oz. of cold water gradually, whilst the meat is being stirred round.

Fill the skins, twisting them into four or five inch sausages. Smoke them for two days, after drying them in an airy place (60°F.) for two to five days according to the temperature and the humidity. They can be kept in a very cool larder for some time.

When you want to cook them, put them into a pan of cold water and bring them slowly to the boil, or rather to the simmer. Leave for five minutes, then serve – if you are not quite ready, take the pan off the heat, but leave the sausages in the water to keep them hot.

Saucisses de Francfort, or de Strasbourg

1½ lb. shoulder and leg of pork, salted in brine 3 days if possible
1 lb. hard back fat
1 heaped tablespoon of salt
1 heaped teaspoon white pepper and coriander
(A tiny pinch of saltpetre, if the meat is unsalted)
1 scant teaspoon of mace (or nutmeg and cinnamon mixed)

Mince the meat twice – the first time fairly coarsely, then add the seasonings, mince again with a finer plate. Stir it well, whilst adding 8 oz. of cold water – an electric beater, at a low speed, is ideal for this part of the operation.

Separate the skins into lengths between a foot and a foot and a half; fill the skins, tie them at each end and twist them in the middle, to make two long thin sausages each.

Hang them up to dry in a cool, airy place, where the temperature is about 60°F. at the most. Leave them for a whole day, then smoke them for eight hours. If timing is awkward, leave them to dry for a longer rather than a shorter time. Eight hours smoking should be enough to produce the deep, tawny brown Frankfurter colour.

You can keep them for several weeks. To cook, lower them into water at the simmer and leave for ten minutes. After that time, draw the pan to one side to keep the sausages hot. Traditionally they are served with *choucroute*, page 158, or a hot potato salad.

LARGE SAUSAGES
(*Saucissons*)

On a row of hooks in the *charcuterie*, above the small, fresh sausages, the *boudins blancs* (page 144), and the *boudins noirs* (page 327), hang the medium-sized saveloy-type *saucissons*, for boiling and eating hot or cold (page 143). Beside them are ranged the very large keeping sausages (*saucissons secs*), which the *charcutier* sometimes makes himself, but which are usually supplied from a factory, as they are to delicatessen shops in this country. They are easy to recognize, meshed in string, wrapped in gold, silver and coloured foils, and cheerfully labelled. Like the fresh sausage, they must be all meat, predominantly pork – if horse-meat, for instance, is used, the label must say so. The more unfamiliar, black-skinned *andouilles*, or large tripe sausages (page 271), hang with them, slicing to a greyish-brown, beautifully marbled surface.

You can buy these sausages whole, for storing from hooks in your own larder, and in miniature for modern, small-family convenience, but mostly they are sold in slices, by weight. Eat them as they are, with hunks of bread and butter; olives go well too and can be bought at most *charcuteries*. A good picnic idea is to heat through some garlic sausage (*saucisson à l'ail*) and a piece of *petit salé* (cooked, pickled pork, page 176) with a large tin of pork and beans french-style (*cassoulet*).

In town *charcuteries* you will often find a variety of regional, national and international *saucissons*. Forget about the ones you know. Buy 50 grams (just under 2 oz.) of as many as you can afford – if they are well wrapped, then re-wrapped after the picnic, they will survive days of heat and car-travel in good condition. Often there will be local names, so point and don't lose heart. French pabietec is endless in matters of food, even in busy shops. Explain that you would like to make an hors d'œuvre of as many kinds of *saucisson* as possible, particularly *les spécialités de la région*. One name that we always remember is *gendarme*, given to flat, strappy, yellow and brown speckled sausages in the Jura.

Buying *saucissons* in small quantities, whilst coping simultaneously with decimal weights and currency, one is only dimly aware of the high cost per pound. With an all-meat sausage you expect to pay more, but in the case of *saucissons secs* there is inevitably a good deal of shrinkage in the processes of drying and maturing, which pushes the price up higher still.

To make these sausages at home, you need skins made from the large intestine. If you have a farmhouse kitchen, with a solid fuel stove and plenty of old hooks attached to the beams, you are well away because the *saucissons* need to be dried at a temperature of 60°F., and a steady temperature at that. You can store them in a cooler larder when the drying is completed, but once again they should hang so that air circulates all round them. Avoid a steamy humid atmosphere.

As well as the right physical conditions, you need patience too because this type of sausage needs at least a month in which to mature, whether or not it is smoked; some kinds need six months. They will be covered with white powdery flowers from about the sixth day: '*cette fleur est constituée par des micro-organismes de la famille des levures, qui préparent le climat idéal pour le développement d'autres microbes qui feront subir à la viande la transformation voulue d'onctuosité et de goût.*' In other words, leave the white organism alone to do its work of maturing the sausage. Don't worry if the sausage shrinks, it will lose up to 40 per cent of its weight.

Saucisson Cuit au Madère

Here first of all is a large sausage that is neither dried nor smoked – in consequence it will not keep very long. Let it mature for two days, then eat it within seven days.

1 lb. good lean pork (fillet)
½ lb. hard back fat
1 oz. Madeira (2 tablespoons, or a liqueur glass)
2 oz. truffles (optional)
8–10 pistachio nuts, blanched
1 heaped tablespoon of salt
Pinches of white pepper, and spices, preferably *quatre-épices*

Mince the meat as finely as possible, two or three times. Season after the first time with salt and spices, then put through the machine again. Finally stir in the Madeira, the chopped truffles and the pistachio nuts.

Put into a nice piece of large intestine, tie each end. Wrap it in a fine muslin and tie it once again, like a parcel, not just at each end.

Simmer for three-quarters of an hour, then hang it up to cool and dry. Tighten up the string and the cloth, an store in an airy place. Like the other *saucissons*, this one is sliced finely and served as an hors d'œuvre.

Saucissons secs

Saucisson de Ménage, or de Campagne

This is the basic sausage mixture, left to dry and mature, instead of being eaten straightaway like a small sausage. It is sliced, and served uncooked.

2 lb. lean pork (neck or shoulder)
1 lb. hard back fat

1 clove of garlic, crushed
2 heaped tablespoons of salt (2 oz.)
1 teaspoon each saltpetre, pepper, *quatre-épices*, sugar

Mince the meat once, mix in all the seasonings, and the saltpetre which will turn the sausage a rosy pink. Fill some large intestine, tying to make one or two sausages as you wish. Remember that they will shrink by about a third.

Hang in a steady, well-aired temperature of 60°F. for three, four or five days according to the season. Keep them away from steam and direct sunlight. Remove them to a hook in a cool, airy place and don't be tempted to try them before a month is up. Better still two or three months. When they start to shrink, squeeze them down from each end so that the inside is well compacted, and easy to slice.

Saucisson à l'Ail (Garlic Sausage)

2 lb. lean pork (neck or shoulder)
8 oz. hard back fat
1 oz. salt
½ teaspoon ground black pepper, 1 teaspoon whole black pepper
½ teaspoon *quatre-épices*
A good pinch cayenne pepper
A small pinch of saltpetre
1 tablespoon brandy, *eau-de-vie*, gin, vodka or *marc*
1 clove of garlic, crushed

Mince the lean meat well, add the seasonings except for the whole black pepper and the hard liquor. Mince again twice.

Chop the pork fat into small dice, and add it together with the whole peppercorns and brandy to the minced lean meat. Mix it well together with your hands for ten minutes. Fill the skins firmly, pressing the mixture down well. Hang from a hook, at an airy 60°F. for four days; then string and store at about 50°F. for five months.

Saucisson de Lyon (a)

There is not a great deal of difference between the large sausages of Lyons, Arles, Lorraine and Burgundy. Sometimes beef is added to the pork, or a glass of liqueur; sometimes the fat is cut in strips, sometimes minced; but the method is the same, and after a maturing period the various types are all eaten raw, in thin slices, with bread, as an hors d'œuvre or snack.

2 lb. leg of pork, weighed without bone or fat
½ lb. hard back fat (green bacon fat would do)
½ teaspoon each of white peppercorns, ground white pepper, *quatre-épices* or spices
1 rounded tablespoon salt
3 teaspoons granulated sugar
Pinch saltpetre

In this *saucisson* the fat is cut into nice little strips, and amalgamated with the finely minced and pounded lean pork, well seasoned and mixed. If you have an electric beater, it takes the hard work out of stirring the lean meat and spices, etc., together.

See that the fat is well distributed, but take care it isn't reduced to a hash like the lean pork.

Stuff the filling well down into the large beef intestine, tying it into 18 inch lengths. Leave in a cool, airy place, hanging from a hook, for four to six months. The temperature should be a steady 60°F. or a little under – no damp, or direct sunlight – for the first three to six days.

After three or four days, take the sausages down and tie them up firmly, so that they keep straight as they mature. Before you start, push the filling of each sausage tightly together from its two ends. Put four lines of string the length of the sausage, then wind the string round and round. Don't cut it into lots of separate bands of string, because you need to pull it up tighter during the long maturing time.

Now put the *saucissons* away in a dry, well-aired larder, hanging from a hook so that they have a good circulation of air all round them, and forget they are there – apart, of course, from an occasional re-stringing. If you are too impatient and try to eat the sausages too soon, they will taste horrible; so leave them for six months.

Saucisson d'Arles

> 2 lb. leg of pork, weighed without bone or fat
> ½ lb. hard back fat (green bacon fat will do)
> ¾ lb. lean beef
> 1½ oz. salt (3 level tablespoons)
> 1 level tablespoon granulated sugar
> 1 teaspoon each ground black pepper, black peppercorns, and
> Quatre-épices

Follow the method of *Saucisson de Lyon*, mincing the lean meat finely and keeping the fat in short strips.

Saucisson de Lorraine

> 1 lb. shoulder of pork, weighed without bone or fat
> ½ lb. lean beef
> ½ lb. fat from the neck
> 1 oz. salt
> 1 teaspoon granulated sugar
> ½ teaspoon each of ground white pepper and *quatre-épices*

Follow the method for *Saucisson de Lyon*.

Saucisson de Bourgogne

> 1 lb. lean neck or shoulder of pork, weighed without bone
> ½ lb. hard back fat (green fat bacon would do)
> 1 oz. salt
> 1 teaspoon white pepper, ground
> ½ teaspoon *quatre-épices*
> 2 oz. kirsch, *eau-de-vie de marc*, brandy, or vodka

Mince lean and fat pork together, stir and season well. Then follow the method of *Saucisson de Lyon*.

Saucisson à Trancher (Slicing Sausage)

> 2 lb. belly of pork, with roughly equal amounts of lean and fat
> 1 oz. salt
> 1 teaspoon ground black pepper
> 1 teaspoon *quatre-épices* (or spices mixture)

2–3 cloves of garlic, according to taste
2 tablespoons chopped parsley

Mince the meat well, flavour with seasonings and fill large intestines, pushing the meat well down. Simmer for two to three hours in salted water, drain, dry and hang up in a steady temperature at 60°F. for at least a month.

See also *Saucisson d'Italie*, page 140.

SMOKED SAUCISSONS
(*Saucissons fumés*)

Saucisson de Ménage (or *de Campagne*) *Fumé*

Follow the ingredients for *Saucisson de Ménage*, on page 135, plus another two teaspoons of sugar, another teaspoon of ground black pepper, and two more cloves of garlic.

Dry from a hook, at a temperature of 60°F. for three to five days, then smoke them until they are a beautiful deep yellowish-brown. This takes a few days. Hang in a cool, airy larder for a month.

Saucisson de Provence

2 lb. lean pork, from neck or shoulder
6 oz. hard back fat
4 oz. lean belly of pork
1 oz. salt
1 teaspoon each black peppercorns, ground black pepper, and
  quatre-épices
2 teaspoons granulated sugar
Pinch of saltpetre

Mince the lean pork and lean belly well, add the fat cut in strips and mix in the other ingredients. Dry from a hook, at a temperature of 60°F. for three to five days, then smoke gently for eight hours.

Saucisson au Foie de Porc

  1 lb. pig's liver
  1½ lb. lean pork, neck or shoulder, weighed without bone
  ½ lb. flair fat
  1 lb. cooked tongue, cut in small dice
  2 oz. chopped onions
  2 oz. salt
  3 oz. truffles
  2 oz. pistachio nuts, blanched
  1 teaspoon pepper, ground, and the same of *quatre-épices*

Mince the meat, liver and fat very small, add the tongue, season, stir well and leave for a day in a covered dish.

Fill large beef intestine, pushing the meat mixture firmly down. Tie at each end. Simmer in nearly boiling water for three-quarters of an hour. Hang up to dry in a steady, airy temperature of 60°F., and leave for five weeks. Smoke it for a few hours, six are recommended, after colouring the *saucisson* with some saffron dissolved in a little white wine.

Saucisson d'Italie

This and the following recipe for *Mortadelle* are given in French *charcuterie* handbooks. Although they are Italian sausages by origin, they have become popular enough to be widely imitated in other countries.

  1 lb. lean pork, neck or shoulder, weighed without bone
  1 lb. lean veal
  ½ lb. hard back fat
  8 oz. pig's blood
  1 rounded and 1 level tablespoon of salt
  1 tablespoon (level) each of ginger, cinnamon, nutmeg
  1 heaped teaspoon ground black pepper
  16 oz. dry white wine

Mince the lean meat; cut the fat into small dice, and add with the blood to the lean. Season. Stir in the white wine and mix everything well. This time the traditional casing is a pig's bladder, but use large intestine as an alternative.

Dry for three to five days, hanging from a hook, in an airy, steady temperature of 60°F. Smoke for four days over a smouldering fire of juniper branches. Brush over with olive oil and keep in a dry, cold place (40°–45°F.), still hanging up.

Leave to mature for at least a month.

NOTE: You can omit the smoking process, and leave the *saucisson* to continue drying on the hook for two months, instead of three to five days.

Mortadelle

I always feel tempted in shops by the pale pink sight of a *mortadelle* sausage, studded with small cubes of white fat and peppercorns – but it never tastes as good as it looks. This recipe should produce a better result.

    1 lb. lean pork, weighed without bone
    ½ lb. hard back fat
    ¾ lb. salted back fat, or green bacon fat
    1 oz. salt
    1 level teaspoon each saltpetre, peppercorns and coriander

Mince to a close fine mass the lean pork and fresh pork fat. Cut the salted fat into small cubes, and mix everything together. Lay a fine cloth on a strainer dish or grid, and let the mixture drain on it, overnight. Traditionally again the casing is a pig's bladder, but you may find a piece of large intestine easier to come by. Tie the two ends and leave in an Italian brine for 10 days (five only, if you are making it in large intestine).

Italian brine is made this way: put 2½ pints of water on to boil with 2 oz. saltpetre, 2½ lb. sea salt (or *unadulterated* rock salt), and 1 oz. of bicarbonate of soda. Stir everything well together and let it boil for a moment or two. Add 2½ pints dry white wine and 1 oz. of mixed spices (peppercorns, cloves, some cinnamon), tied in a little cloth bag. Remove immediately from the heat and let the brine cool down completely before you put the *mortadelle* in. Take out the bag of spices. Whilst you have the brine, you could also cure a boned and rolled shoulder of pork, or a leg (see page 193) in the Modena style.

After 10 days, remove the sausage, drain it well and smoke for four days. It then needs cooking in nearly-boiling water for 3 hours (1½ for smaller *mortadelle* sausages made in large intestine).

Drain it, dry with a cloth and hang up for thirty days to mature.

Saucisson de Lyon (b)

Here is another version of the *saucisson de Lyon* (see also *Saucisson de Lyon* (a)), or *saucisson d'Arles* in that it contains beef. If you make it into large sausages, weighing about 14–16 oz. each, it is a good one to use for *saucisse en brioche* (page 160).

> 1 lb. lean pork, weighed without bone or fat
> ½ lb. fillet steak
> ½ lb. green back bacon fat
> ½ teaspoon ground black pepper
> 1 teaspoon whole black pepper
> ½ tablespoon salt
> Garlic and chopped shallot to taste, e.g. 2 cloves garlic and 4 shallots
> Pinch of saltpetre

Mince the pork and fillet steak together twice, get it as fine as you can. Pounding it with a pestle, or beating it with an electric beater will reduce it to an even mass. Cut the bacon in small dice and mix it in evenly. Add the seasonings, the garlic crushed and the shallots chopped small.

Leave the mixture in a cool place for 24 hours.

Fill the skins, tie them and leave the *saucissons* in brine for six days – three pints of water brought to the boil with half a pound of bay or unadulterated rock salt, and half a pound of sugar, and 1 oz. saltpetre. Leave it to cool before pouring over the sausages, which should be placed for this purpose in a large glass or stoneware pot. Put a board on top, to keep the sausages entirely immersed. Cover the pot. Don't throw away the brine after six days, but turn to page 187, to see how else it can be used.

Drain and dry and smoke very lightly for four days. Hang them up to dry at a temperature of 60°F. Leave them to mature for at least a month, stringing and restringing as they shrink.

In the nineteenth century, sausages were hung up the farmhouse chimney to smoke very gently until they were dry and white. Then they were restrung, and dipped in a mixture of wine lees, boiled with sage, bay leaves and thyme. A day or two on the hook to dry, and a month or two of maturing, wrapped in paper, in a box of wood ashes, and they were ready to eat.

For *saucisse en brioche*, you can treat this sausage as a *cervelas*, drying it for two days after the salting, then cooking for an hour, gently, in unsalted water.

LARGE BOILING SAUSAGES, OR SAVELOYS
(*Saucissons-cervelas*)

As far as mixture goes, there is not much difference between these sausages and the smaller *saucisses* or the big *saucissons secs* and *fumés*. But for size and maturing, they are a half-way stage between the two. Choose skins that will give you a diameter of about 1½ inches, and as you fill them, twist every 8 to 12 inches. Longer, if you want to bend them round and tie together at each end, in a loop. You can smoke them lightly, or not, as you please; you can salt them for three or four days in brine, or just hang them up in a cool place for two or three days.

This is the sausage you find on menus all down the eastern side of France. Served sometimes with a hot potato salad or *choucroute* (pages 155 and 158), it has been simmered gently in hot water or red wine. Try seasoning the dressing of the potato salad with a little grated horse-radish, or a spoonful of French mustard, or serve a proper horse-radish sauce with it – a dessertspoon of grated horse-radish beaten into a 4 oz. carton of cream, with a little salt, sugar and pepper to taste. Sharpen with white wine vinegar or lemon juice.

This sausage is also left to get cold, and then sliced and served as an hors d'œuvre.

Saucisson-cervelas

Enough for one 1 lb. sausage.
½ lb. lean pork, weighed without bone, neck or shoulder
¼ lb. fillet steak
¼ lb. green back bacon fat
Scant teaspoon of ground black pepper
½ tablespoon salt
Half clove of garlic, crushed
2 shallots, chopped
Small pinch of saltpetre

Mince the lean meat, add the seasonings, and re-mince. Chop the bacon into small dice, and mix in well. Fill the skin and tie at each end.

You can either hang up to dry in a temperature of 60°F. for two days, or salt in brine for two to three days; or use straightaway, though I think that it should be left for at least twenty-four hours for all the ingredients to blend their flavours well. It can be gently smoked for 6 hours.

Prick with a sharp needle and simmer in boiling water for an hour, or in red wine.

As the *cervelas* are not keeping sausages, you could use an Abu Smoking Box to give them a smokey flavour. If you want to conduct some experiments in smoking meat, this is a good recipe to try as nothing much is lost if the result is a failure.

WHITE PUDDINGS
(Boudins Blancs)

In contrast to the *boudins noirs* (page 326), these succulent creamy-white sausages are the dearest in the *charcuterie*, and also the nicest. The whitest of pork is used, or chicken, or occasionally rabbit, and cream, eggs, onions and a few breadcrumbs or ground rice to make the mixture as bland and smooth-textured as possible. Like the *boudins noirs,* they have been simmered by the *charcutier,* so all you have to do is fry them, or brush with butter and grill them. Provided you have a sausage-making attachment (or an obliging butcher), you can easily make these delicate *boudins* in England. It's a good way of using up half a roast chicken, provided it was not reared in a battery. If you haven't got a ham or fish kettle with a strainer, use a metal salad shaker or chip basket for the simmering process. *Boudins* need to be lowered into the water, and lifted out, with the minimum of fuss and handling, or they will burst.

Boudins Blancs de Paris

½ lb. roasted chicken, or uncooked chicken breast
½ lb. best pork from the loin
1¼ lb. flair fat and hard back fat
¾ lb. chopped onion
2 oz. breadcrumbs, soaked in 2–3 oz. hot milk or cream
3 eggs
1 tablespoon salt, scant
1 teaspoon finely ground white pepper
1 teaspoon *quatre-épices* or other spices

Mince the meat and fat as finely as possible, season with salt, pepper and spices and put through the mincer again with the onions. Add the breadcrumbs and milk or cream, and the eggs. Beat well – use the electric beater if you have one – and fill the skins, but not too tightly or they'll burst in cooking. Tie into six-inch sausages – twisting is not enough – with button thread.

Set a large pan on the stove with 2 pints of water and 1 pint of milk. Bring it to the boil and lower the strainer-tray or metal chip basket of sausages into the hot liquid. Keep the temperature just below the boil or else they will burst, and prick them with a needle gently as they rise to the surface.

Twenty minutes simmering should be enough, timed from when the liquid returned to just below the boil.

Raise the strainer-tray carefully and leave it to drain completely over a bowl. Next day prick the sausages, brush them with melted butter and grill them – or else fry them gently in butter. Serve with mashed potato.

Boudins Blancs du Mans

This is the usual *boudin blanc* mixture used by *charcutiers*, particularly in Anjou and Touraine.

> ½ lb. lean pork (neck, or leg)
> 1¼ lb. fresh hard back pork fat
> 4–5 oz. cream (single cream will do)
> 1 egg
> Scant tablespoon salt
> Teaspoon of fine white pepper and spices
> 1 medium-sized onion
> 2 heaped tablespoons chopped parsley

Follow the method for the previous recipe.

Boudins Blancs

If you have been using a lot of egg yolks, here is a good way of not wasting the whites.

> ½ lb. pork loin or tenderloin
> ½ lb. white chicken meat
> ¾ lb. flair fat
> 18 oz. milk
> 1 rounded tablespoon ground rice
> 10 egg whites
> 1 teaspoon each finely ground white pepper and *quatre-épices*
> 1 level tablespoon salt

Boil the milk, pour it onto the ground rice, stirring it well to avoid lumps, and return to the pan to cook gently until thick.

Mince the meat and fat two or three times, whirl it in the blender with a little of the milk and ground rice mixture, or put it through a sieve. Mix the rest of the ingredients in thoroughly.

Finish according to the method of *Boudins Blancs de Paris*.

Boudins de Lapin, or de Lièvre

If you have rather a large hare or rabbit, set aside a joint or two for these delicious little *boudins*. Save the blood too, adding a drop of vinegar to prevent it clotting before you use it.

½ lb. rabbit or hare, weighed without bones
¼ lb. hard back fat
¼ lb. pork tenderloin
3 oz. white breadcrumbs
4 oz. milk
2 eggs
2 heaped tablespoons chopped parsley, chives, tarragon
2 shallots and 1 medium onion, all chopped fine
2 tablespoons of blood, and the rabbit liver
1 level tablespoon salt
½ teaspoon each fine white pepper, and *quatre-épices*
2 eggs

NOTE: You don't need skins for these *boudins*, though they can be made in conventional style with success.

First of all you need to make a thick paste of the breadcrumbs and milk. Do this by boiling the milk in a pan, then stirring in the breadcrumbs until the mixture is fairly solid. Cook slowly until the panada comes away from the side of the pan, leave it to cool completely.

Mince the lean and fat meat well together. If you have an electric blender, drop pieces of meat onto the whirling blades and moisten with one or both of the eggs as necessary. Beat this smooth meat mixture up with the cold panada – an electric beater does this well, and saves a lot of hard work.

Melt the chopped onion and shallots in a little butter over a low fire. When they are a golden mush, stir in the blood and liver and go on cooking very gently.

Mix everything together, adding the eggs if you didn't

use them earlier on. If you haven't a beater, squeeze and knead with your hands until everything is well amalgamated.

Make the mixture into little round balls, the usual meat-ball size, and drop them into simmering water to poach for ten minutes. Drain, cool, coat with egg and breadcrumbs, and fry in foaming butter. Serve with mashed potatoes.

SAUSAGE RECIPES USING SAUSAGE-MEAT

Saucisses aux Œufs

A simple version of Scotch eggs, which makes an attractive hors d'œuvre.

Make small flat cakes of sausage-meat, just a little larger in diameter than an egg. Turn them in seasoned flour and fry gently in foaming butter. Drain well and cool.

Hard-boil some eggs, slice them and lay one slice on each cake of sausage-meat. Serve on a bed of young lettuce-leaves, or watercress, and garnish with capers.

Chou Farci

BASIC METHOD

This is one of the great French stand-bys, and I can never think why, in this land of universal cabbage, it isn't an English national dish too. The stuffing can be varied in many unlikely but interesting ways. Here is the basic method, followed by some suggestions for stuffing and accompaniments:

Choose a fine, large, crisp cabbage, a Savoy is ideal.

Make your stuffing, based, usually, on sausage-meat (or the minced remains of a joint of beef); be sure to spice it well with whatever you have to hand – and bind with an egg. Some cooked rice or breadcrumbs make a good addition.

Plunge the cabbage, whole, into plenty of boiling salted water. Let it boil for five minutes. Don't overdo this, you want the cabbage to be pliable, not limp. Drain it well, and lay on a flat surface with plenty of room for manoeuvre.

Very carefully open the cabbage out, leaf by leaf, so that you can spread each one with a spoonful of the stuffing. Start in the middle, and work outwards. Pat the cabbage gently back into shape and tie it up so that it can't collapse all over the pan in the process of cooking.

If you have a deep earthenware pot into which you can fit a metal salad shaker or chip basket, this will make it very much easier to cook the cabbage and remove it in a good shape. I have also wrapped the cabbage in a string netted shopping bag.

On the other hand, if you can cook the cabbage in a pot you can bring to table, all that is required is an initial stringing up.

Having settled the method, put $\frac{3}{4}$ of a pint of liquid into the cooking pot and then the cabbage. Add anything suitable you have by way of carrots, onions, leeks, pig's trotters, small pieces of ham or bacon. The liquid can be half wine and half water with a beef or chicken cube, or stock thickened with a heaped tablespoon of flour dissolved in a tablespoon of butter, or gravy left from the joint flavoured with two thin curls of orange or lemon peel. Use your imagination, and discretion.

Cover the cabbage with buttered or oiled paper, or some slices of all-fat bacon; put on the lid and cook very slowly for three hours at 320°F. (Mark 2). This is a good-tempered dish, which can be cooked longer at a lower temperature to suit your convenience. Don't forget to remove the string before serving, dress with chopped parsley or marjoram, capers, a little chopped red pepper. Be sure, also, to correct the sauce if necessary, and skim off the fat.

If you want to make a really solid meal, add smoked sausages an hour before the end, or a piece of bacon. Frankfurters, or cooked *petit salé* (page 176), should be added twenty minutes before the end. In the last five minutes, slices of garlic sausage or salame can go in, or olives which have been de-salted by five minutes' soak in very hot water.

This dish is, of course, a meal in itself and needs nothing else to accompany it, apart from bread, toast or fried bread.

NOTE: A number of suggestions are made above. Don't follow them all at once.

Chou Farci à la Provençale

4–6 oz. very fat pork or bacon, diced and fried to pale brown
4 oz. cooked rice
1 large onion, chopped and melted in butter
Small packet of frozen peas (or fresh, if available)
1 lb. sausage-meat, well seasoned
½ lb. tomatoes, skinned and chopped
½ lb. spinach and a stalk of celery, chopped together
or
½ lb. chard, chopped
or
A lettuce and a stalk of celery, chopped together
Egg to bind
Extra garlic, if there isn't any in the sausage-meat

Follow the Basic Method.

Chou Farci aux Câpres (from Elizabeth David's *French Country Cooking*)

6 oz. minced pork or pork sausage-meat
6 oz. chicken livers
6 oz. breadcrumbs
1 egg yolk
Seasonings, spices, herbs

Follow the Basic Method.

Cook in a sauce made from 2 oz. flour cooked in 2 oz. butter, and ½ pint stock or tomato juice.

Serve strewn with some capers, and with a small glass of brandy poured over.

Chou Farci au Fromage

1½ lb. sausage-meat
1 large onion, chopped small

1 heaped tablespoon parsley
½ lb. mushrooms, chopped small
2 heaped tablespoons grated parmesan, or well-flavoured cheese

Follow the Basic Method.

Cook in a sauce made of 2 oz. flour stirred into 2 oz. melted butter, moistened with ½ pint tomato juice, or an 8 oz. tin of Italian tomatoes sieved. Sprinkle the cabbage with more grated parmesan and cover with pieces of fat pork or fat bacon.

Serve sprinkled with chopped parsley and the pieces of fat bacon removed. Have a bowl of grated cheese on the table.

Chou Farci aux Saucisses de Francfort

Two Frankfurters per person, plus the following ingredients for the stuffing:

1½ lb. sausage-meat made from half-lean and half-fat pork
4 egg yolks
Salt and plenty of ground black pepper

Follow the Basic Method.

Cook in half a pint of stock, quarter of a pint of dry white wine, with a *bouquet garni*, an onion stuck with cloves and a 6 oz. piece of salt pork.

Twenty minutes before the end, add Frankfurters or other small smoked sausages. Pour off the sauce, skim off the fat, adjust the seasonings and thicken with a tablespoon of cornflour – or less, according to the amount of liquid. It should not be too thick.

Stuffed Cabbage Leaves

When the cabbage has been blanched, the leaves can be carefully broken off and stuffed individually. Tie carefully and braise on a bed of vegetables and diced bacon with half a pint of liquid. An hour and a half will be long enough cooking time. See *Potée,* page 168, and sausage-meat recipes on page 115.

USING SMALL SAUSAGES, FRESH, DRIED AND SMOKED

Saucisses aux Tomates

This is a favourite Saturday lunch dish in France, made with long, chipolata-style, all-meat sausages; and the wonderfully flavoured, large tomatoes you can buy there.

1 lb. tomatoes, plus brown sugar for final flavouring
½ lb. onions, chopped
3 cloves of garlic, chopped, plus two, crushed
1½ lb. sausages
Salt, pepper, parsley, butter, oil

You need two large frying pans; alternatively you can prick the sausages and bake them in a greased dish in the oven, giving your full attention to the tomatoes.

Melt an equal amount of butter and oil together in one of the large pans, add the crushed garlic and the chopped onion. Cook slowly and gently for quarter of an hour, whilst you get the sausages going in the other pan or in the oven.

Skin the tomatoes by pouring boiling water over them, cut them in half and add (cut side down) to the pan of onions. Turn the heat up and brown the onions and tomatoes, or cook gently into a mush – whichever you prefer. Season enthusiastically with black pepper and brown sugar (only a very little if you are using French tomatoes). Finally add the 3 chopped cloves of garlic, stir them in but do not cook, put into a hot dish and lay the sausages on top. A last dressing of chopped parsley or basil, and serve very hot with plenty of bread.

Saucisses au Vin Blanc (or au Cidre)

This recipe greatly improves the flavour of commercial English sausages, but is best made with an all-meat sausage of the size that goes 6 or 8 to the pound.

Prick the sausages and stiffen in foaming butter for five minutes. Transfer them to an oven dish. Swill a large wine-glass of dry white wine or good cider round the buttery pan and pour over the sausages. Cook, covered, in a moderate oven. Allow half an hour, but this is a good-tempered dish which can be hurried a little or slowed down.

Serve with triangular pieces of bread fried in butter.

If you want to make a fine dish, pour off the cooking liquid into a frying pan and reduce it hard over a good heat. Keep tasting. When it is concentrated and interesting, pour it on to a beaten egg yolk, whisking as you pour. Stir in an ounce or two of butter, cut into small dice, and finally a tablespoon of chopped parsley, or sage. Provided you've kept the dish and the sausages very hot, you can pour the sauce over without reheating. If you have to reheat, do it over a pan of almost-boiling water so that it does not curdle.

Tuck the croûtons of bread round the edge of the dish, and decorate with some wedges of lemon.

Friandises (Sausage Rolls)

Make, or buy, some good puff pastry.

Roll out and cut into 4 or 5 inch squares, according to the size of the sausages.

Prick the sausages and blanch for five minutes in almost-boiling water. Skin them.

Lay each sausage on a pastry square, brush the edges with beaten egg or milk and fold the pastry over. Brush with egg, make two diagonal slashes, bake on a greased tray in a hot oven for 10–15 minutes.

See that they don't burn.

Toad-in-the-Hole

Nobody could claim that this is a French dish, but I've given it to many French friends with great success. And it is surprisingly good made with all-meat, well-spiced French sausages, of the chipolata size.

Make the Yorkshire pudding mixture of:

4 oz. flour sifted with a good pinch of salt into a bowl. Form a well in the middle with the back of a wooden spoon and put two eggs in it and a little milk from half a pint. Amalgamate flour and liquid slowly by stirring from the centre, and add the rest of the milk.

Put a roasting pan in the oven, with three tablespoons of lard in it, or oil, or beef dripping. Be sure to use a clear-flavoured fat, not the stale contents of a muddled dripping bowl. The oven should be hot, about 425°F., Mark 7.

Stiffen 1 lb. of sausages, well pricked, in a pan of simmering water for five minutes. Watch the pan of fat in the oven to make sure it doesn't burn, take it out when the fat is smoking. Run a layer of Yorkshire pudding mixture over the base of the pan. It should set slightly and make a bed for the stiffened sausages. Pour in the rest of the mixture and return to the hot oven for half an hour to forty minutes.

The pudding should be puffed up and succulent, 90 per cent crisp outside and no unpleasant semi-liquid dough.

See also the grand version of this, *saucisse en brioche*, made from one large sausage, recipe on page 160.

Saucisses aux Pommes

> Sausages
> 1 lb. eating apples, *reinettes* preferably
> A little good cider, and some brandy or, preferably, Calvados
> Cream, butter

Prick the sausages and fry gently in butter, whilst you attend to the apples in another pan.

Slice the cored apples, but don't peel them; fry in butter

until they are golden brown, but not frizzled, and arrange
them on the serving dish. You can quite well serve the
sausages on them at this stage, but the sauce makes an
elegant dish.

Pour a large wineglass-full of cider into the apple pan and
let it bubble down for a few moments. Stir in the Calvados
or brandy, and then 4 oz. of cream, with the heat turned
down. Cook for a few moments very gently and you will
have a thick, bland sauce of the Normandy type. Taste and
correct the seasoning, before pouring over the sausages and
apples.

If you haven't got cider, use dry white wine or *rosé*.
Whatever you do, don't use the over-sweet gaseous 'cyder'
sold by soft-drink merchants.

Saucisses à la Charcutière

Make a good purée of potatoes, firm but bland, and pile
onto the serving-dish in a forked-up cone.

Fry chipolata sausages in butter, and arrange them upright but leaning against the cone of potatoes.

Serve with a *charcutière* sauce, page 52. Or with a *sauce
Robert,* page 62; or a well-flavoured tomato sauce, page 65.

Onion rings, soaked for an hour in milk, drained and
dipped in seasoned flour and deep-fried in oil, make a good
accompaniment.

Saucisses en Vin Rouge

Fresh sausages should be lightly fried in butter first.

Dried and smoked small sausages, and the larger *saucis-
sons-cervelas,* go straight into the liquid.

Use ½ pint of red wine, Beaujolais if you can, and see that
the sausages bathe in it. Cooking time will vary according
to the size of the sausage, between twenty minutes and an
hour in a moderate oven once the liquid has returned to
simmering point.

Serve with a hot potato salad, made from waxy new

potatoes or firm old ones boiled in their skins and then peeled. Mix the dressing whilst the potatoes cook, so that you can toss them in it whilst they are still hot. For 2 lb. potatoes:

    5 tablespoons of oil
    1 scant tablespoon of wine vinegar
    Freshly ground black pepper, salt, crushed clove garlic
    1 heaped teaspoon French mustard
    Half a teaspoon brown sugar

Don't let the potatoes cook in the dressing, but arrange them whilst still warm on a very hot serving dish. The sausages go in the middle, drained (use the Beaujolais for a casserole), and the dish should be finished with chopped parsley.

This simple and satisfactory dish can be varied by adding 2 tablespoons of raw shallot, or mild onion chopped fine, to the potato salad. Or by finishing with chives instead of parsley. Or by using this dressing instead:

    ¼ lb. fat bacon, fried till crisp, and crushed
    1 large onion chopped small, melted in bacon fat and lard
    1 dessertspoon of cornflour, scant
    1 tablespoon brown sugar
    4 tablespoons wine vinegar
    4 tablespoons water
    1 tablespoon parsley

Stir the water and vinegar into the cornflour and sugar, cook till thickened. Add parsley. Toss the potatoes in this, and gently turn whilst the crisp bacon crumbs are added, and the onion. ·

Quiche aux Saucisses et Poireaux

Make a good shortcrust pastry with, for instance:

    4 oz. plain flour
    2½ oz. butter, or butter and lard
    Pinch of salt
    1 level dessertspoon icing sugar
    And the least possible amount of very cold water to mix.

Line a fluted, 8½ inch flan tin with a removable base. Prick and brush with white of egg. Bake blind, with rice or beans in silver foil to stop the pastry rising out of shape, in a moderate oven for 20 minutes.

Fill this with a purée of 1½ lb. of leeks and like the spokes of a wheel, lay chipolata sausages on top, which you have fried gently in butter for five to ten minutes.

Put back in the oven for the pastry to turn golden-brown. Be sure not to let the *quiche* burn.

NOTE: When making a leek purée, it is simplest to slice the leeks and wash them well, then put them in a thick-bottomed pan with a good lump of butter and a pinch of salt. There will be enough water, even if you drain the washed leeks, to stop them burning – provided you cook them gently with a lid on the pan. A blender is ideal for reducing them to a purée without overcooking, but patience with a sieve and wooden spoon, or less patience and a Mouli-légumes, will achieve a good result. Season the purée, and add some cream and two egg yolks, though this is not strictly necessary.

This is a very pretty dish, with the added advantage of being a complete meal in one.

Saucisses de Francfort au Chou Rouge

Prepare the red cabbage one or two days before you intend to eat this dish. It can be reheated several times without loss of flavour (minus the sausages, which should be added last thing), and it even tastes better for maturing slightly.

Any smoked sausages are suitable, cooked separately in hot water for five minutes to an hour, according to their size. *Petit salé*, hot, and unsmoked sausages are sometimes accompanied by red cabbage. But, be warned, this is a hefty, cold day lunch dish.

There are many recipes for red cabbage. But most people prefer it cooked with an equal or lesser quantity of sliced onions and cooking apples, the three layered together and each layer seasoned with brown sugar, salt and freshly-ground black pepper. Finally a sherry glass of red wine, and the same of wine vinegar, poured over. Cover with a tight-fitting lid and leave in a very slow oven for at least three hours. Correct the seasoning just before serving. Arrange on a hot dish with the separately cooked sausages.

Saucisses de Francfort à la Choucroute d'Alsace

Curnonsky gives this recipe, from Colmar. We probably have to use tinned *choucroute*. Nevertheless it is still worth doing.

    1 lb. *choucroute*
    1 onion, chopped
    2 tablespoons of goose fat (duck, or lard)
    4 oz. dry white wine
    1 good-sized apple, Blenheim, or 2 small Coxes, ideally a
      reinette
    10 juniper berries, tied in a bit of cloth
    ¾ pint of beef stock
    1 lb. smoked streaky bacon
    A liqueur glass of Swiss or Alsatian kirschwasser
    1 lb. potatoes
    A piece of salted loin, cut into chops
    Frankfurter or Strasbourg sausages

In an enamelled cast iron pot, or an earthenware casserole, cook the chopped onion in the goose fat until it is golden. Add the *choucroute*, unwashed if it is fresh from the barrel, or washed very quickly.

Cook for five minutes, stirring with a fork.

Add the white wine, the apple cut in pieces, and the juniper berries tied in the cloth. Pour on enough of the bouillon to almost cover the *choucroute*.

Put on the lid and cook in a gentle oven for two or three hours. One hour before serving add the smoked bacon. Half an hour before serving add the kirsch. Ten minutes before serving add the sausages.

In a separate pot, cook the salted loin chops, simmering

them for half an hour in water, unseasoned, so that they are ready with the *choucroute*.

Heat a big, round serving dish, and arrange the drained *choucroute* on it (having removed the juniper berries), together with the smoked bacon, cut into slices, the sausages and the chops. Serve with potatoes, boiled in their skins, then peeled.

Choucroute Soup

The above recipe can be adapted for soup, by cooking ½ lb. of peeled potatoes with the *choucroute* and increasing the stock to 2 pints. Remove the smoked bacon and juniper berries before putting everything else through a sieve, or Mouli. Cut the bacon up into small pieces, and the sausages – omit the salted loin chops altogether – and heat through with the soup. Simmer gently for ten minutes. Just before serving stir in 3 oz. of unsalted butter or cream.

For other soups, using salt pork and sausages, see *Potée*, pages 168–9.

NOTE: Cumin seeds are often used for flavouring *choucroute* instead of juniper berries.

Saucisses aux Pois Chiches

Soak 1 lb. split green or yellow peas overnight. Next day cook peas and liquid with an onion stuck with four cloves, a piece of salt pork or green bacon weighing up to 8 oz., a *bouquet garni* and some salt and pepper. When the peas are cooked, drain them and remove the onion, bacon, etc. Sieve the peas and reheat slowly with some butter – about 2 tablespoons, and a little milk.

Cook the sausages in butter; or simmer them for five minutes in hot water if they are the smoked Frankfurter type, or dried. Put the purée of split peas into a serving dish and arrange the sausages on top.

Saucisses aux Lentilles

Follow the recipe above, using lentils which can be cooked exactly like the split peas. The piece of salt pork should be kept for another meal, or else neatly sliced and served with the sausages.

USING SMALL AND LARGE SAUSAGES

Saucisse en Brioche à la Lyonnaise

Sausage baked in brioche dough is a speciality of many high-class *charcuteries* throughout France. For English cooks the main problems are the dough itself (the *charcutier* obtains his from the *pâtissier* as a rule) and the timing of the various quite simple procedures. For these reasons I quote the whole of Elizabeth David's recipe from *French Provincial Cooking*: there is no better version, though I would underline the necessity of using a hard flour, not the usual soft plain cake flour, for a satisfactory result. 'The sausage used in Lyon, where this dish is a renowned speciality, may be one of three kinds; it may be one of the routine cooking sausages, very coarsely cut and interlarded with large cubes of fat; it may be a *cervelas*, a close-textured sausage, very lightly smoked; or it may be a *cervelas truffé*, an unsmoked sausage of coarsely-cut pork generously truffled and spiced. Whichever it is, it will weigh in the region of 12 to 14 oz. and be about 1½ inches in diameter, and because the pork for these sausages (as indeed for the majority of fresh or partly cured French sausage) is either brined for a night and a day or has saltpetre added to the mixture before the skins are filled, the colour of the finished sausage is a good red instead of the pinkish-grey characteristic of our own sausages.

'Randall & Aubin, in Brewer Street, Soho, sell a coarsely-cut garlic-flavoured sausage which is not unlike the Lyon sausage, and the Italian shops of Soho supply *cotechino*, the Modena boiling sausage which is also suitable for this dish; and at Harrods' butchery counter there is a special pure pork luncheon sausage, English in character, which is admirable for this dish and for the two which follow, for I see no reason why we should not adapt these splendid French dishes using the ingredients which are available to us here. And no doubt many readers will be able to persuade their own local butchers to obtain the right casings for these large sausages and to fill them with their own favourite sausage mixture. But it should be borne in mind that if you are going to wrap a sausage in a brioche dough or even a flaky pastry, as for our own sausage rolls, it is really preferable to have a pure meat sausage. If you use a sausage containing the usual English mixture of 35 per cent bread or rusk, it means you are going to eat a rather doughy dish.

'Now for the recipe.

'It must be given in some detail and will take up a good deal of space, but I trust that its rather formidable length will not deter readers from trying it, for in many ways it makes the almost perfect hot first course dish, the majority of the work being done well in advance and the timing of the final cooking such that it can be put in the oven a few moments before your guests are expected and, in half an hour, is ready to emerge, a beautiful, golden roll of brioche enclosing the delicious savoury sausage. The procedure is as follows:

'(1) If the sausage is to be served at lunch, the brioche dough is made the previous night; if for dinner, in the early morning of the same day. It is extremely easy, for this is a simplified brioche dough. First you mix to a paste a scant ½ oz. of baker's yeast and 2 tablespoons of barely tepid milk. In a bowl you then put 6 oz. of plain flour, a half teaspoon of salt, and 1 of sugar. Make a well in the centre. Into this break 2 whole eggs, and add the yeast mixture. Fold the flour over the eggs and yeast and knead all together until the mixture is smooth. Now beat in with your hands 4 oz. of the best butter, softened but not melted. Knead again and shape it into a ball. Put it in a clean bowl, a wooden one for preference, in which you have sprinkled some flour.

Make a deep crosswise incision across the top of the ball of dough with a knife. Cover it with a clean, folded muslin. Put the bowl in a warm place, such as a heated linen cupboard or near the boiler, or in the plate drawer of the cooker with the oven turned on to a very low temperature. Leave it for 2 hours, by which time it should have risen to at least twice its original volume and will look and feel light and spongy. Break it down, knead it lightly once more into a ball, cover it again, and this time put the bowl in a cool larder and leave it until next day, or until the evening.

'(2) Put your large sausage (the quantity of dough is enough for a 12 to 14 oz. sausage) into a pan in which it will lie flat. Cover completely with cold water. Bring very gently to simmering point and thereafter let it cook with the water barely moving, for 45 minutes to an hour. Take it out and put it on a board or dish until it is cool enough to handle. Now remove the skin, very carefully.

'(3) Allowing yourself half an hour the first few times you do this dish (afterwards it will be much quicker) make the final preparations. Very lightly rub a baking sheet with butter. Put your dough on this, sprinkle it with flour, and with your hands spread and pat it out into a rectangular shape on the baking sheet. Turn it over (by this time you can, or should be able to, handle the dough as easily as if it were a piece of material). Put your skinned sausage, still warm, in the centre. Gather up the edges of the dough and, having dipped your fingers in cold water, pinch the edges lightly together, along the top and at the ends, so that the whole thing looks rather like a small bolster. Now dip a pastry brush in cream and paint the whole of the exposed surface with it (cream makes the best glaze for these sorts of dishes – not so shiny as egg and smoother than milk). With the back of a knife lightly mark a few criss-cross lines on the dough. The sausage and its brioche can now be left for 15 to 20 minutes, ready on its baking sheet, before it goes into the centre of a preheated oven at Gas No. 5, 375–80°F., to bake for 30 minutes. When you take it from the oven, leave the brioche standing for 5 minutes before transferring it, with the aid of a flat fish slice, to a serving dish, and carving it deftly into thickish slices, starting in the middle and working outward. It will be ample for four.

'One should not perhaps expect this dish to come exactly right the first time, except for those accustomed to working with yeast doughs. But although it may sound complicated, after one or two tries it becomes a matter of timing rather than of any special knowledge, and you get a splendid-looking delicious dish with absurdly little trouble. It is mainly a question of assembling all your ingredients and utensils before each of the two main operations – the original mixing of the dough and the final wrapping of the sausage in it. Points to observe carefully are:

'(1) Brioche dough is very much more liquid than bread dough, but if after the initial mixing it is really too soft to handle, it may be because you have added a little too much milk to the yeast, or because the eggs were unusually large, or because you are using a soft flour. A little more flour sprinkled in will put matters right.

'(2) The sausage is to be put into the dough while it is still warm, because if it is left to get quite cold it will separate from the brioche when it is cut; but if it is too hot the fat running from it will make your dough liquid and difficult to handle.

'(3) Be sure to join the edges of the dough well together round the sausage without drawing it too tightly or the sausage will burst through during the baking. This does not detract from the taste of the dish, but rather spoils its appearance.

'(4) It is essential that the sausage be cooked right through to start with; once inside its casing of brioche, it will heat but will scarcely cook any more.'

Cassoulet

The tastiest form of baked beans is *cassoulet*, a rich slowly-cooked dish of dried white haricot beans, goose, salt pork, sausages large and small including the Toulouse sausage (page 126), small squares of pork skin to make the sauce smooth and bland, and breadcrumbs to form the crusty golden top. Languedoc is the native home of *cassoulet*, more specifically the small town of Castelnaudary on the Canal du Midi, whose classic version was described by Anatole France as having 'a taste, which one finds in the paintings of old Venetian masters, in the amber flesh tints of their women'. At Toulouse and Carcassonne cooks add mutton and partridge.

Cassoulet in a *cassole* and a *toupin*

This dish needs careful planning and preparation. It is not cheap. The ideal time to choose for it, is when you are able to have a goose: keep the legs to one side, turn them over daily in a mixture of 2 oz. unadulterated salt and a small pinch of saltpetre. Invite your guests and assemble the other ingredients.

Good beans are worth an effort. Most grocers sell dried white haricot beans vaguely described as Foreign. Better quality and a creamier texture are to be found in Soho, where grocers import beans from France, varieties known as Soissons and Arpajon from the market-gardening centres near Paris where they were first developed. Like geese, dried beans are at their best in the autumn; with time they become drier and harder and harder and drier, so beware the grocer with a slow turnover.

The other main requirement is a deep wide earthenware pot in which all the ingredients are finally amalgamated. Correctly a *cassole* or *toupin*, any earthenware or stoneware casserole will do, provided it is deep and wide.

BEANS

1 lb. haricot beans

A good-sized piece of pork or bacon skin, cut into squares

Knuckle of pork

1 lb. salt belly of pork

Large onion stuck with four cloves

1 carrot

4 cloves garlic

Bouquet garni

PORK AND GOOSE, OR MUTTON RAGOÛT

1 lb. boned shoulder of pork

1½–2 lb. preserved goose (*confits d'oie*, page 318), or duck, or either made up to weight with boned loin or shoulder of mutton

3 large onions, chopped

6 cloves of garlic, or according to taste

Bouquet garni, salt and ground black pepper

4 large skinned tomatoes, 3 tablespoons tomato extract

Beef stock

Goose or duck fat, or lard

SAUSAGES

1 lb. Toulouse sausages (page 126), or *saucisses de Campagne* (page 125), or a large 1 lb. boiling sausage of the all-meat *cervelas* type (page 143), or the pork boiling rings sold in delicatessen shops

1 lb. *saucisson* à *l'ail* (page 136)

PLUS

Plenty of white breadcrumbs to form a top crust

Soak the haricot beans overnight. Drain and put them in an earthenware pot with the other ingredients; cover with water. Bring to the boil, and cook in a gentle oven for an hour and a half, or until the beans are tender but not splitting.

Meanwhile prepare the pork and goose ragoût. Put the chopped onions on to melt to a golden hash in a large frying pan (preferably cast iron). Cut the various meats into eating-sized pieces, or joints, and add them to the onions. Turn up the heat a little so that they can brown, without burning. Pour off any surplus fat, then add the tomatoes skinned and chopped into large chunks, and a little stock, about quarter of a pint, to make enough sauce for the meat to continue cooking in. Flavour with concentrated tomato extract and seasonings, push the *bouquet garni* into the middle. Cover the pan, and keep the contents at a gentle bubble until the beans are ready – about half an hour.

Add the large *saucisson à l'ail* and the *cervelas* to the beans, so that they have half an hour's simmering. If you are using sausages, stiffen them in a little goose fat or lard for ten minutes.

When the beans are cooked, drain off and keep the liquid; remove the onion, carrot, *bouquet garni*, and knuckle bone, and slice the salt pork and knuckle meat. Use the bacon skins, or pork skins, to line the deep earthenware pot you intend to use for the final cooking. Put in half the beans, then the pork and goose ragoût, the sliced meats from the bean cooking pot, the small and large sausages, and the rest of the beans. Pour over $\frac{1}{4}$ of a pint of the bean liquid, and finish with a half inch layer of breadcrumbs dotted with pieces of goose fat or lard.

Cook very slowly, about 320°F., Mark 2, for $1\frac{1}{2}$ hours. The crust will turn a beautiful golden colour, and traditionally you should push it down with a spoon three to seven times, so that it can re-form with the aid of another sprinkling of breadcrumbs.

The point of this last cooking is to blend all the delicious flavours together gently, without the meat becoming tasteless and stringy. Everything has, after all, already been cooked. If you find that the *cassoulet* is becoming too dry, add a little more of the bean liquid, but don't overdo this.

The quantities can be varied, the essentials are beans, sausages, pork and goose (or goose and mutton, or a small roasting duck). Pork and beans alone are very good (see below, and recipes for Boston baked beans, etc.), but it is the goose or duck that makes the difference.

This is an ideal dish for a winter's Sunday lunch-party – it pleases everybody from children to grandparents. The cook should be pleased too, because her guests should not be allowed to eat too much beforehand, and can't eat much afterwards, so her labours are cut to a minimum.

Cassoulet au Beurre de Gascogne

Here is a simple family version of *cassoulet*. An excellent filler on a cold day, which can be prepared after breakfast – if you omit the sausage, or use small ones – and left to look after itself until half an hour before lunch.

1 lb. haricot beans
1 lb. piece of *petit salé*, uncooked, or brine-pickled pork belly (page 187)
1 large French sausage of the boiling type, or small smoked sausages
Pieces of fresh pork skin

Beurre de Gascogne

8 cloves of garlic
3 oz. lard, goose, duck or chicken fat
2 tablespoons chopped parsley

Soak the beans overnight.

Next day line the casserole with the fresh pork skin, outside down, and put the piece of pork on top. If you use *petit salé*, make sure that the salt is washed off first. Pack in the beans around and on top. Just cover with water, and put on a close-fitting lid. Give it three hours in a slow oven, Mark 2, 320°F. Add no salt at this stage.

If you use a large sausage, add it one hour before the end of cooking time. If you use small sausages, add them half an hour before. Taste the *cassoulet* whilst you do this and add salt, pepper, etc. Make the *beurre de Gascogne* by blanching the cloves of garlic in salted boiling water for five to ten minutes. Pound them to a paste adding the 3 oz. of fat and finally the parsley.

Just before serving, strain off the liquid from the beans and pork, taste again and adjust the seasoning. Mix in the *beurre de Gascogne* at the last moment before serving.

NOTE: If you have no pure fat, or dripping, use olive oil or butter.

Potée
BASIC METHOD

Potée is basically a cabbage soup, in the way that *cassoulet* is basically beans and pork. But the addition of other vegetables as well as sausages and pickled meat makes it a complete meal in one pot, again like *cassoulet*. In the southwest of France, this thick soup is called *garbure* and contains, inevitably, *confits d'oie* (page 318). Country housewives use what they have to hand in their own kitchens and attic store, so the ingredients vary; but here is a suggested list and basic method:

    1 good crisp savoy cabbage
    3 leeks, sliced
    12 new carrots, or 4 old ones cut in pieces
    6 medium sized potatoes
    4 small onions
    Green beans and peas, if in season
    1 lb. salt belly of pork, or green streaky bacon in a piece (page
        176)
    Toulouse or Country sausages, or dried or smoked sausages
    A piece of garlic sausage, or boiling sausage (*saucisson à l'ail*)
    Large piece of pork skin

Cut the cabbage into quarters, plunge it into boiling water to blanch for 10 minutes. Leave it to drain.

Put the pork or bacon and pork skin in a pot and cover with water. Don't add salt. Simmer for half an hour.

Add the potatoes, carrots and onions, and any other root vegetables you want to use. Simmer for half an hour. Add the garlic sausage, peas and beans – and the smoked or dried sausages if you are using them. Simmer for half an hour.

Meanwhile slice up the blanched cabbage, stiffen the fresh sausages for ten minutes in lard or butter, and add them to the *potée* five minutes before serving. Remove the piece of salt pork, so that it can be sliced too, then returned to the pot. Taste, and correct seasoning.

One French custom is to add thick slices of wholemeal bread just before serving the soup, but it is usually best to leave people to do this for themselves in case they are watching their weight. A more popular tradition is the addition of a glass of red or white wine to the last few spoonsful of soup in one's plate – this is known as a *goudale* in the Béarn, where much *garbure* (see below) is consumed.

Potée: economical recipe

Use a large piece of pork skin, omit the pork, and stuff some of the larger leaves of the cabbage with half breadcrumbs, half minced pork, ham or bacon, bound with egg. Tie each stuffed leaf into a little package with some tape and add with other green vegetables half an hour before the end of the cooking time (see above). Remember that even a very small piece of smoked sausage gives a good flavour.

Garbure

Follow the recipe for *Potée*, above, but add some *confits d'oie* (or the remains of roast goose or duck) and a little goose fat, when you put in the garlic sausage.

In deepest winter, instead of green vegetables, add half a pound of haricot beans, which have been soaked overnight, cooked and *drained* (see *Cassoulet*, page 163). Even a tinned red pepper or two make a difference, or try half a pound of chestnuts, shelled and roasted. All these things need to be added half an hour before the end of cooking time, but don't try them all together – or rather don't use beans and chestnuts together.

Sieve a few pieces of root vegetable, or haricot beans, if you like the liquid itself thickened.

NOTE: Once you have blanched the cabbage, you may find it more convenient to pack all the ingredients into a huge pot, cover them with fresh water and leave in a slow oven for three hours. But if you have the time, the basic method is more popular, most people preferring cabbage to be slightly crisp – *al dente,* like spaghetti or rice – rather than a mush.

See also Frankfurter and *choucroute* soup (page 158), and the chapter following on salt pork for *petit salé*. Recipes for making the sausages required are given earlier in this chapter, on pages 125 and 136.

Salt Pork and Hams

Of all *charcuterie*, the most easily rewarding to make, from an English housewife's point of view, is salt pork and unsmoked ham. Everybody nowadays knows about pâté, but produce a hot, glazed joint of salt pork, or a cold dish of delicate *jambon de Paris*, and you cause a sensation.

This enthusiasm has a long historical tradition. Dumas, in his *Grand Dictionnaire de Cuisine*, tells of the not-so-stupid Emperor Claudius, Robert Graves's Claudius, who walked into the Senate one day crying, 'Pères conscrits, dites-moi, je vous prie, est-il possible de vivre sans petit salé?' To which that noble body promptly replied, 'Oui, seigneur, plutôt mourir que de se passer de lard'. And from then on senators ate large quantities of salt belly of pork and cabbage (*petit salé aux choux*, page 177) to keep alive and flatter Claudius.

Or perhaps they meant it, for the Romans sustained their enthusiasm, beyond their own resources, by imports of ham from Gaul. It was Strabo who early recorded the excellence of French *charcuterie* in his *Geographia*, Book 4, written in the first century A.D.: 'Food they (the Gauls) have in very great quantities, along with milk and flesh of all sorts, but particularly the flesh of hogs, both fresh and salted. . . . And their herds of swine are so very large that they supply an abundance . . . of salt-meat, not only to Rome, but to most parts of Italy as well.' At the same time Romans in Britain were enjoying their favourite salt-pork in another Celtic area: one cremation site of the first century A.D., excavated recently near Winchester, disclosed to the diggers 'a tray set with cutlery for a meal, a pig's trotter and a Bath Chap'. A vivid but anachronistic description; or were pig's jaws cured *à l'Aquae Sulis*, even then? (The tray is on view in Winchester Museum.)

When I buy kilo bags of *sel marin de Bretagne* from our
Trôo grocer, I like to reflect that Strabo's hams were cured
in this same grey salt, evaporated nearly two thousand
years ago from the same cold Atlantic.

Earlier still, northern meat had to be preserved by burial
in pits, or by drying in the wind, because our fitful sun
could not sustain a salt industry on Mediterranean lines,
where, then as now, huge glistening heaps of white salt
dried on low shores, in brilliant light. But with the increased
technological skills and achievements of the Iron Age,
Northern Europeans overcame their salt problem by arti-
ficial means. The method they used has left red fertile

Saloirs, or brine-crocks

mounds, easily to be seen around Maldon, in Essex, where
excellent sea salt is still produced. Shallow earthenware
trays on legs were filled with sea water and fires were lit
beneath. The water boiled away leaving a deposit of salt
to be scraped off the trays. Naturally there was a high
wastage of such friable equipment. New trays were set up
on top of the broken pieces, and reduced in their turn to
coarse red powder, betraying now, by large, slightly raised

circles of red soil in brown ploughed fields, and by lumps of *briquetage* fused with jade-coloured vitrifications of sand, the sites of this ancient, essential industry.

The problem of salt is still with us (though not, in these days of refrigeration, as a means of preserving meat for winter use). The flavour of sea salt is vastly better than the flavour of refined rock salt. In London continental grocers in Soho stock good salt, and so does Elizabeth David, at 46 Bourne Street, S.W.1, but in smaller towns it may only be available in Health Food shops. Polythene bags of sea salt which keep well in a dry place, can be brought back from France. Refined rock salt is all right for brine and dry salting, but the flavour of the ham will not be quite so good; all grocers stock refined rock salt. Be careful not to buy free-running table salt, as chemicals are added, to prevent it forming lumps, which make it unsuitable for curing.

The other things needed are easily come by. A large crock, preferably of stoneware, although a plastic bucket will do. A piece of boiled wood which fits right into the crock, to keep the floating pieces of pork below the surface. Household soda for cleaning the crock. Saltpetre (to be bought from any chemist) to give the meat an appetising pink colour. Sugar to counteract the hardening effects on the meat of salt and saltpetre. A maximum and minimum thermometer is not essential, but it gives accurate information about the fluctuations of surrounding temperature, which can be deceptive.

As you will see from the brine recipe on page 193, white wine can be used, and flavourings of herbs and spices, but from the actual preserving point of view salt is the only absolute necessity. Brine will keep for several weeks, indefinitely if you strain it off from time to time, clean the crock, and boil up the brine again. In bacon factories the brine in huge white-tiled curing baths is eternal, perpetually being drained off and added to, but never thrown away. A vintage blend, with as many strains as a fine brandy. Details of temperature and length of time in byrne are given in the appropriate section on page 185, but any fresh pork recipe is greatly improved in flavour if the joint first spends a clear 12 hours in the crock. This applies even to a delicate truffled loin of pork, or to the famous pork with prunes of Tours.

Smoking is an additional, but not an essential means of preserving meat which has already spent a few days in brine, or else been dried from a hook at a steady temperature of 60°F. (see *saucissons* recipes on pages 139 to 143). It is a difficult process for the amateur to attempt, and obviously a start should be made with small, inexpensive items like sausages. Maintaining a steady smoke is also extremely tricky, sometimes involving sleepless nights on account of visits to the fire. The point of smoking is firstly to remove the moisture from the meat very slowly, like drying, and secondly, unlike drying, to give additional flavour and preservatives. Unless you have an experienced friend to guide you, my advice is to take hams to be smoked at the nearest bacon factory, once you have pickled them in brine. This applies particularly to hams intended to be eaten raw (the most famous French one is Bayonne ham – in fact cured at Orthez, near Bayonne, although many districts have their own, and one should always inquire in the *charcuterie* for a *jambon cru de la région*).

Living in the country, three miles from the nearest butcher, I find that the brine crock has taken many anxieties away. Unexpected visitors can cheerfully be welcomed, and given something more interesting than scrambled eggs. After a little initial planning, this is what I have found best to keep in the *saloir*:

1. A 5 lb. loin of pork (*noisettes,* chops, or a large glazed joint – most useful of all cuts).

2. A boned leg of pork (boiled salt pork, or a *jambon de Paris*), and a hock (*jambonneau*).

3. 2 lb. piece belly of pork (fatter end to be used bit by bit for improving shin of beef and oxtail stews, the leaner end to be simmered in water and served as *petit salé*, page 176).

4. A shifting population of trotters, ears, tails, pieces of

pork skin – anything the butcher throws in for a copper or two.

Replace the joints as you use them, and remember that they can spend up to five weeks in brine – though this is not really a good idea for small pieces. If you can rely on a dry airy temperature which will not rise above 60°F., and will stay fairly steady, you can remove the meat from the brine and wrap it tightly in clean linen or cotton and hang it up to dry. Incidentally, there is an excellent chapter on 'Pig Curing and By-products', pages 241–63 of *Farmhouse Fare*, published for the *Farmers' Weekly* at 6s. Many English methods of curing and recipes for brine are given there. If you have room for extensive meat curing beyond the range of the average household, consult chapters III and IX of *Sausage and Small Goods Production*, by Frank Gerrard, M.Inst.M., M.Inst.R., M.R.S.A., published by Leonard Hill at 20s. Although it is subtitled 'A practical Handbook for all in the Meat Trade', a farmer and his wife for instance, with space and meat supply to hand, could follow some of the methods Mr Gerrard describes. I would also recommend this book to anyone who is really concerned about the meat products on sale to the public. Apart from the pleasure of reading practical and interesting information, there's the side bonus of discovering what care is taken by manufacturers in achieving their twin targets of perfect hygiene and perfect nonentity. No wonder most sausages on sale in this country are not worth buying. Mr Gerrard also gives this explanation of the different effects of dry-salt curing and brine-curing: 'When a piece of meat is placed in a strong solution of salt the fluids in the meat begin to flow out and mix with the salt solution. Meanwhile the salt has begun to penetrate the meat and to bring about changes within the meat. These changes slow down the outward flow of fluid from the meat, and finally the flow is reversed. Water as well as salt now flows into the meat from the strong salt solution. The stronger this solution the longer it takes before the reversal of flow takes place. . . .

'If solid salt or solid sugar is used, no action takes place until they have dissolved in the fluid exuding from the meat. Thereafter the changes are similar to those occurring when meat is immersed in strong solutions but occur more slowly, the rate depending upon the speed at which the fluid can exude from the meat.'

If you are not used to salting meat, I suggest you begin with dry salting, and make your experiment with a lean piece of belly of pork or spare ribs.

DRY SALT CURE
(*Salaison à Sec*)

Petit Salé

Flavoured salt (*sel aromatisé*) is the first requirement:
  To every 2½ lb. salt (enough for 12 lb. meat in fact)

  1 oz. saltpetre
  1 oz. granulated sugar
  1 teaspoon peppercorns
  1 oz. juniper berries
  4 bay leaves, crushed
  Thyme leaves from two sprigs, crushed
  4 cloves

Mix it all well together. Put about ¾ lb. in the bottom of a stoneware pot.

Take the piece of belly of pork and rub a good handful of salt firmly into the skin side. Turn it over and rub some more into the flesh side, but not so vigorously. Lay it on the layer of salt, flesh side down, skin side up, and pack the rest of the salt round the sides and over the top. Put a piece of boiled wood on top (or a scrupulously clean plate) and a light weight.

Leave in a cool, dark place for at least 4 days per inch thickness of meat. You can leave the *petit salé*, on the other hand, in salt for much longer – one handbook recommends two months. You will find that the meat juices turn the salt to brine.

Cook the *petit salé* in plenty of plain water, bringing it slowly to the boil, and timing it from then. As belly of pork is never very thick, an hour is the maximum time required; 40 minutes is usually enough. Taste the water, and pour it away after five minutes simmering, if it is too salty. Alternatively, if the meat has been salting for several weeks, soak in tepid water for 2 hours before you start cooking.

Whichever you do, saltiness is easy to remedy, so don't panic. Serve hot with mashed potato, or arranged in slices on top of *choucroute* (page 158). Cold, the way the *charcutier* sells it, it makes a delicious meal with salad.

Petit salé is an excellent accompaniment, in the English style, to roast chicken or turkey. It is often an ingredient of *cassoulet* and cabbage soups and stews, *potée* for instance, on page 168.

Petit Salé aux Choux

Here is the good Roman dish, so approved of by the Emperor Claudius.

Choose a crisp, savoy cabbage, cut it in quarters and remove the hard stem part. Whilst the *petit salé* is simmering away, plunge the cabbage into another pan of fast boiling water, and leave it there for ten minutes. Drain it well. Pour away the blanching water and remove enough liquid from the *petit salé* pan to give a $\frac{1}{4}$ inch depth in the cabbage pan. Twenty minutes before the *petit salé* is ready, bring this liquid to the boil and put in the cabbage to cook quickly, with a knob of butter as well.

Cut the *petit salé* in slices and serve on top of the cabbage, which should still be slightly crisp and not a mush.

NOTE: Many recipes tell you to cook the cabbage in with the *petit salé*, but the above method gives a much pleasanter result.

Petit Salé aux Pois Secs

Wintry *petit salé* is delicious with a purée of dried peas, which you should have soaked overnight and cooked in with the meat. When they are done, remove them from the liquid and sieve. Reheat in a separate dish with a good knob of butter, and a little meat jelly if you have some, or a spoonful or two of the *petit salé* liquid.

Serve, too, with purées of other dried vegetables, *aux lentilles*, for instance, or *aux haricots blancs*.

It is a good idea to soak the *petit salé* beforehand, and then cook with just enough liquid to cover it and the dried vegetables. This gives you a thick soup, like the *potées* and *garbures* on pages 168 and 169, in which *petit salé* can also be used.

Petit Salé aux Petits Pois

Serve the *petit salé* on a purée of green peas, which can be old ones, if they are cooked in the French style:

Cook one large chopped onion in 2 tablespoons of butter until it is golden, but not brown. Add the heart of a lettuce, $\frac{1}{2}$ teaspoon of salt, $\frac{1}{4}$ of a pint of boiling water and a dessertspoon of sugar. When it is all boiling away together, pour in 2 or 3 lb. of peas shelled. (*If your peas are tender, new ones, omit the water.*) Cover and cook gently. Drain and put through a sieve, correcting the seasoning if necessary.

Serve the *petit salé*, sliced, on top.

Petits Pois au Lard

This is a delicious way of using up, or stretching, a smallish piece of *petit salé* (which is, in effect, a mild green bacon or *lard*).

Soak the *petit salé* in tepid water for several hours, if it has been in salt longer than three or four days. Drain and dry it, then cut into small dice. Melt some butter in a large thick pan and gently fry the dice until they are a golden colour. Remove them whilst you make a *roux* with a tablespoon of flour. Pour in half a pint of stock, stirring all the time to avoid lumps. Cook for two minutes, then put back the *petit salé*, and add 2 or 3 lb. of peas, shelled, a chopped onion and a *bouquet garni*. If your peas are on the hard side, and flavourless, add sugar. Bring the pan back to the boil and after five minutes gentle simmering, taste to correct the seasoning. Add plenty of freshly ground black pepper with it and some chopped sage leaves. Simmer until cooked.

Pommes de Terre au Lard

Follow the above recipe, only use large potato dice instead of peas. A good glass of wine improves this dish. Naturally you omit the sugar.

Petit Salé aux Poireaux

Cook the *petit salé* (page 176).

Meanwhile prepare a leek purée. Slice the leeks and wash them well. Shake them free of surplus water and put them in a pan with a large knob of butter and a pinch of salt. Put the lid on, and set over a low heat until the butter has melted and a fair amount of water has exuded from the leek slices. Then cook as quickly as you can, and either sieve or purée in an electric blender. Add salt, black pepper, more butter, cream, a dash of sugar, as you think fit. Grated or cream cheese are good additions.

Serve the *petit salé*, sliced, on top of the purée.

Petit Salé aux Pommes

Cook the *petit salé* in the usual way (see recipe, page 176), and serve hot on a dish of apple rings fried in butter, or on a purée of apples.

Petit Salé aux Champignons

Serve the *petit salé*, sliced, on a bed of potato purée, flavoured with nutmeg, and surrounded by sautéed mushrooms. Sprinkle with parsley before setting on the table.

Petit Salé aux Marrons

Serve *petit salé* with a purée of chestnuts, or with brussels sprouts and chestnuts cooked together.

Nick the chestnuts, put them on a baking tray in a hot oven for eight minutes. Remove a few at a time and shell them. Simmer them in stock until they are soft and purée them, or else mix them with cooked brussels sprouts. Potatoes are unnecessary.

Hochepot

Like *cassoulet* or the thick *potées* and *garbures, hochepot* is one of those delicious all-inclusive dishes in which pork makes a telling appearance. Our Lancashire Hot Pot is reduced to solo mutton, and the last thing one needs to do to it is to shake (*hocher*) the pot. In Northern France the liquid is served as a soup, and the meat afterwards, like the more widely known *pot-au-feu*.

MEAT

1½ lb. boned ribs of beef
½ lb. mutton, best end of neck chops (weighed without bones)
½ lb. veal, scrag end of middle neck (weighed without bones)
½ lb. piece of *petit salé*
2 pig's ears
Some all-pork country sausages, or pork sausages (pages 115 and 125)

VEGETABLES

The crisp heart of a savoy cabbage, blanched for 10 minutes in boiling water
2 or 3 leeks tied together with
3 sticks of celery
2 or 3 small white turnips, cut up
½ lb. small onions
½ lb. carrots, sliced
1 large parsnip (½ lb.), cut up
Potatoes, small new ones are the best

SEASONINGS

Juniper berries (about 10)

4 cloves
Pepper and salt, and a *bouquet garni*

You will also need a large, deep casserole, filled with 4 or 5 pints of water.

Put the beef into the cold water, bring it quickly to the boil and skim. Keep it bubbling away whilst you brown the rest of the meat in some lard, except for the *petit salé*, which must be blanched in boiling water for ten minutes – this could be done with the cabbage.

Keep skimming the big pot, and when the various other meats are browned or blanched, add them to it with the seasonings and the vegetables – except the potatoes.

Bring the pot to the boil again, and reduce the heat so that a simmer is maintained. Cover the pot and leave for ¾ of an hour. If you have potatoes and sausages, add them a quarter of an hour before the end – in other words, after the pot has simmered for half an hour. If you do not have new potatoes, cut old ones fairly small.

This soup tends to be fatty, so skim off as much as you can. I usually pour off the liquid into a bowl and let it settle, so that the fat has a chance to rise. Reheat when you have dealt with it, and put some slices of bread in the bottom of the soup tureen.

Whilst the soup is reheating, slice up the meat into nice pieces and arrange on a serving dish with the vegetables, which should have been well drained and (in the case of leeks and celery) cut up. Keep warm in the oven whilst the soup is being drunk, then serve sprinkled with chopped parsley, on very hot plates.

Quiche Lorraine

Whether you prepare *petit salé* by dry salting or brine cure, you can slice and use it for *quiches* instead of commercial bacon.

Shortcrust pastry (4 oz. flour, 2½ oz. butter and lard, 2 teaspoons icing sugar, pinch salt, water)

4–6 oz. *petit salé*, washed, sliced and cut into small pieces
4 egg yolks (or 2 eggs)
½ pint cream (double or single)
Grated nutmeg or mace
Freshly ground black pepper, salt

Those shallow, fluted French tins are the best to use for
quiches. They have a removable base that can be pushed
gently up to ease out the tart when it is cooked. Grease
lightly and line with shortcrust pastry. Everybody has their
own ideas on avoiding a soggy base – I usually brush the
whole pastry lining with white of egg.

Next make the filling. First prepare the *petit salé* in one of
two ways – either blanch it for five minutes in simmering
water, or else fry it gently in butter for five minutes.
Distribute it evenly over the pastry.

Beat the egg yolks, cream and seasonings together lightly,
and pour over the *petit salé*.

Bake in a moderate oven for about 40 minutes. Remember
that a *quiche* is really a savoury custard tart; it mustn't cook
too quickly or it will curdle. Like sweet custard tart, it is
best eaten warm, so let it cool down for about twenty
minutes before serving.

This recipe can be adjusted in various ways. For instance,
when you arrange the *petit salé* on the pastry, add 4 oz. of
Gruyère cheese cut into small dice.

Or as well as the Gruyère, add 4 oz. of chopped onions
which have been softened to a golden transparency in some
butter. For economy instead of cream, use half milk and
half cream – or even all milk. It cannot be denied that flavour
and texture both suffer, but the result is quite pleasant.

Or cook in small individual tins or patty pans. More
pastry will be required, and a shorter cooking time, according to the size.

Jambons (Hams) par Salaison à Sec

The mildest and most delicious English and American
hams are cured the dry salt way at first, even if some of

them later spend a period in brine. Although their names refer to various localities (Virginian, Kentucky, Suffolk, York), it is no absolute guarantee that that is where they were cured, but only that they were cured in the Virginian etc. style. This accounts for the puzzling ubiquity of *jambon d'York* all over France. *Jambon de Paris* is another example of this.

The wetter the cure the quicker the salt penetrates the meat, so a dry cure has a gentler, more prolonged effect. With a brine cure sugar is often added to counteract the quick, harsh effects of the salted water, though this was of course out of the question in Cato's day. He described the method used by contemporary Northern Italians – or rather, Romans – about 200 B.C., and it is not very different from the method recommended in modern *charcuterie* handbooks, as well as in Bulletin 127 of the Ministry of Agriculture and Fisheries:

'When you have bought your hams, cut off the hoofs. Take half a peck (10 lb.) of Roman salt, ground fine, for each. Lay salt over the bottom of the tub; then put in a ham, the skin-side looking downwards. Cover it over with salt. Then put another ham on top, taking care that meat does not touch meat. So deal with them all. When you have got them all snug put salt over them, so that no meat is visible, and make the surface level. When they have been in salt five days take them all out and the salt with them. Then put them in again in reverse order so that those which were before on top are now at the bottom. Cover them over and make them snug in the same way as before. After twelve days, at most, take the hams out, rub off all the salt and hang them up in a draught for two days. On the third day wipe them well over with a sponge and rub them with oil. Hang them for two days in the smoke. Then take them down, rub them well with a mixture of oil and vinegar and hang them up in the meat larder.'

Jambon de Campagne

Use flavoured salt (*sel aromatisé*), which should be prepared beforehand:

    2 lb. salt
    3 oz. saltpetre
    6 oz. sugar
    1½ oz. peppercorns
    1½ oz. *quatre-épices* (or mixed spices)
    Level tablespoon cloves
    Level tablespoon juniper berries
    20 bay leaves
    20 sprigs of thyme

Mix it all together.

Prepare the ham from a newly-killed pig by removing the thigh bone (leave the knuckle bone, so that you can hang the ham up), and beating it with a wooden mallet so that it exudes any remaining blood and juice. Tie a strong, clean piece of cord round the knuckle bone and hang the ham up in a dark airy place, with a plate beneath to catch any further liquid which drips out. Leave it for three days, but make sure to wipe it with a clean cloth twice a day. Next rub the ham over with the cut side of half a lemon, and then with the flavoured salt. Having cleaned your crock with washing soda and boiling water, and then rinsed it with fresh boiling water, put it to drain and dry in a warm place.

Put a layer of the salt in the bottom, then your ham, skin side down, and pack the rest of the salt round and over it. Make sure that there is some salt in the ham where the thigh bone was; salt should also be forced down the knuckle bone as much as possible. Lay a boiled piece of wood on top and a weight on that, to keep the pork entirely submerged in the brine. Leave the crock in a cool (38°–45°F.), dry place for 10 to 15 days according to the temperature and humidity of the weather.

If the weather should still be on your side – or you can provide artificially a steady drying temperature between

50° and 60°F. – you can wash the ham with a clean nail-brush and tepid water and hang it up for 10 days.

If you are dubious about these conditions – and have no intention of keeping the ham for any length of time anyway – you can proceed straight to the cooking.

If you have embarked on the drying process with confidence, you can either cook the ham after the ten days, or go on further and smoke it (see page 194). Stored in a close-fitting linen or cotton bag, and hung in a cool dark place, or submerged in a box of cooled wood-ash, these hams will keep for months before you need cook or eat them raw.

Cooking instructions for all hams and salted pork, apart from *petit salé,* are given from page 202 on.

BRINE-CURES
(Salaison par Saumure)

I can recommend this method as the easiest and most successful of all, from the family cook's point of view. Small joints can be used, and turned into mild, delicate hams and picnic hams without any of the anxieties involved in smoking or dry salting. Even if your *jambonneaux* don't have quite the beautiful conical, pear-shaped form of the *charcutier's,* they will taste quite as good and be a lot cheaper. Boned and rolled shoulder or blade bone, loin and leg of pork can be turned into excellent *jambons de Paris.*

In fact, of all the recipes in this book, those in this section are the ones I would most recommend.

Saumure Anglaise pour la Fabrication du Jambon d'York

This English brine produces a good *jambon blanc* (white ham – another name for *jambon de Paris*). A joint of pork left in it for two or three days is greatly improved – recipes on page 187. This is the best one to keep in an all-purpose brine crock.

    5 pints of soft or rain water
    ¾ lb. sea salt
    ¾ lb. granulated or brown sugar
    2 oz. saltpetre

Put all these into a large pan and bring very slowly to the
boil, giving them an occasional stir.

Meanwhile cut a small square of clean cotton, linen or
muslin, large enough to hold:

    1 level teaspoon juniper berries
    A small piece of nutmeg (ungrated, a good way of using up the
        last fragments of a nutmeg)
    1 bay leaf
    3 sprigs of thyme
    1 level teaspoon peppercorns
    4 cloves

Tie up the cloth, so that nothing falls out.

Clean the crock with soda and boiling water. Rinse
thoroughly with boiling water, and dry with a clean cloth.

By now the pan of brine should be boiling away. Skim
off the murky froth, and take the pan away from the heat.
Put in the little bag of spices and herbs and leave to get
quite cold in the pan. Pour the brine through a cloth-lined
strainer into the crock and put the meat in.

The cooling down takes much longer than you might
suppose. You can hurry it up a little by pouring the boiling
brine straight into the crock through a cloth-lined strainer,
and adding the bag of seasonings then. It should be
removed before adding the meat to the quite cold brine.

Put a board on the top, to keep the meat below the surface, and weights (I use a reddish lump of igneous rock; for
this purpose stones must not be porous or crumbly).

After three days stir the contents of the crock with a
boiled wooden spoon or copper stick. Remove joints required for immediate use as boiled, salt pork (recipe given
below), or *fromage de tête* (page 239).

After six days, you can remove some of the thinner pieces
– belly of pork, for instance, to make *petit salé* (recipes,

page 176), or a boned loin to make *jambon blancs*; small hocks, too, for *jambonneaux*.

After seven days, leg and shoulder of pork should be ready for *jambon blancs,* for immediate use.

Reinforce the brine if you want to cure leg and shoulder for long-keeping hams, with a pint and three-quarters of water, boiled up with 7 oz. of salt, and 3 oz. of juniper berries added whilst the brine cools. Wait till it is quite cold before adding to the crock.

NOTE: Every time you remove a joint from the brine crock, you remove salt as well. This doesn't matter with a couple of trotters, but with a really large joint the curing power of the brine may be seriously weakened. A concentrated solution of salt and water can be added. This is what many professional meat curers do when their brineometers indicate the necessity. For most of us, preparing food in the uncertain hygiene of a family kitchen, it is prudent to remove the other joints as well as the large one. They can be kept in a cool dry place for a few hours, until a new lot of brine has been prepared and the crock has been cleaned with boiling soda water and rinsed with boiling water.

Salt Pork, using Saumure Anglaise

All joints of pork can be salted, from the *parties nobles* (legs and loin), to cheaper joints such as belly of pork, hand and blade, trotters, tail, ears and head. After 12 hours in brine, joints can still be roasted; but if they've been pickled for several days, they should be simmered in a *court bouillon,* for about 30 minutes to the pound, then skinned, glazed and put to bake in a moderate oven for a further 20 minutes.

I think there is no better way of cooking pork; the result is tender, full of flavour, and particularly delicious cold.

The two finest pork recipes of all *enchaud de porc* (boned, truffled loin of pork) and *noisettes de porc aux pruneaux de Tours* (pork *noisettes* with prunes), are improved if the meat spends 12 hours in a *saumure anglaise* first (recipes, pages 226 and 227).

BASIC METHOD

Put the joint of pork in brine, boned or not as you please.
Leave it for a minimum of 3 days or a maximum of 30.

When cooking time comes, weigh the joint and tie it into
shape if it has been boned. Place it in a large pan, cover with
cold water and bring slowly to the boil. Simmer for 10
minutes and taste the liquid – if it is unpleasantly salty,
throw it away and start again. If it is all right, add 2 carrots
cut up, an onion or two stuck with three cloves each,
peppercorns, and a *bouquet garni*. Allow 30 minutes to the
pound cooking time, taken from the start of simmering.

The next and final operation is glazing. Mix up some
French mustard, brown sugar and orange juice (or wine or
cider or hard liquor) to a thick but smearable paste. Skin
the joint, place it on an ovenproof dish and cover with the
glaze: this is the point for imagination, though I cannot
recommend going as far as some Americans do in mixing
honey and cherry juice together. Bake in a moderate oven
for 20 to 30 minutes. Watch it to see the edges of the fat
don't burn, and baste occasionally.

A sauce can be made from the glazing juices; boil down
a little of the cooking liquid, add it to the pan juices with
some cream or wine, taste frequently and season.

Serve with plainly boiled potatoes, tossed in butter and
chopped parsley or sage, followed by a green salad.

There are many ways of varying this recipe. You can, for
instance, omit the glazing, serve with a purée of dried peas
(pease pudding, page 177), lentils, or haricot beans.

You can omit the glazing, and serve *à l'anglaise* with
buttered young broad beans and a well-made parsley sauce
(page 60). Or else leave the joint to cool in the simmering
liquid, skin and press when cold. Toast some white breadcrumbs and roll the salt pork in them whilst they are still
warm. A pleasant half-way stage between cold pork and
ham. Don't use yellow commercially packaged crumbs.

Jambon de Reims en Croûte

An excellent way of using cold, pressed salt pork, given by Curnonsky.

Cut ¼ inch thick slices, and make (or buy) a large quantity of puff pastry. Roll the pastry out and cut two rectangles for each slice of pork. Brush the edges of one rectangle with beaten egg, score a square lid on the other, and sandwich a slice of meat in between, pressing the edges together to close them. Brush the scored top with beaten egg, and lay on a baking sheet. Complete the other slices of pork *en croûte*, and bake in a hot oven for 20 minutes until the pastry is golden and well risen.

Carefully lift off the scored lids, and pour in some of the delicious port wine sauce given on page 62, serve the rest separately. Be sure that everything is very hot, sauce, plates and pork *en croûte*.

Many of the ham recipes given later in this chapter can be adapted for salt pork, so can some of the recipes in the chapter on fresh pork.

UNSMOKED HAMS USING ENGLISH BRINE

Jambon de Paris, or *Jambon Blanc*

A leg of pork, about 5 lb.
Court-bouillon including:
2 carrots, sliced
2 onions, each stuck with three cloves
Bouquet garni
Salt, pepper, *quatre-épices*
Odd scraps of pig's skin, bones, a pig's trotter.

Bone the leg and leave it in brine at least ten days, at most thirty. Assemble the ingredients for a *court-bouillon*, but don't put them into the cooking pot.

Roll the leg of pork into as even a shape as possible and tie it at frequent intervals to keep it tidy. Wrap it firmly in a cloth, and tie again. Weigh it.

Put the bundle into a large pan, cover generously with cold water and bring slowly to the boil. Simmer for ten minutes, and taste the water. If it is very salty indeed, throw it away and start again. When you are happy on this score add the ingredients for the *court-bouillon*.

For small hams of this type, 20 minutes per pound, plus 20 minutes, is quite time enough. Reckon from the start of simmering.

Let the ham cool in its liquid, then leave it – still wrapped up – overnight under a weight.

A fine piece of boned loin makes a good *jambon de Paris*.

Jambon à l'Américaine

Smithfield hams come from a small village in Virginia, and have nothing to do with Smithfield Market in London. They are famous for their mild, sweet cure. This is the kind of ham to serve with pickled peaches (page 60), or spiced apples (page 46), or pineapple, and here is a simplified method:

A leg of pork weighing 5 lb. or over, boned
1 lb. white sea salt (Tidman's, or Maldon salt, not *gros sel*)
6 oz. saltpetre
½ lb. granulated sugar
English brine (page 185)

Mix together the salt, sugar and saltpetre, and rub the boned leg with it. Pay particular attention to the part of the leg which is not covered by the skin. Leave the meat in the salt.

Next day do the same thing all over again, and the two days following. Four days of dry cure in all.

Scrape off any salt that is still clinging, and put the leg into English brine for six or seven days. String it firmly into a neat tubular shape.

If you have a good drying place (cool, airy, the temperature between 50° and 60°F., without violent fluctuations, no direct sunlight), squeeze the ham of as much moisture as possible and hang it up, in a boiled string bag, for twenty days.

If you can't be sure of drying the ham properly, let it hang for several days only.

Cook like a *jambon de Paris*, page 187.

(This ham can be smoked, but only to give it a light golden colour.)

Jambon d'York

> Leg of pork, at least 5 lb., not boned
> 1 lb. white sea salt
> 7 oz. granulated sugar
> 2 oz. saltpetre
> English brine

Mix salt, sugar and saltpetre together and rub the leg of pork well with it, push the mixture down the bone as far as possible. Leave the meat in the salt overnight, then rub it all over again.

Scrape off surplus salt, when the ham has been in the mixture a total of 24 hours, and put it into a crock of English brine for a fortnight.

At the end of this time, remove it from the brine, squeeze out as much moisture as possible with the aid of a clean board and hang the leg up to dry in an airy place (temperature between 50° and 60°F.) for several days.

(This ham can be smoked after drying, over oak, or beech chips, or over branches of juniper and rosemary.)

Cook in the same way as *jambon de Paris*, page 187.

Jambonneau (Picnic Ham)

This pretty little rounded cone, nicely breadcrumbed, with a stalk of white bone sticking out, is one of the most charming sights in the *charcuterie*. Here's a way of making one:

Buy a forehock and salt it in an English brine (page 185) for 8 days.

Jambonneaux

Put it into a large pan with a *bouquet garni,* a large onion stuck with five cloves, 2 medium carrots sliced, and a level teaspoon of saltpetre (to give it an extra rosy colour). Cover with water. Bring to the boil and simmer very gently for two hours.

Let it cool in the cooking liquid for one hour.

Remove it onto a large dish, skin and pat it into the best shape you can manage. Push down the meat at the point of the cone to expose a small piece of bone – you should aim at a large pear shape – and trim off any uneven bits.

Toast plenty of white breadcrumbs on a baking tray in the oven, and whilst they are still warm roll the *jambonneau* firmly over them until it is completely covered.

Leave overnight, and eat within two days – this is not a keeping ham.

Épaule Roulée (*Rolled Shoulder Ham*)

Buy a whole hand of pork and bone it. Use bits of meat from the fleshier part to pad out the thinner part and roll the joint up, after sprinkling it with pepper and spices. Tie firmly and leave in brine twelve days.

Hang up to dry in a cool, airy place (60°F.), away from direct sunlight or humidity. It will be ready after four days.

(This ham can be smoked after drying.)

This is an especially good ham for *Jambon de Reims en Croûte,* page 189.

Saumure Italienne

Alcohol makes an excellent preservative, so it is not sur-
prising to find it used for curing pork, along with the
processes of salting, drying and smoking. In Scotland, beer
is used to make a rich sweet brine (page 194); and at the
other end of Europe, the Italians use their plentiful dry
white wine, particularly in the Northern plain around
Modena. There the hams are cut squat and thick, and spend
a month to five weeks in a brine of this type:

    2½ pints of soft water, or rain water
    2 oz. saltpetre
    2 lb. white sea salt
    1 oz. bicarbonate of soda
    2½ pints dry white wine
    1 oz. whole spices

Put the first four ingredients into a large pan and bring to
the boil, giving an occasional stir As it bubbles, add the
wine and spices, and take off the heat immediately, so that
the brine does not boil again, once the wine has been added.
Leave it to get quite cold, then strain through a muslin, or
piece of white sheeting, into the scrupulously clean crock.

A rolled shoulder of pork, prepared in the same way as for
the previous recipe, is a good joint to cure in this brine.
Give it a fortnight (10–12 days, if the weather is hot) in the
brine, then hang from a hook in a cool, airy place, where
the temperature is between 50° and 60°F., for four to six
days. Cook in the usual way – see *Jambon de Paris,* page 187,
and serve with a white wine sauce, page 63.

A leg of pork would give you a Modena type ham; four
weeks in brine, four days to dry, then store in olive (or
pure vegetable) oil – not unlike a Mediterranean *confit de
porc,* substituting the local form of fat for lard.

(Both shoulder and leg can alternatively be smoked,

rather than preserved in oil, for eating raw. Again I would repeat my warning not to rely on the safety of home smoking unless you can do it under the care of an expert.)

Saumure Écossaise

> 2 pints of good strong beer
> 1 lb. sea salt
> ½ lb. rock salt (*gros sel*), or block salt
> A small piece of salprunella, crushed, or 1 level teaspoon saltpetre
> ½ lb. soft, dark brown sugar
> Teaspoon freshly ground black pepper
> Teaspoon freshly ground allspice

Bring all these ingredients to the boil in a large pan and let them cool overnight. Strain carefully.

Rub the ham with 2 oz. dark brown sugar and 1 oz. saltpetre, and leave it overnight.

Next day rub the ham over again with the 2 oz. sugar and 1 oz. saltpetre, put it into a deep dish and pour the beer brine over it. Leave to cure for a month, but every day turn the ham over and rub the brine well in, particularly down the bone.

(This farmhouse cure was intended for hams which would be spending some time up the big kitchen chimney being smoked – but without this, you will get a delicious result.)

SMOKED HAM
(*Jambon Fumé*)

Smoking involves three major problems – space, advanced standards of hygiene, and expertise. Smoking, that is to say, for preservation over a fair period of time. A smokey flavour can be induced by small apparatus of the Abu Smoking Box type (available at Habitat Ltd, 77 Fulham Rd, London S.W.3); but this is only suitable for small objects like sausages, in any case.

From an English point of view, the main purpose of smoking hams would be to produce a *jambon cru* of the Bayonne type, which is either not widely available in this country, or very expensive. The best solution for most people would be to make arrangements with the nearest bacon factory for smoking, and then get down to the actual pickling process at home.

If, however, you want to experiment with smoking, order a copy of Bulletin 127 of the Ministry of Agriculture and Fisheries, *Home Curing of Bacon and Hams,* from your local public library. It is out of print, so you will not be able to buy it. See also pages 35–8 of *Sausage and Small Goods Production,* by Frank Gerrard. Less easily obtainable are French handbooks on *charcuterie*, which deal more fully with smoking on the farmhouse scale, as this is still widely carried on in country districts. The most useful, I find, is *La Charcuterie à la Campagne,* by Henriette Babet-Charton, published by La Maison Rustique, 26 rue Jacob, Paris VIe.

She suggests three ways of smoking, firstly by hanging the pieces above the mouth of the bread oven, secondly by suspending them from an iron bar placed high up across a wide farmhouse chimney, and thirdly by building a special smoke box which can be fixed against the chimney breast when required: the illustrations give an idea of the last two methods.

Many French houses still have a bread oven in the large fireplace, like English farms. The idea is to hang the joints and sausages, once cured, above the opening so that the smoke from the fire inside the oven billows up and around them in a gentle steady waft. This system ensures that the temperature of the smoke never rises above 90°F., at which point the fat begins to melt, and the hams are spoilt. By burning green branches you ensure plenty of smoke – for extra flavour burn juniper, pine, sage, bay, and heather. In the past Breton hams were smoked in fires of seaweed. Beat the fire down to keep it smouldering, not burning in flames. The first day, smoke the hams for half an hour, then take them down and rub them whilst they are still warm with pepper, spices, thyme, crushed bay leaves, which will cling to the softened fat. Leave them to cool and dry for 48 hours. Then smoke them for one hour. Leave them again for 48 hours, and smoke again for one hour. This should be enough for a light flavour.

If you have a wide old-fashioned chimney, which you are not using to cook in as many French farmers' wives do, you can either stretch wire between two hooks high up, or else make use of a permanently fixed iron bar. The fire will be

French farmhouse meat smoking

more subject to draughts caused by household comings and goings, and will therefore need more attention. The best plan is to confine the smoking to a couple of hours every day, over a longish period, when you can be sure of attending to the fire without too many interruptions. In the bacon factory, a series of smoking rooms are supplied from a furn-ace room for so long each day, and the whole business is carefully controlled; but don't be discouraged, after all factory curing is a newcomer against the long history of smoked meat. Allow at least three weeks for fireplace smoking.

If you are handy, the best method of all is to fit up a fireplace with a smoking box, fitted onto the wall above the fire. The first requirement is a sheet of metal across the whole chimney, with a piece of bent piping going through it and through the wall up into the smoking box. Another piece of bent piping goes out of the top of the box and back into the chimney. Leave the meat in the box for eight days, and smoke for two hours every day.

Weight loss is a good indication of whether a ham is properly smoked. It should lose about a quarter, which means that an 8 lb. ham will end up at 6 lb. more or less. Then there is the strong smokey aroma, and the beautiful deep golden brown colour that we all know from Christmas hams and sides of bacon.

The next problem is storage. French country hams and sausages are kept in deep boxes of wood ash, prunings from the vineyard perhaps, or the ashes of a beech. Lay a sifted layer in the bottom of the box, arrange hams and sausages wrapped tightly in strong clean canvas or thick cotton, then sift more ashes over the top. You can repeat the process until everything is tidily layered away. Naturally the box must be kept in a clean dry place, preferably raised up off the floor.

Looking romantically back into the mists of agriculture, most people see the farmer's kitchen decorated with head-banging hams, suspended from heavy iron hooks at the far end of the room, away from the heat of the fire, but still dry and contented. And if you have a large kitchen, this is an excellent solution to the storage problem. Although it may be gratifying to glance occasionally at a golden ham, it is really much safer to sew it into a canvas, linen or calico covering, and limewash it three times. But if you can rely on the steady, dry temperature produced, for instance, by an Aga stove, hams can be stored without wrapping. Remember that the temperature should not rise above 60°F., nor go down below 32°F. No sunlight. Have you ever noticed that cheese and ham rooms are always north-facing? Do not rely on a cellar (dark it is true, but often humid), or an attic (dark also, but subject to rapid fluctuations of temperature and stuffiness). An inadequately dried piece of meat soon grows mould, so watch for the slightest sign of moisture.

Another point is this. Home-cured hams are much

stronger and saltier than the mild, sweet cures of commercial ham and bacon, which can be stored in low temperatures, and will in any case not be stored for very long. William Cobbett's provident cottager required his great side of bacon to last for many months; it had to, it was the only major source of protein for the whole family during winter months. Nowadays we can lay on the salt with a lighter hand, but not so lightly as the factory with its rapid cures by injections of brine. Home-cured hams therefore will require long overnight soaking, if they are to be cooked.

But there are, notably, three hams of international reputation that nobody would think of boiling. These are the Parma, Westphalia and Bayonne hams, bought at great expense (like smoked salmon) to be served in thin, thin slices with curls of unsalted butter, *and no bread*, or fresh, ripe figs, or melon. In France, Bayonne ham (cured really at Orthez, about 40 miles away) is more widely on sale in *charcuteries* than Parma or Westphalia hams; and there will often be local *jambons de campagne* too – of coarser, heartier flavour, but much cheaper, and closely approximating to the kind of result you can achieve by home-curing and home or local bacon factory smoking.

Jambon de Campagne Fumé

    1 fine leg of pork
    5¼ pints of water
    2 lb. salt
    1 tablespoon granulated sugar
    1 teaspoon saltpetre
    1 scant teaspoon whole cloves
    2 level teaspoons peppercorns
    4 bay leaves
    3 sprigs of thyme

Bring the water to the boil, and add the salt when it bubbles hard. Draw it off the fire, stirring in the herbs and spices. When the brine is absolutely cold, strain it and whisk in the saltpetre and sugar.

Lay the leg of pork, skin side down, in the stoneware crock and pour the brine over it. (If you are curing two legs, lay them flesh to flesh, not skin to skin.)

After three days take the leg out (using kitchen tongs, not your hands), and press it firmly with a boiled piece of wood. This is necessary to squeeze out any blood which still remains, and would spoil the finished ham. Put the ham back in the brine for another three days, then fortify with some more brine ($\frac{3}{4}$ pint water brought to the boil with $1\frac{1}{2}$ oz. salt, take it off the fire and add $\frac{3}{4}$ oz. crushed juniper berries; let it cool and strain into the brine crock).

Leave the ham another week, before taking it out and drying it well for ten days, on a board, in a cool, airy larder.

Smoke it in the chimney – or take it to the bacon factory.

(If you do not smoke the ham, and still want to keep it for a while, scrape it well when you take it out of the brine crock and dry it off. Then rub all the part uncovered by skin with some brandy or other hard liquor.)

NOTE: Before you start to slice your *jambon de campagne*, and send out invitations to the feast, make sure that it is sweet and wholesome. It should smell good, and when you stick a larding needle or metal knitting needle down the bone, it should come out as clean and fresh as when it went in, with slight overtones of smokey ham.

Filet de Porc Fumé (Smoked Loin of Pork)

4–5 lb. piece of fillet of pork
5 pints water
$1\frac{1}{4}$ lb. salt
2 oz. brown sugar
$1\frac{1}{2}$ oz. saltpetre
Bouquet garni
$\frac{1}{2}$ teaspoon peppercorns

Bring the water, salt, sugar and saltpetre to the boil. Take off the fire, add the *bouquet* and peppercorns, leave to cool.

Put the fillet of pork into a stoneware brine-crock – the tall jars are best for this joint – and strain the cold brine over it. Put a clean board on top, lightly weighted with a clean stone, to keep the meat below the surface. Don't disturb it for eight or nine days.

Hang it up to dry in a cool, airy place, suspended in a boiled string bag, for four days.

Smoke it for 24 to 30 hours.

This ham can be eaten raw, in thin slices, like the more conventional leg hams.

Alternatively you can simmer it for 2½ hours, once boiling point has been reached. Serve it with *choucroute* (page 158), lightly cooked buttered cabbage, or a purée of dried vegetables.

NOTE: This is a good recipe to try if you want to practice your smoking technique. It's a short programme of curing, so you don't build up hope for weeks, only to find that you have a large mouldy flop on your hands.

Jambon de Bayonne

Here is a simplified version of the process, to be attempted after the hay harvest in a dry summer:

1 leg of pork

DRY-SALTING
2 lb. salt
1 scant ounce saltpetre
½ lb. granulated sugar

BRINE
2½ pints red wine
2½ pints soft or rain water
1½ oz. saltpetre
1 lb. white block salt
¾ lb. sea salt
6 sprigs rosemary
¼ pint olive oil

If you have a ham from a newly killed pig, you will have to beat it with a piece of clean wood – one of those old-fashioned butter pats are excellent for this. This brings out a certain amount of blood, and also smooths out the wrinkles in the skin. Thread a piece of strong string through the knuckle so that you can suspend the ham over a dish, in a dry and airy place, for three to five days – according to the temperature. You will find that a pinkish liquid runs out, mop it off twice a day at least.

If you are buying the leg straight from the butcher, tell him what you want it for. You will probably not have to go through the above performance.

The next step is to remove the bone, which is not too difficult provided you have a small, very sharp knife, and plenty of elbow room.

Mix the dry-salting ingredients well together. Don't overlook this stage, as the brine has no sugar in it at all and a certain amount is needed to counteract the hardening effect of the salt and saltpetre. Rub the mixture well into the ham, particularly into the hollow left by the bone and other areas of exposed flesh.

Pat the ham into a nice shape after this vigorous operation and leave it overnight, whilst you make the brine and leave it to cool down.

The brine is made in the usual way, by boiling everything together *except the oil*. After a moment's bubbling, remove the pot from the fire, strain it directly into the clean, empty crock, and pour in the oil. Stir everything round and leave it to get quite cold.

Next day take the ham out of the dry-salt mixture and put it in the brine. Weight with a board and stone.

Leave it for twelve days, making sure that the crock inhabits a steady dry temperature, never exceeding 60°F.

Drain the ham, hang it up for forty-eight hours whilst you go searching for newly dried hay, and suitable wood for the smoking fire.

Wrap the ham up in plenty of hay, holding it in place with string, and put it to smoke until it is deep golden brown.

COOKING HAM AND SALT PORK

Once again I would repeat the warning – with home-cured ham particularly, make absolutely sure that it is still good before you cook it. It should smell unsuspicious and appetizing – push a larding or metal knitting needle right into the middle of the ham, it should come out clean and sweet.

SOAKING

The point of soaking is to remove excess salt, and to restore moisture to the dried-out tissues.

It follows therefore that salt pork and very lightly cured hams (*Jambons de Paris*, page 189) need no soaking.

On the other hand home-cured hams, which have been subjected to a prolonged curing followed by smoking, need to be left in water overnight.

With commercial hams, follow the instructions provided with them. Otherwise make enquiries from the supplier. For mild cures four to six hours soaking may well be enough.

Very large hams need longer than small hams cured in the same way.

But don't worry. You will have a further chance to rectify saltiness in the cooking process.

COOKING UTENSILS

Borrow or buy a ham kettle.

If this is impossible, try to find a pot large enough to hold the ham with *plenty of water*. In the case of a large ham, a washing copper is a good solution. This also enables you to suspend the ham, by a strong clean cord, so that the more quickly cooked knuckle end is out of the water.

COOKING

Weigh the salt pork, or soaked ham. Calculate the cooking time. *Salt pork and smaller hams, up to 4 lb.*, reckon 30 minutes to the pound, plus an extra 30 minutes. But watch the joint – the last 30 minutes may be unnecessary: if so, take the pot to the side of the stove and leave the joint in the liquid to keep hot. Or glaze it in the oven.

Hams of 5 lb. and over, up to 10 lb., 20 minutes per pound, plus 20 minutes.

Hams of 10 lb. and over, the period of time gets progressively less. This diagram from Bulletin 127, Ministry of Agriculture and Fisheries, *Home Curing of Bacon and Hams*, gives you the answer.

Draw a vertical line from the lb. to the diagonal, and a horizontal line from the point where they intersect to the hours' scale. In other words a ham just over 16 lb. needs four hours cooking.

Put the joint or ham into the pot, cover with plenty of cold water and bring slowly to the boil. Count your cooking time from now, and keep the water at a simmer. After 10 minutes or quarter of an hour, taste the water. If it is un-pleasantly salty, throw it away and start again, reckoning the cooking time from the second boiling point, *less* 10 *minutes or quarter of an hour*.

FINISHING — COLD HAM

When the ham is cooked, leave it to cool for an hour or two in the liquid. Then remove it, and take off the skin. Toast plenty of white bread crumbs and press them into the fat of the ham whilst both are still warm.

(If the ham was cooked boneless, let it cool for an hour in the liquid, remove the skin, and press the ham, either with a board and weight, or with a weight into an appropriately-shaped mould. Remove string afterwards, and cloth, if it was cooked in a cloth.)

Leave the ham to set in a cool place for 12 hours. This makes it much easier to carve.

FINISHING — HOT HAM

The simplest and most attractive way to finish a hot ham is to glaze it.

Remove the ham from the cooking liquid half an hour before the end of cooking time. Peel off the skin, and smear the ham with, for instance, a mixture of brown sugar and French mustard, or brown sugar and mustard powder, moistened with a little of the cooking liquor.

Put it in a moderate oven for the rest of the cooking time.

There are endless variations and complications on this theme. Some of them are given later on in this chapter. You can invent more for yourself, remembering that the most successful glazes combine sweetness and spiciness. One attractive finish is achieved by scoring the fat of the ham in a lattice pattern, studding the intersections with cloves, and then smearing the glaze on gently. Be careful not to score right through the fat to the lean. The juices from the glazing can be turned into the sauce, with a little extra liquid from the boiling operation, or cream, or a wine like Madeira, Marsala, port, sherry, etc.

CARVING

The essential requirement is a very sharp knife, preferably one with a long, thin blade.

Remember that there are right and left hams, if your ham has been cooked on the bone. If the ham is boneless and pressed, you will carve it straight down, so right and left are of no consequence. The knuckle must lie towards the carver – to his left for a right hand ham, and to his right for a left hand ham. Cut each slice from alternate sides, as thinly as possible with an even smooth movement of the knife – this prevents a ridgy appearance.

Carving ham

Jambon à l'Anglaise (or *en Chausson*)

Three-quarters cook the ham, leave it to cool for an hour in its own liquid, then peel off the skin.

Meanwhile make a large quantity of short-crust pastry (12 lb. ham needs 3 lb. plain flour, 1½ lb. butter, or butter and lard, mixed with as little very cold water as possible, and salt to season). Roll out the pastry and put the ham, rounded or right side down, in the middle. Gather up the pastry and seal it together.

Grease the baking tray with lard and turn the ham over on to it, so that the sealed side is underneath. Brush with beaten egg and decorate with leaves, flowers, or abstract shapes of pastry. Brush the decorations with beaten egg, and make a small hole at the highest point of the ham – this allows steam to escape during the cooking, and a glass of Madeira or other suitable wine to be poured in at the end.

Bake in a moderately hot oven for three-quarters to one hour. Pour in the small glass of Madeira (up to 3 oz.) and serve. Everything can be eaten – except the bone.

VARIATIONS

Make sauces of increasing luxury and complication (Madeira sauce, port sauce, Périgueux sauce, wine and cream sauces, pages 59–64), and pour a few spoonsful into the steam vent, serving the rest separately.

Line the pastry with a suitable forcemeat – preferably containing truffles; or at least mushrooms, chopped and fried in butter with finely chopped onions, and a final addition of white breadcrumbs. Very homely, but good – make the pastry of flour and water. Don't eat the crust, it's a juice conserver only.

Jambon persillé de Bourgogne

This is the famous and beautiful Eastertide dish of Burgundy. The major requirements are plenty of white wine, the ham, plenty of parsley, and one of those old-fashioned bedroom wash-bowls. I use a leg of pork cured in the York or American style, or a 3 lb. piece of gammon. It goes into a ham kettle with plenty of cold water, which is slowly brought to the boil to draw out excess salt. Pour off the water if it is very salty and start again. When the water is once more at the boil, simmer the ham very gently for three-quarters of an hour.

Remove from the water and cut the meat off the bone in sizeable chunks. Put them into a pan with a large knuckle of veal, chopped into pieces; 2 calf's feet, boned, and tied together; a few sprigs of chervil and tarragon tied together with a bay leaf, 2 sprigs of thyme and 2 sprigs of parsley;

8 peppercorns tied into a little bag. Cover with dry white wine and bring to a gentle boil. Skim off fat as it rises, and leave the ham to cook very thoroughly, as it will need to be mashed and flaked with a fork.

Jambon persillé

However before you do this, attend to the jelly. Pour off the cooking liquid through a strainer lined with a piece of clean cotton sheeting. Taste it to make sure it is not too salty. Add a tablespoon of white wine vinegar, and leave it to set a little.

Meanwhile crush the ham into a bowl.

Before the jelly sets altogether, stir in plenty of chopped parsley – at least four tablespoons, and pour over the ham. Leave to set overnight in a cold place. Turn out the *jambon persillé*, and serve. When it is cut, it will display a beautifully marbled, green and pink appearance. If you like you can keep back some of the parsley jelly, remelt it gently next day and pour over the ham in an even green layer.

Jambon au Madère

Cook the ham in a bouillon for three-quarters of its cooking time – reckon 20 minutes to the pound, plus 20 minutes, from the time it reaches simmering point. See page 203.

Skin the ham and transfer it to a closer-fitting pot. Pour

over ¾ of a pint of Madeira, put on the lid and cook in a moderate oven for 50 minutes or the rest of the cooking time – whichever is the longer.

Transfer the ham again to a shallow dish, sprinkle it with icing sugar, or a brown sugar, spices and French mustard glaze, and put it to melt in a hot oven. See that it doesn't burn but turns to a succulent golden sheen.

Meanwhile deal with the sauce. Taste the braising liquid – add some stock or Madeira, reduce it or leave it alone, according to your judgement. Thicken it by adding a little knob of *beurre manié* (tablespoon flour kneaded into half a tablespoon of butter).

VARIATIONS AND ACCOMPANIMENTS

(i) Use another fortified wine – Marsala, port, sherry, or any heavy wine, instead of Madeira.

(ii) Serve with a cream sauce made by reducing the braising liquid and adding half a pint of double cream. Surround the glazed ham with little piles of vegetables cooked in butter (new carrots, tiny onions, mushrooms, young peas, young green beans). This is *jambon à la crème*.

(iii) Serve *jambon à la crème* with a purée of spinach, or spinach and sorrel, instead of the little piles of vegetables. Get the spinach as dry as possible and flavour the purée with a little sugar, salt, pepper, cheese, cream as you think fit – spinach varies so much that you have to use your discretion. If you do grow sorrel, add a few leaves for their sharp, spring flavour.

(iv) Belgian chicory (*witloof* or *endive de Bruxelles*), blanched for fifteen minutes in boiling water, then braised in butter in the oven, makes a good accompaniment to *jambon au Madère*.

(v) Most popular of all, *jambon au Madère*, or *à la crème*, served with young green peas and new potatoes in the early summer.

Saupiquet de Jambon

Saupiquet – not to be confused with *salpicon*, a dice of vegetables or meat or both, bound with thick sauce – was the name of a medieval sauce made of wine thickened with bread. Nowadays it means a piquant but delicate cream sauce. I find that Elizabeth David's version, *Saupiquet des Amognes (French Provincial Cooking)* is the most successful, with its hint of juniper and bland sharpness.

She recommends it with slices of uncooked ham or gammon, soaked for half an hour, then fried in butter. Or else with slices of cooked ham, arranged on a plate and covered with the sauce, then put to heat through in the oven. I serve it with a whole boiled ham at Christmas time – the time for extravagance.

Whichever version you choose, make sure that the serving dishes, the sauce boat, and the plates are very hot. Cream sauces soon lose their charm on tepid china.

8 oz. beef or veal stock
2 tablespoons butter
2 tablespoons flour
4 shallots
6 tablespoons wine vinegar
3 crushed juniper berries
6 tablespoons white wine
7 oz. double cream (2 pots of 3¾ oz. each)
Extra butter

Chop the shallots almost to a hash; put them with the juniper berries and wine vinegar into a little pan. Boil away the vinegar until the pan is practically dry.

Melt the butter in another pan, make a *roux* with the flour, and cook until it turns pale coffee colour. Pour in the heated stock carefully, stir all the time until the sauce thickens. Add the white wine and the shallots. Simmer gently for half an hour at the side of the stove. If this is impracticable, a double saucepan, or a basin over a pan of just boiling water, works very well. This long gentle cooking contributes everything to the smooth maturing of the sauce.

Near the time of serving, sieve the sauce into a clean pan or basin, add the cream and season. Finish with a small knob of butter and reheat without boiling. Stand the pan in another pan of hot water while you deal finally with the ham.

Jambon au Foin

Hay and ham suggest hay-boxes and folk-dancing, but in fact combine excellently, the hay being used to give the ham a scent of coumarin, the substance (hydroxy cinnamic lactone, to be precise) which occurs in Sweet Vernal Grass and makes new-mown hay so fragrant (it is also found in Tonka beans, from Guiana, with which snuff is perfumed). The French farmer's wife beds the ham in sweet, newly dried hay, covering the ham and hay with water. I follow Eliza Acton's method, wrapping the ham (best for this is tubular stockinette sold in rolls by bicycle shops) and covering with one part white wine and two parts water. The ham is then simmered until cooked. Let the ham cool in the liquor. Serve with unsalted or lightly salted butter and new bread with a good crust; and white wine, or cider.

HOT RECIPES USING COOKED HAM

Saupiquet des Amognes

The best way, and the most delicious, of reheating cooked ham. Lay the slices in an ovenproof dish, pour over the *saupiquet* sauce, page 209. Ten minutes in a gentle oven and it is ready to serve.

Omelette au Jambon

For one person, chop 2 oz. cooked ham into small dice, and fry gently in an 8-inch omelette pan with a little butter. When the ham's well heated through and turning golden, pour on two lightly beaten eggs, seasoned with some pepper and a pinch of salt.

As the eggs cook, draw up the solid parts to one end of the pan, so that the liquid runs down and cooks in its turn. But be careful not to overcook. Omelettes should still be liquid inside, when they are served, though firm on the outside and lightly browned. Sprinkle with chopped parsley, and rush it to table on a very hot plate.

Soufflé au Jambon

½ lb. lean cooked ham
1 oz. butter
1 oz. flour
Generous ¼ pint milk, or single cream
3 egg yolks
3 egg whites
Salt, pepper

Mince the ham twice and pound to a smooth mass in a mortar. Make a very thick white sauce with butter, flour and milk or cream, cooking until it comes away from the side of the pan. Use a wooden spoon for stirring. Add the ham and season well.

If you have an electric blender, mince the ham once or chop it roughly. Put it in the blender goblet, with the thick white sauce and whirl at top speed. Reheat in the pan, but not to boiling point. The egg yolks should now be added, one by one.

Beat the egg whites until they are stiff, fold lightly into the pan mixture with a metal spoon, and pour into a soufflé dish with an oiled greaseproof collar.

Bake in a moderate oven for 25 minutes. Serve immediately – remember to remove the paper collar – to seated guests.

This soufflé can be cooked in small individual soufflé dishes. They will only take about 10 minutes to cook, and the oven should be hotter than for a large soufflé.

Quiche au Jambon

Follow the recipe for *Quiche Lorraine*, page 181, using ham instead of *petit salé*.

It is, in brief, a flan tin lined with short-crust pastry, filled with a layer of chopped ham and half a pint of cream beaten up with 3 eggs, and seasoned. Bake for half an hour to forty minutes in a moderate oven. Serve warm – not hot, and not cold, but warm. Or cook as *petites quiches* in small tins.

Diced Gruyère cheese can also be added with the ham.

Croque-Monsieur

This delightfully named hot sandwich, can be served as an hors d'œuvre.

Choose good bread, milk loaf, *pain de mie* or *pain brioché*. Cut thin slices, butter them, and make them into sandwiches with a layer of Gruyère cheese and a layer of lean ham on top. Cut into elegant triangles, and fry in half butter, half oil, until they are golden brown, on both sides.

VARIATION

Fry slices of bread on one side only, butter the unfried side, lay thick slices of ham on top and cover with a paste made of grated Gruyère cheese, French mustard and thick cream – enough to make the mixture spread. Grill gently until gold and bubbly – serve on very hot plates.

Jambon au Sauce Moutarde, or au Gratin

Arrange the ham in not-too-thin slices on an ovenproof serving dish, and cover with the following sauce:

  2 heaped tablespoons French mustard
  1 heaped tablespoon grated cheese, Gruyère or mild Cheddar
  2–3 tablespoons thick cream

Mix these three ingredients together and add to some rich *Béchamel* sauce, made from 1 oz. each butter and flour, and half pint of milk or ¼ pint milk and ¼ pint cream. Season.

Pour over the ham, top with grated cheese and brown under the grill, or in a hot oven.

More elaborately, you can cook a wineglass of heated white wine into the butter and flour *roux*, when making the *Béchamel* sauce, before adding the milk.

Croquettes de Jambon

Like ham cornets, this dish can be homely or grand, according to inclination and resources. Piled in a pyramid on a very white cloth and silver dish, accompanied by a fine Madeira sauce, they made a popular appearance at nineteenth-century banquets; sprinkled with parsley on an earthenware dish, with a friendly bowl of tomato sauce. they are not out of place in the nursery. Here is a basic recipe, to which you can add Madeira, truffles and so on, or which you can leave alone:

    2 oz butter
    2 oz. flour
    ¾ pint good milk
    ½ lb. ham
    ¼ lb. mushrooms
    2 egg yolks
    Salt, pepper, and mace or nutmeg
    Egg and breadcrumbs to finish

Make a *Béchamel* sauce with the first three ingredients. Do not season it, but leave on the side of the stove (or a low heat) to reduce by half – you should end up with a very thick 8 oz. This operation should not be rushed, nor side-stepped by halving the amount of milk.

Chop the mushrooms and cook them in a little butter. Mince the ham twice and add it to the mushrooms. If you are adding alcohol, do so at this stage.

Add the ham mixture to the *Béchamel* sauce, when it has

reduced to the right amount, and sieve. If you have an electric blender, now is the time to use it.

Reheat to just under boiling point, and add the egg yolks, beating them in well for two or three minutes.

Pour the mixture into a buttered inch-deep dish to cool.

When you want to serve the *croquettes*, cut the mixture into even pieces, roll them lightly in flour; then in egg; then in breadcrumbs; and fry quickly to golden brown in boiling oil. A chip-basket helps.

If you are feeling fanciful, and have nothing better to do, cut the mixture into shapes – crescents, triangles, circles, rings, and so on. Serve with Madeira sauce (page 59), or tomato sauce (page 65).

Timbales de Jambon

For timbales, you need small soufflé dishes, or dariole moulds. Mince half a pound of ham twice – do not use all lean ham, but a normal amount of fat as well. Mix it with 3 oz. of double cream, in the blender, to a smooth consistency. Season with salt, pepper and French mustard.

Butter the moulds and line them with the ham mixture, break an egg into each one and set them in a shallow pan of hot water. Put them into a moderately hot oven until the eggs are cooked but not hard – about 20 minutes.

Sprinkle with a little parsley and serve with triangles of hot, thin toast.

You can turn the timbales out on to circles of fried bread or toast or a bed of spinach purée, and serve with a mornay sauce (page 59) as *timbales florentines*.

Endives au Gratin

Have as many heads of chicory as slices of ham. Blanch the chicory for fifteen minutes in boiling salted water. Drain well, wrap each one in a slice of ham and lay side by side in a buttered gratin dish. Pour over enough mornay sauce (page 59) to cover (try to use a dish which just holds the chicory, as they should not be swamped in liquid), sprinkle with grated cheese and brown in the oven, slowly for twenty minutes and fast for ten.

Jambon Persillé au Gratin

Prepare a stiff well-flavoured potato purée. Do not stint the butter. Stir in plenty of chopped parsley and turn out onto a buttered plate to cool. You will need about 3 oz. of potato purée for each slice of ham, which should be rolled round the potato and laid in a buttered dish close to its neighbour. Pour over mornay (page 59) or cream (page 54) sauce, sprinkle grated cheese (preferably Parmesan) over the top and bake in a moderate oven for three-quarters of an hour. Brown under the grill, or turn the oven up.

This is a simple dish, but not to be despised provided the potato purée and sauce are made with care and discrimination.

Vol-au-Vent (Croustade) au Jambon

Smallish amounts of left-over ham can be attractively stretched with vol-au-vent cases or *croustades*.

Make a *salpicon* of ham, by dicing it and mixing with a little rich *Béchamel* sauce, and chopped fried mushrooms.

This mixture can be as simple as you like, or as luxurious (*Béchamel* sauce made with butter, flour and single cream, or a brown sauce flavoured with Madeira).

Make *either*

One large vol-au-vent case of puff pastry, or several small ones. Roll out the pastry, not too thinly. Cut out a large circle, and mark a smaller one inside that does not go right through the pastry. Brush with beaten egg and bake in a hot oven. Remove the inner circle, which will form a lid, put in the hot ham *salpicon*, lay the lid on top and serve.

Or

Fry some soft bread rolls in deep fat until they are crisp

and golden. Let them cool a little, then scoop out the inside after cutting out a lid. Put them into the oven to reheat and dry. Fill them with the hot *salpicon,* put the lids on top and serve.

Ham and Fruit

The use of pineapple and peaches with ham is American. The French are used to the more subtle combinations of orange, prunes and apple with pork and ham. Their juice, or the alcoholic liquors made from it, can be used in the glaze and the sauce. Lightly fried orange and apple rings, or prunes simmered in white wine make good accompaniments.

See the recipes in the fresh pork chapter, page 219.

RECIPES USING COLD COOKED HAM

Jambon en Cornets

Take some large thin slices of ham and form them into a cone shape – like the improvised bags in old-fashioned grocer's shops. Use cocktail sticks to hold them in shape, or some aspic or Madeira jelly which is on the verge of setting.

Fill the cornets with a *salpicon* of diced vegetables, or vegetables and chicken, bound with mayonnaise. Olives, capers, anchovies, red peppers, can be used for additional spice. Cream cheese, whipped with cream and a little aspic jelly, with walnuts folded in, make the cornets into a more substantial luncheon dish.

Or you can pipe into the cornets, with a forcing bag, some of the mixture kept aside from next day's

Ham Mousse

½ lb. cooked ham, with no fat
6 oz. aspic or Madeira jelly
½ pint thick cream

¼ pint thick white sauce (page 49)
2 egg whites
Salt, cayenne pepper

Mince the ham twice. Whirl it in the electric blender with the white sauce. If you have no blender, pound the ham alone in a mortar.

Put the ham mixture into a bowl, stir in the slightly melted but cool aspic jelly, and then the cream whipped. Season well.

Beat the egg whites until they are very stiff. Add the ham mixture when it is almost set, folding it in carefully with a metal spoon.

Tie a lightly oiled collar of greaseproof paper or silver foil round the soufflé dish, and pile in the mixture lightly. It should come well above the edge of the dish, so that when it is firmly set and the collar removed it has the appearance of a soufflé hot from the oven, and well risen.

Leave in a refrigerator to set, and serve chilled.

NOTE: Chicken, or chicken and tongue, or ham and tongue can be used, instead of all ham.

Ham or Cold Salt Pork, with Swedish Mayonnaise

Cut the meat into slices, arrange on a dish and serve with green salad, boiled new potatoes tossed in butter and chopped parsley, and a bowl of the mayonnaise and apple purée sauce given on page 68.

This is an unusual and always popular sauce to serve with cold ham and pork.

Ham with Orange and Chicory Salad

Arrange some sliced ham on a dish, and serve with the following salad:

3 heads of chicory, sliced
3 large oranges, peeled and sliced
½ large mild onion, sliced
Vinaigrette sauce, page 70

Cut the orange slices in quarters, mix with the chicory, and turn in the dressing. Top with onion rings and a sprinkling of chopped parsley.

Black olives can be added as well.

Fresh Pork Cookery

THE most obvious, visible difference in the French cooking of fresh pork – apart, of course, from the elegant butchery – is the lack of crackling. In the *charcuterie*, the *porc rôti* will be a neat boneless cylinder, pale pink from its night in brine, studded with an occasional clove of garlic, and sold by the succulent slice.

The outer layer of fat and skin will have been used in pâtés, sausages and *crépinettes*. If the *charcutier* is the butcher as well, you will see nicely-cut oblongs of white fat barding the lean roasts of beef. If you want to buy a fillet of beef for roasting, you can also buy fat to cut into larding strips. The skin, *la couenne*, is available too, for additional flavour and texture in beef casseroles. As you can see from the recipe on page 317, crackling is not unknown in France, but it is served quite separately from roast pork.

The finest roasting joint of all is the loin, usually divided into two on account of its length. The leg end is known as the *filet* or *longe*, and the smaller end as the *carré*. When the *filet* is cut into chops it becomes escalopes, or the small round *noisettes*. When the *carré* is cut into chops, it becomes *côtes* and the smaller *côtelettes*.

The leg, together with the loin, are the *parties nobles* of the pig, but the leg is most usually turned into ham. The French for both is *jambon* (though *gigot* is often used for a fresh roasting leg), and the adjective *frais* to designate an uncured leg is often omitted. Be careful of this when using a French cookery book, or an English one derived from French sources. Read the recipe very carefully before visiting the butcher, and decide which is most likely – fresh leg of pork, gammon or cooked ham.

The cheaper joints of pork benefit even more than leg and loin from being salted in brine before they are cooked.

Boned shoulder of pork (*épaule desossée*), for instance, spare ribs (*échine*) and blade bone (*palette*), and the often despised belly of pork (*poitrine*), gain in flavour and tenderness for three days in *saumure anglaise* (page 185). They can then be stewed or braised to advantage, or simmered in water and finally glazed. Try combining belly of pork, salted or not, with shin of beef in the casserole on page 230; the pork supplies a bland smoothness which greatly improves the flavour and texture of the sauce.

The extremities of the pig can also be eaten fresh, but they have been dealt with in a separate chapter, page 239.

ROASTING

Unlike beef or lamb, there is nothing to be gained by undercooking pork. Indeed it is neither desirable nor safe to do so. Pork should be well and gently cooked, whatever the cut and whatever the method of cooking used.

Prepare a joint of pork for roasting by boning, salting, marinading or seasoning. Then weigh it, and reckon 30 minutes cooking time for joints up to and including 4 lb. Add 20 minutes a lb. for each lb. over. Put the joint on a rack in the roasting pan, and set it in a low oven, 325°F., Mark 3. There is no need to add fat or water. Test the joint near the end of the cooking time with a larding or knitting needle. The liquid which oozes out should be colourless. If it is pink the joint is not ready.

Make a sauce from the pan juices after pouring off excess fat, according to taste and recipe.

Longe (*Carré, Gigot*) de Porc Truffée

Truffles are the finest flavouring of all for pork. Even a ¾ oz. tin makes a remarkable difference to a 4 lb. joint. If you want to eat the pork cold, follow the pot-roasted version of this recipe on page 226.

Open the tin of truffles, cut them into small pieces, and

reserve the juice. Bone the joint (which will taste even better after 24 hours in brine, page 185). Make incisions in the fat, and put pieces of truffle in. Save some for the bone cavity. Roll and tie the joint. Cook the joint according to the basic roasting method. Make the sauce by pouring a large glass of white wine into the pan juices – remember to strain off the excess fat first into a separate basin, it will be deliciously truffle-flavoured. When it has thickened a little add the truffle liquid from the tin and cook the sauce very gently, with barely a bubble, for five minutes. Do not obscure the delicate flavour of this dish by hearty accompaniments and garnishes. Some plainly boiled new potatoes, tossed in butter and parsley, are all that is required. Follow with a green salad.

Longe de Porc aux Pistaches

Follow the above recipe, but stud the pork with blanched pistachio nuts.

Longe de Porc Rôtie

Stud the pork with slivers of garlic. Serve plainly garnished with watercress, or with *sauce Robert*, or *sauce piquante*, *sauce diable* or *sauce à la charcutière*.

Longe de Porc à la Normande

Baste and make the sauce with good cider. Serve with unsweetened apple purée made with *reinettes*, Cox's or Blenheim apples.

Or salt the pork and serve with a cream *sauce normande*, page 54.

Longe de Porc Clamart

Roast pork served with the Clamart or St Germain garnish of young green peas and artichoke hearts, finished in butter. One of the best combinations with pork or ham.

Porc Rôti à la Bourgeoise

An hour before the pork is cooked, add small new carrots
and tiny onions to the roasting pan. Turn them over from
time to time so that they glaze. Serve the vegetables round
the meat, garnish with parsley.

If small new potatoes are cooked in the pan as well, you
have pork *à la bonne femme*.

Porc Rôti à la Berrichonne

Shell and simmer 1 lb. chestnuts for 20 minutes, blanch
1 lb. of small onions, and add them with a few rolls of
bacon to the pork three-quarters of an hour before the end
of cooking time.

An attractive way of serving chestnuts with pork or ham,
is to cook them to a purée, flavour with pan juices from the
pork or crumbs of crisply fried bacon, and serve it in small
barquettes or *tartelettes* of short pastry, baked blind.

Porc Rôti aux Herbes

Sage is not often associated with pork in France, but if you
grow it, here is a way of combining it with pork in the
French style (don't use dried sage):

Make incisions in the joint of pork and insert small
sprigs or leaves of sage. Mix a tablespoon of salt, a tablespoon
of thyme, and half a bay leaf crushed, and rub this over the
fat and boned sides of the joint. Leave overnight. Rub the
seasoned salt in again next morning, before tying up the
joint for roasting.

In Provence, plenty of crushed garlic, breadcrumbs and
some olive oil are mixed together into a paste, and this is
spread over the joint three-quarters of an hour before the
end of cooking time. It forms an appetizing golden crust.

Porc Rôti aux Choux Rouges

In Northern France pork is accompanied by red cabbage, *choucroute* and purées of dried vegetables, all cooked separately from the meat, but served round it on the same dish. A sprinkling of green herbs lightens the appearance.

This is a heavy way of serving pork. Like *petit salé aux choux* (page 177), *potée* (page 168), *garbure* (page 169), *hochepot* (page 180) and *cassoulet* (page 163), it is most wisely eaten in cold weather at midday.

Carré de Porc au Fenouil

This recipe was given to me by Madame Champy, the owner of the *Tabac* at Trôo. Fennel grows wild on the cliff there, but it is easily cultivated in English gardens, see page 36.

Rub the pork over with salt and fennel leaves. Put a branch or two of fennel in a dish and leave the joint on it overnight. Next day insert some slivers of garlic into the fat of the pork, and roast in the usual way.

Skim excess fat off the pan juices, and make the sauce by adding white or *rosé* wine to them and reducing. Serve with potatoes sautéed in lard, flavoured with a sprig of fennel, and serve them with a sprinkling of chopped fennel.

Glazed Roast Pork

In the absence of crackling, glazing is the logical extension of basting when applied to roast pork. It involves a combination of spiciness (French mustard, cloves, or ground spices) and sweetness (orange, in juice or marmalade form, redcurrant jelly, brown sugar) which not only mingle their flavours harmoniously with the pork, but also provide it with an irresistible coat of gleaming golden brown. The pan juices are enriched, making a variety of sauces possible beyond the conventional range. The glaze can be the consistency of thick cream, or a virtual paste (*pommade*), which extends its use to grilled chops.

Porc Rôti à l'Orange

Insert some slivers of garlic into a roasting joint of pork, and two or three small sprigs of rosemary. Don't overdo either herb: orange must be the predominating flavour.

Roast the pork as described on page 220, but half an hour before the end of cooking time, skin the joint and glaze it with a mixture of:

    1 tablespoon French mustard
    1 tablespoon, heaped, Oxford-type marmalade
    Juice of one orange
    Dessertspoon brown sugar

Skim excess fat off the pan juices at the end, and make a sauce by adding to them white wine, orange juice and Madeira or Marsala, orange juice and a little Curaçao, so that you have a piquant, not too sweet sauce.

Cut two oranges into thin slices, heat them through carefully in the sauce and serve round the joint of pork. The sauce is finally poured over the joint. The lightest sprinkling of parsley makes an attractive finish.

Porc Rôti aux Pommes

Glaze the pork with a mixture of French mustard, melted redcurrant jelly, and a little brown sugar and ground cloves.

Serve with apple rings, peeled, cored and fried lightly in butter. Or cored eating apples baked in the roasting pan beneath the rack.

NOTE: If you would like a crustier glaze, incorporate breadcrumbs in the mixture.

BRAISING, POT-ROASTING AND STEWING

The first two methods amount to much the same thing in the case of pork, as the meat is moist enough to require very little additional liquid. What moisture there is, is conserved by covering the pot with a tight-fitting lid, which means that it is a good method for cheaper joints of pork. If you tell the butcher that you wish to braise a joint *en casserole,* he will probably give you a piece of *échine* (spare ribs and blade bone joint); or the fillet end of the leg.

Here is a typical way of pot-roasting very popular in small French villages, where not everybody has an oven:

Choose a heavy cast-iron pan, melt some lard in it, or butter and oil, and brown the neatly-tied joint of pork all over, including the two ends. Warm some *eau-de-vie de marc,* brandy (or vodka) in a small pan, set alight to it and pour over the browned pork.

Add a *mirepoix* of carrots and onions, some crushed garlic and a large glass of *rosé* wine – about $\frac{1}{4}$ of a pint. Grind salt and pepper over, put on the lid and turn the heat down low enough to keep the liquid gently bubbling. Allow half an hour to the lb.

Turn the meat over from time to time. Add new potatoes for the last half hour.

Taste the sauce and adjust the flavour and seasoning as you like. Skim off the fat. The French like their *jus* or gravy to be concentrated and well-flavoured – this means that there can't be a vast quantity of it, just a spoonful or two for each person.

Some farmers say that if the pork is accompanied by a hash of onions, sautéed in butter and flamed in brandy, it will keep you sober through a day's hard drinking. Recommended for market-day breakfast.

Use a cast-iron pot which has been enamelled if you can – otherwise the sauce turns a disconcerting blackish colour, due to the wine. It tastes all right, but the appearance may put people off.

Carré (Échine) de Porc en Gelée à la Vendômoise

Follow the method described above, but omit the *mirepoix* and add the bones. Increase the quantity of liquid to one pint, by adding ¾ of a pint of water or stock. Let the pork cool in the liquid, scrape off the fat and keep it for frying potatoes, or bread on another occasion, and serve the pork sliced, surrounded by chopped jelly.

The pork can be seasoned in many of the ways suggested earlier in this chapter. I think of it stuffed with long purplish black *Trompettes des Morts* fungi from the woods near Trôo, and served at the midday *vendange* picnic.

Enchaud de Porc à la Perigourdine

This south-western version of our Vendômois pork is one of the two best recipes for pork that I know. The other is *noisettes de porc aux pruneaux de Tours*, on page 227.

Buy a really good piece of loin of pork about 5 lb. in weight. Ask the butcher to bone it for you and remove the skin.

Leave the joint in brine, *Saumure Anglaise*, page 185, for 24 hours. This is where I depart from Elizabeth David, who gives the recipe in *French Provincial Cooking*.

Next day drain the pork well and dry it with a clean cloth. Lay it out, boned side up, on a board and season with pepper, and the truffles from a small tin cut into pieces, and a few slivers of garlic. Salt, too, if the pork did not soak in brine.

Roll the meat together and tie at frequent intervals with fine string. Put the joint into a deep dish, surround it with the bones and pieces of skin. Let it cook uncovered for half an hour in a low oven, Mark 3, 325°F. The fat will turn pale gold. Pour in ¼ pint of white wine and ¾ pint of water, or 1 pint clear, hot meat stock, together with the juice from the tinned truffles. Cover with the lid or a double sheet of silver foil, and leave the meat for 2 to 2½ hours, to cook, at the same temperature.

Remove the bones, skin, etc., and leave the meat to cool in the liquid. Next day remove the fat and treasure it for spreading on bread. Serve the pork in slices surrounded with its jelly, chopped. This dish smells wonderful, tastes wonderful – and looks wonderful, the pale pink meat contrasting with the black nuggets of truffle, and creamy white fat.

Gigot de Porc en Sanglier

If a leg of pork is soaked for 2 to 4 days, depending on the temperature, in the cooked marinade given on page 72, it can then be braised and served as a passable imitation of wild boar. It is perhaps more usual to treat legs of mutton *en chevreuil*, like venison, but with pork it works just as well.

After the four days soaking, brown the pork in lard then remove to a heavy, lidded pan whilst making the sauce.

Stir a heaped tablespoon of flour into the lard in which the pork browned, and add the strained marinade gradually so that no lumps form. Dilute the sauce with hot stock until it is the consistency of single cream. Pour it over the leg of pork and put the lid on the pan.

Cook in a low oven for 2 to 3 hours according to the weight of the pork.

The sauce will need to be reduced, after you have skimmed off the fat. Taste it continuously, and season until you are satisfied.

Chops and small cuts like *noisettes, escalopes,* and the pork undercut known, in England, as tenderloin, can be braised too. One of the best pork recipes ever invented gives a good idea of the basic method:

Noisettes de Porc aux Pruneaux de Tours

This bland combination of pork, prunes, cream and the white wine of Vouvray embodies what Henry James described as 'the good-humoured and succulent Touraine'.

The wine is made – as the best white wines are – from grapes which are almost rotting on the vines. As local *vignerons* say: 'They piss in your hand'. The first time I made this dish I couldn't afford the Vouvray, so I improved on the very ordinary white wine in the larder by using Christmas prunes, which had been steeping in a mixture of half *marc*, a crude *eau-de-vie*, and half syrup. Delicious, if unorthodox.

½ bottle white Vouvray (drink the other half with the dish)
1 lb. large Californian prunes (unless you can find prunes from Agen)
½ pint thick cream
1 tablespoon redcurrant jelly
Salt, pepper, a little flour
2 *noisettes* or 1 chop per person
Dash of lemon juice

Put the prunes to soak overnight in the Vouvray. Next day pour off about 2 oz. of the liquid, and put the rest of it with the prunes into a slow oven to cook. Three-quarters of an hour is enough, but in fact you can leave them there for up to an hour and a half provided they simmer slowly enough. Cover them so that the juice does not evaporate.

Season and flour the *noisettes*. Cook them gently in the butter on each side, making sure that the butter doesn't go brown. Add the 2 oz. of steeping juice and leave the pork to cook for 40 minutes with a lid on the pan.

Pour on the juice from cooking the prunes. Cook for three minutes then remove the pork to a large flat serving dish, and arrange the prunes around the *noisettes* whilst the sauce in the frying pan boils down to a thinnish syrup. Add the redcurrant jelly. Then the cream bit by bit, stirring it in well so that after each addition it is properly amalgamated. Because English cream doesn't have that slightly sour tang of French cream, I add a dash of lemon at the end before pouring the sauce over the *noisettes* and prunes. Leave in the oven for five minutes. Serve this dish on its own.

Côtes de Porc à la Vosgienne

Here is another recipe for pork and plums, this time the pretty little yellow *mirabelles* which grow in gardens all over France, not just in the Vosges where this dish is supposed to have originated:

    1 lb. *mirabelle* plums
    ½ pint white wine
    1 tablespoon white wine vinegar
    1 large onion
    4 pork chops, thick ones
    1 small beef bouillon cube
    3 oz. butter

Chop the onion, fry it gently in the butter, and when it is half-cooked, add the chops to colour slightly on both sides. This is an operation demanding care as the butter must not catch, or the delicate flavour will be lost. Add 3 oz. of wine to the pan, put the lid on and simmer until the chops are cooked.

Meanwhile cook the *mirabelles* in just enough water to stop them catching. Don't let them overcook, so that they collapse into a mush. As English plums will not be so naturally sweet as French ones, add a very little sugar.

Arrange the chops and plums on a dish and make a sauce with the pan juices, the extra white wine and the bouillon cube, which should be crumbled first, then added bit by bit as required.

NOTE: This method can be adapted in many ways, using different herbs and spices. The small amount of sauce has a fresh flavour which makes a change from the more meditated piquant sauces, that have been quietly maturing on the side of the stove for hours.

Stewed Pork (*Ragoût de Porc*)

The fattiness of pork means that it needs careful attention when stewed, to make sure that all excess fat is removed both at the beginning and end of the cooking.

Pork tails and bones are successful cooked in this way, also shoulder and belly of pork; although in the latter case the best result is achieved by stewing it with shin of beef.

This is the method:

Cut 2-3 lb. of meat into regular pieces and roll them in seasoned flour.

Melt a little lard in a heavy frying pan and brown some sliced onions. Add the meat and brown on all sides. Pour off the fat, then sprinkle in a tea poonful of sugar which will caramelize and help to give the sauce a good colour.

Heat ¼ of a pint of *rosé* wine and add it to the meat and onions. Whilst it is bubbling away, heat ½ pint of good stock, then add that. Depending on the quantity of meat you may require more or less liquid; the pork should be hardly covered.

Season with salt, pepper, crushed juniper berries, thyme, sage, garlic – whichever you prefer, cover the pot and simmer until the meat is tender and dropping off the bones.

Strain off all the sauce into an upright glass jar – I use a 2-pint tumbler from a pub sale – so that the fat can rise and be skimmed. Check the seasoning, reduce the sauce if necessary and pour over the meat, which you have arranged in a clean dish. Serve with a light dressing of parsley, and boiled potatoes.

Jarret de Bœuf en Daube

Use equal quantities of shin of beef and belly of pork.

To 1 lb. of each use two large onions. Follow the method given above, substituting red wine for *rosé*. Season with more pepper than you would use for pork. Serve with boiled rice or potatoes.

NOTE: Like all stews, these are better made one day and heated through the next. The long wait overnight in the wine sauce acts as a marinade in maturing and tenderizing

the meat. Remember to heat through thoroughly by
bringing to the boil, then simmering for half an hour, or
longer if the stew was only half-cooked the previous day.

.

FRYING AND GRILLING

These methods involve the small cuts of pork, and are
virtually interchangeable according to your circumstances.
If you have really good pork chops, grill them. If you are in
the least bit dubious, fry or braise them (see pages 227-9).
Either method should be applied gently – unlike fillet steak,
pork chops will take about 20 minutes under the grill, or in
the sauté pan.

Filets Mignons de Porc Sautés

Buy a tenderloin, the undercut of bacon pigs, which looks
like a pallid, miniature fillet of beef, and cut it across,
slightly at an angle, into slices about half an inch thick.

Beat them out gently, season, dip them in egg, then roll
in breadcrumbs, and fry gently in butter for about 4
minutes each side.

Serve garnished with watercress and lightly fried apple
rings.

Pour over a little sauce made from the pan juices, by
stirring in some white wine and stock. There should not be
a lot of sauce.

NOTE: Tenderloin can be cooked in a great variety of
ways. Use it for *porc aux pruneaux de Tours*, page 227, but
reduce the cooking time for the meat.

Wrap it in bards of hard back fat and roast it for half an
hour.

Split it not quite in two lengthways, flatten, stuff and
roll it up; roast for three-quarters of an hour.

Keep the garnishings and accompaniments light – young
green peas, very small new potatoes, or onions or carrots.
Don't overburden a delicate cut.

Côtes de Porc Sautées à la Gasconne

This is a good dish for amateurs of garlic and olives, from *Larousse Gastronomique*. Don't be frightened of the quantity of garlic.

Buy thick pork chops. Two hours before you intend to cook them, pique each one with a sliver of garlic, sprinkle with thyme and bay leaf, crushed, salt, pepper, oil and lemon juice. Leave them to marinade.

Meanwhile prepare the olives and garlic. You require six of each per chop. Stone the olives, peel the cloves of garlic. Get ready two small pans of water, bring them to the boil and plunge the garlic in one, the olives in the other. Leave them for two minutes at a galloping boil, remove and drain. Chop the garlic roughly.

Now attend to the chops. Fry them quickly on both sides in duck or goose fat, or butter. Three minutes each side is enough. Add the chopped garlic, turn it over in the fat, and leave to cook with the chops slowly, with a lid on the pan. This will take from half an hour to three-quarters depending on the quality of the chops. Arrange the cooked chops on a mound of mashed potatoes, with the olives, and put them into a low oven while you attend to the sauce. This is made by pouring white wine into the cooking pan, and some concentrated beef stock, and reducing them. Pour the sauce over the chops, without straining, bits of garlic and all. Sprinkle with chopped marjoram, or parsley.

Côtes de Porc à la Bayonnaise

Larousse Gastronomique also gives this recipe which is particularly good if you can find edible ceps (*boletus, bolet comestible, cepe de Bordeaux*).

Marinade the chops as in the previous recipe.

Meanwhile prepare some small new potatoes; and the ceps, which you do by slicing them across, and removing the yellow spongy under-layer, as well as any small forms of animal life.

Fry the potatoes gently in lard for five minutes, and the ceps in a little oil. Give the chops a brisk five minutes in lard, on each side, then put them with the vegetables to cook together in a lidded earthenware dish. Simmer in a low oven for three-quarters of an hour. Sprinkle with chopped parsley.

Côtes de Porc au Vin Blanc

After a long day's work, or excursion, grilled pork chops are everybody's solution to the evening meal. With a little forethought, you can improve on everybody else's solution and enjoy a much better meal.

Season the chops. Put previously cooked potatoes into a pan with milk, to heat through for mashing.

Grill the chops fast for one minute, then lower the heat and give them 9 minutes. Turn over, and repeat with 1 minute fast, and 9 minutes slow.

Deal with the potatoes, adding plenty of butter and nutmeg or mace; arrange the chops round them and put the dish into the oven whilst you make the sauce.

Take the rack out of the grill pan, pour in some white (or *rosé*) wine, bubble it all together on top of the stove. Taste and season.

Be sure to scrape in all the little brown bits. Pour over the chops and serve. Have French mustard on the table.

(Watercress always makes a good appearance with pork chops.)

Côtes de Porc à la Charcutière

Make the *charcutière* sauce the previous day, page 52, but don't put in the gherkins until just before serving.

Follow the above recipe, but reheat the sauce in the grill pan, add the gherkins and herbs, and serve in a separate sauce boat.

(All the piquant sauces are delicious with pork chops. And *sauce Bercy*, see page 50.)

Côtes de Porc Vallée d'Auge

Score thick chops lightly on each side. Spread one side with a mixture of chopped shallots and chopped parsley. Dot with melted butter and grill. Turn the chops carefully over, spread the other side with shallots and parsley and butter, and grill.

Heat 4-5 oz. cider in a small pan whilst the grilling goes on. Transfer the chops to a serving dish and pour the hot cider into the grill pan. Bring to the boil over a strong heat on top of the stove and let it reduce to a good sauce. Stir in all the little bits and juice from the chops.

If you have any Calvados, add some with the cider. Pour over the chops, and serve with mashed potatoes and a green salad. (Elizabeth David's recipe.)

Côtes de Porc Avesnoise

A delicious way of serving pork chops from Avesnes-sur-Helpe in the very north of France. The method can be adapted for use with other glazing mixtures, see pages 188 and 223; but this French rarebit style is the best of all.

Grate a quantity of Gruyère or Emmenthal cheese (2 oz. is enough for three chops), mix it to a thick paste with half-and-half French mustard and cream. It should spread but not run.

Grill the chops on both sides as in the recipe for *côtes de porc au vin blanc*. When they are done, spread one side of each chop with the Gruyère paste and set under the grill. The mixture will melt, bubble and turn gold.

One of the most appetizing ways of serving pork, the smell is irresistible and draws the whole family into the kitchen.

Côtes de Porc Ambassadrice

    4 pork chops
    4 chicken livers
    4 large mushroom caps
    4 slices of truffle (optional)

3 oz. Madeira
About 3 oz. butter
Meat glaze or concentrated beef stock
Salt, pepper

Sauté the seasoned chops in the butter gently, until they are cooked. Arrange them in an ovenproof serving dish and keep them warm. Sauté the chicken livers next, arrange them on top of the chops, then the mushroom caps and put them on top again. If you are using truffles, they should be put on last of all.

Swill the frying pan round with the Madeira, scraping all the delicious bits that have stuck to the pan into the juice. Add some meat glaze or concentrated stock to make a little sauce. Correct the seasoning, then pour over the chops and garnish with a light sprinkling of parsley.

(In earlier times, the dish would have included cocks' combs and kidneys, for the full *ambassadrice* garnish.)

OTHER SUGGESTIONS FOR SERVING PORK CHOPS

À la Ratatouille. A stew of onions, peppers, courgettes, aubergines and tomatoes.

Provençale. A thick purée of tomatoes, well spiced, and finished with strips of red blanched, or tinned, pimentoes and stoned, blanched black olives.

Aux Haricots Verts. Green sliced beans, finished with chopped almonds fried in butter.

Aux Marrons. Chestnut purée, or cooked chestnuts and Brussels sprouts in *sauce mornay,* page 59.

Aux Poireaux. Leek purée. Cook the sliced leeks in a little butter. Whirl them in the electric blender (or sieve), adding fresh cream, salt, pepper, and a good pinch of sugar. Serve the chops on top.

Aux Champignons. Surrounded by mushrooms sautéed in

butter, tiny glazed onions, and diced sautéed bacon. Flavour with thyme.

Soubise. Sauce given on page 64.

À l'Orange. See page 224, or *Sauce Bigarade*, page 50. With small pats of some of the butters given on page 51.

SUCKING PIG
(*Cochon de Lait*)

Sucking pig is killed, as its name suggests, when it is from 2 to 6 weeks old. It makes a good festival dish either hot, or cold in a galantine. One of the special delights of roast sucking pig, in France and England alike, is the beautiful crackling. To this end it should be basted with olive oil so that the skin becomes *croquante*.

Cochon de Lait Rôti

First make a light herb and vegetable stuffing – this is a good one:

2 large onions, chopped
4 sticks celery, chopped
4 oz. butter, plus 2 extra ounces
Grated rind and juice of 1 lemon, plus juice of another
Plenty of chopped parsley
2 sprigs of thyme
8 oz. breadcrumbs
Salt, pepper
2 large eggs

Simmer the onion and celery in 4 oz. butter very gently for 15 minutes. They should not brown at all, but melt to a golden transparency. Put the contents of the pan into a bowl, add the extra butter, the grated rind and juice of one lemon, the herbs, breadcrumbs and beaten eggs. Taste and season. Add the juice of the second lemon if necessary; you need a good tang.

Stuff the pig and sew it up with button thread. Make three or four scorings on either side of the backbone, at an angle, like arrow heads, and brush the pig over with olive oil. Set in on its side on a rack in a large roasting pan and cook in a moderate oven for 2½ hours, turning over at half time. Be careful of the crackling as you do this. Some recipes suggest brushing the crackling with thick cream 20 minutes before the end of cooking time, but this should not be necessary.

To make the accompanying sauce, pour the liquid from the roasting pan into a tall heavy glass jar. This makes it easy to skim or siphon off the fat. Return the gravy to the stove, adding a large glass of white wine and the same of good stock. Boil it down a little, tasting and correcting the seasoning.

No vegetables are necessary apart from plain, boiled potatoes, finished in butter and parsley, and watercress. Some people like an unsweetened purée of eating apples.

NOTE: Many cookery-book writers are anxious that the sucking pig should be presented on the table with an American mortician's skill. 'Truss the legs and tail in a lifelike position, a small red apple in mouth and cranberries in the eye sockets'. 'Try and preserve as nearly as possible the animal's original shape and form'. But do not over-emphasize these effects: few people have the robust constitutions required to look a small creature in its cranberry eye.

Galantine de Cochon de Lait

A sensational dish for a large party, but not one which will keep, on account of the jelly.

    6 oz. lean veal
    6 oz. hard back fat, plus 3 oz.
    6 oz. breadcrumbs, soaked in a little milk
    2 large eggs and 1 egg yolk
    4 oz. ham
    Small tin of truffles

BRAISING

Carrots, onions, veal knuckle bone, garlic, *bouquet garni*, salt
    and pepper, 2 or 3 cloves
$\frac{3}{4}$ pint of white wine
$\frac{3}{4}$ pint of beef stock
plus
$\frac{1}{2}$ lemon

Mince the veal and 6 oz. of hard back fat, plus any trimmings from the sucking pig. Squeeze the soaked bread, mix
it with the meat and add the truffles and the eggs. If you
want to make a particularly splendid farce, add slivers of
almonds and pistachio nuts (blanched).

Cut the ham and the extra back fat into matchsticks.

Line the cavity of the pig with stuffing, then a layer of
ham and back fat. Stuffing again, then the ham, etc.
Finish with the stuffing. Sew the pig up with button thread.
Truss the front and back legs together, rub all over with the
cut side of half a lemon and tie or sew into a cloth.

Chop the carrots and onions into large dice, and put with
all the other braising ingredients into a large pan. Lay the
sucking pig on top and cover over, either with a lid or a
double layer of silver foil.

Bring to the boil and simmer gently for four hours (three
may be enough for a very small pig). Leave the pig to cool
in the pan, and don't unwrap until it is cold. Melt the
braising liquid, strain, skim, reduce and season. Clarify
if necessary, page 48. Brush a layer of jelly over the pig
when it is almost set, and serve the rest, chopped, around it.

THE HEAD

PIG'S head, like the other extremities, is sold cheaply in this country. It makes an excellent brawn (*fromage de tête, hure*) or galantine, if suitable attention is paid to its preparation. Anyone can grill a steak or chop; the cheaper cuts require careful and sophisticated cooking. This does not mean that the methods are difficult or tortuous, but they do require judgement and care over detail. Lack of proper care, above the statutory requirements of hygiene, and insensitivity to flavour make many manufactured meat dishes in England uneatable. This commercial debasement of brawn, black puddings, meat pies and sausages has misled people into feeling that only the expensive parts of a pig are worth eating.

There is little difference between *fromage de tête* and *hure* and *galantine de porc*. *Fromage* is a mixture of the meat set in jelly, *hure* is a mixture of the meat enveloped in the skin of the head, galantine is a mixture of the meat with hardly any internal jelly, but a coating of jelly round the outside.

Fromage de Tête

½ pig's head	2 sprigs parsley
1 trotter	2 sprigs thyme
2 onions	8 peppercorns
2 carrots	2 tablespoons wine vinegar
2 leeks	Water to cover
2 cloves garlic	½ bottle white wine
2 bay leaves	lemon juice to taste
To finish – toasted breadcrumbs, parsley	

Half a pig's head makes enough for the average family; but try and acquire the whole brain for a separate dish. Ask the butcher to chop the head into two or three bits, so that it will fit easily into a pan.

Deal with the brain immediately, see page 249.

Put the pig's head and trotter into the brine tub, page 185, if you have one ready. This makes a great improvement in the flavour of the brawn. Even twenty-four hours makes a difference; if you leave them there for two or three days you will need to bring them to the boil in a pan of cold water to draw off excessive salt before you start the proper cooking.

You can cook several trotters at once with the head, to be eaten on another occasion. If you do this, bind them up tightly in cheesecloth so that they keep their shape. Reckon five hours cooking time.

Once you've drawn off the salt and thrown away the scummy water, add all the other ingredients to the meat in the pan, except the wine and lemon juice. See that the new water really does cover all the meat. Bring slowly to the boil, and wedge the lid on tightly. Use silver foil, and a weight (I have a lump of red rock for this) to keep the lid down.

Simmer as gently as you can for four to eight hours. The length of time will depend on your success in keeping the simmer down to a bare bubble. The slower and steadier the better. Do this on a low heat, or in a low oven. The meat is cooked when it drops easily off the bone.

No salt yet. Wait until you've drained off the liquid, put $\frac{3}{4}$ of a pint of it into a clean pan with the white wine, and boil it down to $\frac{3}{4}$ of a pint again. Then taste, and season with salt and lemon juice if you think it needs further sharpening. The point of this operation is to make a well-flavoured jelly. Remember that cold food loses flavour, so allow for this. The secret is to keep tasting the liquid as it reduces.

Meanwhile pick out the meat from the solid remains. Throw the bones and vegetables away. Keep the tongue whole, chop the rest of the meat into smallish dice. There's no short cut to this. Whatever you do, don't put the meat through the mincer, or you'll end up with a nasty jellied mush. Season the meat with spices – *quatre-épices* if possible, otherwise a mixture of allspice, cloves and nutmeg. Don't overdo it.

Add the meat to the pan of reduced bouillon, simmer very slowly for twenty minutes. Taste again, and put the pan in the larder to cool down. Keep tasting as it cools and correct the seasoning. Just before it sets, put a layer of chopped meat in the loaf tin, add the tongue whole along the middle, and then add the rest of the chopped meat. Spoon off some of the liquid if you think there's too much of it.

When the *fromage* has set, unmould it and cover with home-toasted breadcrumbs, not the yellow commercial ones. Put a few slices of white bread in the oven to dry to a pale brown. Crush them between sheets of greaseproof (or in a pestle and mortar), then press them gently onto the *fromage* when they are nearly cold. Surround with parsley, and put the dish in the refrigerator to chill.

VARIATIONS

The *court-bouillon* can be flavoured with whatever you have to hand: turnip, celery, onion studded with cloves, orange and lemon rind, a few crushed juniper berries or allspice berries and nutmeg if you are unable to buy the French *charcuterie* spice-blend, *quatre-épices*. You could line the mould with slices of hard-boiled eggs (don't cover with toasted breadcrumbs at the end), put them in layers with the chopped meat in which you have included the tongue chopped, or use the eggs whole as for a veal-ham-and-egg pie.

Serve with – French mustard (to my mind essential with most pork dishes, particularly the smooth, gelatinous ones), hardboiled eggs, green salad dressed with 2 tablespoons of raw chopped mild onion and 2 tablespoons of chopped parsley as well as oil and vinegar and seasonings. Mashed potato is a standard accompaniment to *charcuterie* – slimmers might prefer thin toast, or wholemeal or rye bread.

Hure

Here you are dealing with the whole head. If you are feeling adventurous and have sharp knives, you might like to bone it before cooking. Or perhaps you have a skilful butcher who would do it for you. Then you could proceed to a *tête de cochon farcie*, or a simulated boar's head (given by Alexis Soyer in *The Modern Housewife or Ménagère*, 1850, and quoted in André Simon's *Concise Encyclopaedia of Gastronomy*).

But first an easier way.

Remove the ears and tongue, but leave the head whole. Put everything into the brine tub, if you have one ready, for three days, page 185. Assemble the ingredients for a *court-bouillon*, similar to the one described in the previous recipe: vegetables, wine vinegar, wine (in this case to be included from the beginning); and find a pan large enough to take the head comfortably. An old boiling fowl makes a useful addition, but it is not necessary. It is no good whatever using a young roaster, because it has little flavour compared with the good strong taste of a mature hen.

The point of using the whole head is to end up with a large area of skin (*couenne*) in which to envelop the cooked meats. Wrap it up tightly in a cheesecloth or napkin, and place it in the pan, with the boiling fowl if you decide to use one. The ears and tongue can then be fitted into the spaces with the vegetables. Add plenty of water to cover the ingredients, and set the pot to boil. Keep at a gentle simmer for between five to eight hours, removing the tongue after two.

Remove the head, unwrap it, and let it cool down a little so that you can handle it. Keep the strained liquid boiling away gently. Take the bones out of the head, and the meat as well. Lay the skin outside down on a clean piece of cloth, and cut the meat into strips and dice, including the chicken, but excluding the tongue. Season well with spices. You can augment the meat with home-made sausage meat.

Arrange your meats as elegantly as possible in the skin,

with the tongue in the middle; fold the skin completely round the chopped meats so that you end up with a sausage-like pudding which can be tied up firmly in the cloth. Simmer this for an hour in the liquid. Remove and squeeze gently to get rid of the juice. Unwrap. You can either ease the *hure* gently into a mould, or leave it under a weight to cool. If you do put it into a mould, put a piece of wood on top and a weight. Finish with toasted bread-crumbs.

Serve with – the accompaniments suggested for *fromage de tête*, except in the case of *hure à la pistache* which is a dish on its own.

VARIATIONS

A delicious and elegant variation is *hure à la pistache*. You follow the above recipe until you get to the meat chopping stage, then you chop the tongue too. Arrange the chopped meats as before, but this time include whole pistachio nuts. Their pale green and lavender beauty adds a sensational effect, when you slice the marbled *hure*; their texture and flavour go well with the bland meat. Serve simply with salad, as the delicate flavour must not be drowned.

Tête de Porc Farcie

If you feel like boning the head before you start cooking (or you can persuade your butcher to do so), try this recipe. Should you come to disaster and pierce the skin, you could always lay your largest piece of it out flat on a cloth and roll everything up as for *hure*.

COURT-BOUILLON

    1 calf's foot (2 trotters would do instead)
    3 onions stuck with cloves
    4 carrots cut in rounds
    3 cloves of garlic

$1\frac{1}{2}$ pints white wine
Salt and pepper to taste
Extra water to cover

Set all this to boil whilst you make the stuffing.

STUFFING (FARCE)

Tongue from the head, sliced
Home-made sausage meat (according to the size of the cavity), page 115
$\frac{1}{2}$ lb. minced veal if possible
Parsley

Stuff the head, sew up the neck. Tie it up in a cloth, and add it to the pan of *court-bouillon* with the bones. Simmer very gently for at least five hours.

Remove from the liquid, which you leave to boil down for the jelly; leave it to cool a little, then unwrap. Push carefully but firmly into a mould, filling the gaps with the reduced liquid. I find that it is necessary to use a board and weight.

Galantine

Ingredients for *court-bouillon* as above.

1 pig's head
A few parings of truffles, or whole truffles

Cut the meat off the head, and chop it into thin slices. Chop the tongue and ears too. Leave for twenty-four hours with 3 tablespoons of salt, freshly ground pepper and the spices you prefer, in an earthenware dish in a cool place.

Next day tie the meat up in a cheesecloth, and simmer it for at least five hours very gently in the *court-bouillon*, to which you have added the bones. Do not salt the bouillon for the first two hours, then taste and see if it requires it.

Take the meat out, and let it cool a very little. Leave the liquid to reduce on a hard flame, but do not let it get too salty. Unwrap the meat and pack it into the mould very tightly leaving no gaps. Should you be able to afford the truffles, mix them in at this stage. Put a board and weight on top to keep everything pressed down; leave to get cold.

In the autumn instead of truffles you could substitute the black mushroom called Horn of Plenty (*craterellus cornucopioides*), as they often do in France for the pâtés eaten during the grape-picking and harvest supper afterwards. Then they are mixed in with the raw meat and baked with it, but five hours simmering with the galantine would be far too much. I just simmer them in a tablespoon of water at the very end of the cooking time, and mix them with the meat when everything is ready to go into the mould.

Whilst the galantine is setting, attend to the liquid. Strain it off and leave to jelly. A certain amount of scum separates itself, and you may find that the jelly is clear, once you have removed the opaque layers. If it needs clarifying, turn to page 48.

Here is the recipe for the English Bath chap, made from the jowl of the pig (*bajoue*). I have never seen anything similar in the *charcuterie*, but it is worthy of a place there.

Bath Chap

> *Court-bouillon* as for the recipes above
> Half the lower jaw of the pig
> Breadcrumbs to finish

Ask the butcher to cut off the jaw as for a Bath chap. I usually cook it in with the rest of the head, wrapped up tightly in a cloth so that it doesn't lose its shape. It must be salted in brine for two to three days first, however, see page 185.

Simmer gently for four hours. Unwrap it and carefully remove the bones. Mould the jaw into a nice Bath chap shape, and leave it to cool with a weight on top. When it's quite cold, cover with toasted breadcrumbs and cut the end of the snout off, as it upsets some people. Chill.

VARIATIONS

You can alter the flavour of the *court-bouillon* as suggested for the other recipes, but I don't think this makes as much difference to the chap as it does to *fromage* or *hure*.

Bath chap

Serve – chilled and sliced thinly, with the usual accompaniments: hard-boiled eggs, green salad, mashed potato, French mustard, perhaps pickled walnuts, capers, or gherkins.

PIG'S EARS
(*Oreilles de porc*)

Pig's Ears are one of the most appetizing delicacies in the *charcuterie*, lying swathed in jelly on their white tray. Expensive too, you will find. Here in England your butcher will very likely give them to you free. If you buy a whole head, to use in the various ways suggested, ask if you could have some extra pairs of ears as well; then you will have the making of a separate dish for the whole family. Clean the ears well, and see that the hair is properly singed off; you need not soak them in the brine tub, but here again the flavour is greatly improved if they are pickled for two or three days.

NOTE: The whole of the pig's ear can be eaten. The cartilage has an agreeably contrasting bite, which goes well with the blandness of the meat.

Oreilles de Porc Grillées Sainte-Ménéhould

Pig's ears, cleaned and pickled
Court-bouillon (wine unnecessary)
Breadcrumbs to finish

Simmer the pig's ears gently for about one to two hours. Watch that the delicious gelatinous covering does not fall off the cartilage – take the ears out before this happens. Put them to cool under a weight.

About half an hour before you are ready to eat, cut the ears in half lengthways, dip them in melted butter, then in white breadcrumbs. Grill them gently until the coating is crisp or put them in a hot oven. It is this method of finishing that is known as Sainte-Ménéhould, the name of a small town in the Marne famous for its pork products. In earlier days the pigs wandered in the surrounding wooded plateau of the Argonne, eating themselves to a pitch of succulence in ideal conditions.

VARIATIONS

Serve them hot from the *court-bouillon*, accompanied by a vinaigrette sauce: 1 tablespoon wine vinegar, mustard, sugar, salt, pepper mixed well together – then beat in slowly 5 tablespoons of oil, and add chopped onion, parsley, garlic, shallots, capers or gherkins to taste.

Cool the ears, cut in strips, dip in batter and fry.

Cool the ears, cut in strips, dip in beaten egg, then breadcrumbs, and fry.

Oreilles de Porc au Diable

When the cooked ears have cooled down, cut them in two, lengthways. Brush them with French mustard, dip in

melted butter and breadcrumbs, then grill. You can equally
well put them in a brisk oven, if this is more convenient,
but don't let them go beyond the point of crispness.
Charred ears are not attractive. Serve with *sauce diable*
(page 55), or any other piquant sauce.

Oreilles de Porc aux Lentilles

This is a favourite French way of serving pig's ears. You
can cook them separately, and serve with the lentil purée;
or you can cook everything together:

> Pig's ears
> 1 lb. lentils, soaked overnight and drained
> 2 medium carrots, diced
> 2 medium onions, chopped
> 1 large onion stuck with 4 cloves
> *Bouquet garni,* salt, pepper
> 2 oz. butter

Take a large pan that will hold everything comfortably.
Sauté the chopped onion in the butter first, then add the rest
of the ingredients and cover with water. Bring to the boil
and simmer until everything is done. This takes a good hour.

To serve, cut the ears lengthways in two or three strips
and lay on the drained vegetables.

Oreilles de Porc Braisées

A grander recipe for devotees.

> 4 pig's ears
> 1 lb. of diced vegetables, onions, carrots, celery
> 4 oz. diced bacon fat
> Large glass (5 oz.) white wine or Madeira
> 1 pint beef stock
> 4 oz. chopped onion
> 4 oz. sliced mushrooms
> 4 oz. chopped mushrooms
> 4 oz. butter
> 2 oz. flour
> Paprika pepper

Butter a fireproof dish, lay in the diced vegetables and bacon fat. Put the pig's ears, well-cleaned, on top. Pour over the wine or Madeira, bring to the boil and simmer for two minutes. Pour over the heated stock, bring to the boil, cover the dish and transfer to a moderate oven for a good hour.

When the ears are nearly cooked, set about making the sauce and, first of all, the garnish: fry the chopped onion in 2 oz. butter until it is pale gold, add the sliced mushrooms and cook them for two or three minutes. Keep warm.

For the sauce, melt the remaining 2 oz. of butter in a small pan, cook the 4 oz. of chopped mushrooms in it until the juice runs. Sprinkle on the tablespoon of flour and cook gently for two minutes. Add bit by bit enough of the braising liquid to make a smooth sauce the consistency of thick cream. Season.

Arrange the ears, cut in two lengthways, and the sautéed onions and sliced mushrooms on an ovenproof serving dish. Pour over the sauce, sprinkle with paprika and brown in a hot oven or under the grill.

BRAINS
(*Cervelles de Porc*)

In France, brains for sale lie on a white tray, ringed with parsley, and neatly finished with a high price ticket. In England, they lurk messily on a sodden piece of greaseproof paper in a corner, and the price is much lower.

So do not be put off by their appearance. An hour in salted water, and the membrane holding the blood vessels is quite easy to remove. Simmer them in salted milk, or a light stock for 15 to 20 minutes, remove with a perforated spoon and leave to cool on a meat dish with a strainer tray. Once prepared, you can do many things with them.

Here are five recipes from which you can develop further ones of your own:

Cervelles de Porc à la Sauce Béchamel

Simmer the brains in milk, and use it to make the sauce. Melt a good ounce of butter in a pan, stir in a heaped tablespoon of flour. Add the simmering milk bit by bit until you have a smooth white sauce. Use extra milk if necessary. Season well and pour over the brains. Sprinkle with chopped parsley and surround with triangles of fried bread or toast. This is a very bland dish, excellent for children, or invalids, or for a late supper.

Cervelles de Porc au Beurre Noir

Slice the cooled brains and sauté to golden brown in some butter. Remove to a serving dish to keep warm, while you make the *beurre noir*. Melt 3 oz. butter in a pan, cook to golden brown (not black, as the name suggests), pour over the brains. Quickly swill the pan round with a tablespoon of white wine vinegar, and pour this in its turn over the brains. Garnish with chopped parsley and serve with baked bread (or toast, if you have a helping hand to make it while you are dealing with the *beurre noir*).

Cervelles de Porc en Matelote

If you want to make a good substantial main dish out of several sets of brains, this is a splendid way of doing it.

The secret of all good *matelotes* – whether of eel, fish or brains – is to cook the sauce slowly for at least an hour before adding the main ingredient. Red wine sauces improve with long gentle cooking; you can quite well prepare them the previous day, and reheat when required for the final preparation of the dish.

Sauté an assortment of diced vegetables (8–12 oz.) in 3 oz. butter – choose leeks, carrots, onions, celery. Pour on a pint of red wine (or half red wine, half stock) and simmer for at least an hour, covered. Remove the lid and boil hard until the liquid has reduced to about half a pint.

Strain into a clean saucepan and thicken with *beurre manié* – a heaped tablespoon of flour kneaded into a level tablespoon of butter, added in little knobs to the hot sauce gradually until it thickens to the consistency of thick cream. Stir all the time and keep just below the boil.

Sauté some tiny pickling onions and button mushrooms in butter. Arrange them on a serving dish with the sliced, prepared brains. Strain the *matelote* sauce over them and leave in a low oven for 10 minutes. Chopped parsley makes a good finish, and toast a good accompaniment.

Bouchées à la Reine

The *reine* was Marie Leszczinska, gourmet queen of Louis XV, and although her *bouchées* are correctly filled with morsels of chicken in a cream sauce, brains as well as sweetbreads are often used in French homes instead of, or as well as, the chicken. As most of the preparations can be done well in advance, *bouchées à la reine* make a good starting course for a dinner party.

Use 1 lb. puff pastry to make a number of small vol-au-vent cases, or one large one. Store them in an air-tight tin, if you are making them well in advance of consumption.

3 sets of pig's brains, prepared
4–8 oz. mushrooms, sliced
½ pint *Béchamel* sauce (page 49)
4 oz. pot of double cream
Optional extra: small amount of cooked chicken, or sweetbreads
Salt, pepper, lemon juice

Heat the *Béchamel* sauce, add the mushrooms and cook slowly for at least 20 minutes, add the brains, and other meat if you are using cooked chicken and sweetbreads, diced, and the cream. Keep the pan over a low flame until the brains are heated through, and set the vol-au-vent cases on an ovenproof serving dish in a hot oven. Season the mixture in the pan with salt, pepper and a dash of lemon juice, fill the cases and serve very hot.

Brains and pastry are an excellent combination – try

them baked in puff pastry like apple dumplings (*cervelles en chausson*); or as a filling with cream sauce for short-pastry *barquettes* and *tartelettes*, which have been baked blind in advance – capers, and small strips of lemon peel or anchovy, on top give a sharp contrast.

Soufflé de Cervelles

In the case of pig's brains, you will need two sets. Prepare them in the usual way and put them through a sieve when they are cooked. Make the quantity up to half a pint with some cream and some *velouté* sauce (page 66). Melt a good ounce of butter in a pan, add a heaped tablespoon of flour and cook for a few moments. Add a quarter of a pint of milk and stir until the mixture is thick and comes away from the side of the pan. Mix in the half pint of brain purée. Season well. Bring the mixture up to the boil and remove from the heat. Beat three egg whites to a stiff foam. Then add the three yolks one at a time to the pan, beating them well in. Finally fold the beaten whites in gently and lightly. Pour the mixture into a soufflé dish, buttered, and collared with greaseproof paper to contain the rising soufflé. Cook in a moderate oven for 20 minutes, remove the greaseproof paper quickly (for this reason it is prudent to have tied the string with a bow rather than a knot), and bring it straight to the table.

If you wish to make this delicious soufflé into a more showy affair, add 3 oz. grated parmesan cheese and a tiny tin of truffles cut into thin strips just before you add the egg yolks, and bake the soufflé in tiny soufflé dishes or ramekins. They only take about 10 minutes in a medium to hot oven. The name of this soufflé (*soufflé de cervelles à la chanoinesse*) is a reminder of the very high standard of convent cooking in the past. Vows of holy poverty did not exclude truffles it seems.

THE TONGUE
(*Langue de Porc*)

Any recipe for ox-tongue can be adapted for pigs' tongues. Similarly salting, even for one day, is a great improvement to the flavour and quite practical. When you bring the tongues home, rub them over with a good handful of *gros sel* (bay salt, Tidman's sea salt, or Maldon salt) and a pinch of saltpetre and leave them to rest in a dish with the remaining salt. Before you go to bed, turn them over. Next day they are ready to be braised or poached. But first, here is a recipe which does not demand prior salting, and which makes a delicious standby for feeding unexpected visitors.

Langue de Porc en Rillettes (Potted Pig's Tongue)

You need the tongue, the two cheeks and the neck, plus 2 lbs. of all fat, or very fat, pork.

Scald the tongue, remove the skin and cartilage. Skin and bone the neck. Chop all the meat, but keep the fat separately.

Take a heavy iron pan, heat the chopped fat pork in it until the melted lard runs out. Pour it off into a basin, and add the lean pork. Cover, and cook for four hours.

Season well with salt, pepper and *quatre-épices*. Pound in a mortar, or whirl in the electric blender with some of the melted fat poured off in the beginning. The best texture is obtained by pounding the meat for a while, then transferring it to a sieve over a bowl and tearing it apart with two forks, until all is reduced to a mass of fine fibres.

Sterilise some small stoneware pots – in Touraine special brown-glazed thick mugs are traditional – pile in the *rillettes*, leave them to cool and cover, with a half inch layer of melted lard. When this has set firm, cover with silver foil. *Rillettes* will keep in a cool place for several weeks without benefit of refrigerator or deep freeze.

See other kinds of *rillettes*, page 323.

Braised Tongue (*Langue de Porc Braisée*)

It sometimes seems to me that the most important thing about braising is the pan, and attention should be paid to this before you start cooking. The success of braising depends on the small amount of liquid used and the slowness of the cooking. It follows that the pan must be thick, the lid air-tight, to avoid burning. If you aren't too sure about the lid of your pan, make a flour-and-water paste to secure it. The French, who developed the art of braising to a pitch of excellence, have a special *braisière* or *daubière*, a rectangular or oval vessel with a deep well-fitting lid – see the many 'en daube' recipes to be found in French cookery books. When the philosopher Jean-Jacques Rousseau perfected his recipe for braised beef, *Daube à la Montigny-en-Vexin*, he would have used an iron or earthenware pot buried in hot ashes, with a flat lid to hold hot charcoal. Nowadays the *braisière* is more conveniently produced in tinned copper or enamelled cast iron, (see page 29), as well as fireproof porcelain or glass, and unless you are feeling experimental on bonfire night, make use of a slow oven rather than red-hot ashes and charcoal.

If you have a suitable metal pan, all the cooking from first to last can be done in it. Otherwise you must prepare the *mirepoix* and sauce in a heavy frying pan, then transfer everything to the braising pot.

First remove your tongues from the salt, wash and plunge into boiling water for five minutes. This enables you to remove the skin and small bits of cartilage and bone.

Dice half a pound of lean rashers of bacon.

Chop, roughly, one onion, two leeks, one carrot.

Fry the bacon gently in a tablespoon of butter; when it turns transparent add the chopped vegetables, and more butter if it seems necessary.

When the onion has turned transparent in its turn, and golden, season with salt, pepper, a clove of garlic crushed, one sprig of thyme and two of parsley.

Continue frying until the vegetables and bacon are nicely

browned. Stir in two level tablespoons of flour, cook until it takes on a pale brown colour. Then add gradually, stirring all the time, a ¼ pint of red wine (5 oz.) and a ½ pint of stock. Bring to the boil, add a bay leaf.

If you are not using a metal braising pan, this is the moment to transfer the *mirepoix* and liquid from the frying pan to whatever dish you intend to use.

Lay the pigs' tongues (enough to weigh between 2 and 3 lb.) on top of the vegetables, cover the pot closely, and put into a low oven for two to three hours to simmer gently.

When the tongues are cooked, remove them. Pour the sauce through a sieve into a clean pan, skim, taste, reduce by boiling hard. Keep tasting.

Meanwhile arrange the cooked tongues nicely on a serving dish, surround with mashed potatoes, put into the oven to keep warm. Flavour the reduced sauce with tomato purée, for instance, or Madeira, or sherry – pour some over the tongues, put the rest into the sauce boat and hand separately.

Langues de Porc Pochées

Wash the salt off the tongues. Plunge them for five minutes into fast boiling water so that the skin and small pieces of cartilage can be removed.

Unsalted tongues should soak for three hours in cold water, before skinning and trimming as above.

Put the tongues into a pan, cover with light stock and bring slowly to the boil. Add a *bouquet garni*. They will need about two hours gentle simmering.

A bland parsley sauce is the traditional accompaniment to this mild dish. For a contrast, try any sauce made with wine, mushrooms, tomato or piquant ingredients. In some parts of France, *choucroute* (page 158) is served with it.

Langue de Porc Garnie

The time taken to poach or braise tongues leaves the cook free to prepare an attractive garnish, which will be arranged round the tongues on a large serving dish at the last moment.

For a family lunch on a cold day, buttered pasta or buttered rice are ideal – plenty of butter, and an accompanying tomato sauce. More elegantly, for a dinner party, surround the tongues with braised chestnuts, fried mushrooms, tiny glazed onions and small sausages, and a final scatter of chopped parsley. Serve Madeira or sherry-flavoured sauce.

Here are two excellent ways of using up – or stretching – cooked tongue. It doesn't matter whether it has been braised or poached.

Langue de Porc, Sauce Diable

Cut cold cooked tongue into slices about $\frac{1}{4}$ inch thick. Spread them lightly on both sides with French mustard, dip in melted butter and breadcrumbs. Lay them on the rack of the grill pan, dribble melted butter over and brown them on both sides under a gentle heat. Serve with *sauce diable* (page 55) on a bed of mashed potato.

Langue de Porc, Sauce Duxelle

Slice cold cooked tongue thinly. Cut an equal number of ham slices to the same shape and arrange on a flat oven dish in a circle, alternating with the slices of tongue. Butter the dish first. Cover with a Duxelle sauce (page 56), to which some of the liquid from cooking the tongues can be added. Scatter an even layer of breadcrumbs over the top, dot with tiny pieces of butter and brown under the grill or in a hot oven.

Langue de Porc à l'Écarlate

In England we are normally accustomed to pickled ox-tongue of a deep and wonderful red. Pigs' tongues can be pickled in the same way. In France this is known as Scarlet Tongue – *langue* (*de bœuf*, or *de porc*) *à l'écarlate* – and the addition of sugar to the brine, as well as spices and herbs, results in a much more subtle, less angry flavour.

Soak the tongues in cold water whilst you make the brine.

Put six pints of water into a large pan. Stir in 1½ lbs. of *gros sel* (unrefined salt, or sea salt, see page 42), 1 lb. dark brown sugar and 2 oz. saltpetre. Season according to inclination with a bay leaf, whole peppercorns and crushed juniper berries. Bring to the boil, gallop for five minutes, and set aside to cool – this takes several hours.

When the brine is nearly cold, remove the tongues from the cold water and plunge them into fast boiling water for five minutes, so that they can be skinned and trimmed. Prick them all over with a larding or darning needle. Lay them in a plastic bucket or bowl (or a stoneware salting jar, if you have one) and strain the cold brine over. You will need to weight the tongues down with a scrubbed piece of wood, as they must be entirely submerged. Cover the whole thing over with a clean cloth to keep the dust out and leave for five days in a cool, dry place.

To cook the tongues, put them in a roomy pan and cover with cold water. Bring slowly to the boil and simmer for two hours. Taste the water after half an hour's simmering; if it is unpleasantly salty, pour most of it away and add fresh hot water to cover. This should not be necessary, but if you have had to leave the tongues in brine for longer than five days, it is as well to know what to do.

When the tongues are cooked, leave to cool under a light weight. Serve with green salad and potatoes, mashed, boiled or cooked in their jackets.

Langues de Porc à la Mode de Troyes

Troyes is an old town on the Seine in Northern Burgundy, worth visiting for its viciously flamboyant rood screen in the church of St Mary Magdalene – and for its *charcuterie* (see

Andouillettes de Troyes, page 275). Tongues treated in the Troyes manner make a very pretty cold dish for a buffet supper.

Follow the recipe for *langue de porc à l'écarlate* above, but only pickle the tongues for three days.

When the tongues are quite cooled under a light weight, stuff them into lengths of intestine and tie at each end to make a sausage-cum-cracker shape. Plunge the encased tongues for a moment into a pan of fast-boiling water which will make the intestine cling to the shape of the tongue. Cross-garter with thick string, brush either with caramel (not to be confused with sugar burnt black and tarry) or cochineal (be light-handed and discreet). Leave for two or three hours, then remove the string and you will find the *langue de porc* attractively patterned.

To make the caramel, boil 8 tablespoons of sugar and three of water in a pan, without stirring. Watch it. Remove from the heat when the colour is deep golden brown.

Langue de Porc Fumée

If you are interested in smoking meat (see page 194), you could make a start with pigs' tongues. Like sausages, they are not very expensive, so if the first experiments are a disaster you will not be seriously out of pocket.

Soak, clean and pickle the tongue as for *langue à l'écarlate* on page 256, but remove it from the brine after 48 hours. Stuff into a piece of intestine, tie at both ends and hang in a fresh draught of air for two hours. Plunge into fast-boiling water for a moment, so that the intestine clings to the shape of the tongue. Smoke for three days.

Provided you hang the tongue in a cool, dry place, with a steady temperature of not more than 60°F., it will keep for several weeks. When the tongue is required for cooking, put it in a roomy pan and cover well with plenty of cold water. Add an onion stuck with five cloves, a carrot, a clove of garlic, eight whole peppercorns and a *bouquet garni*. Bring to the boil slowly and simmer gently for two to three hours. Test it with a metal skewer after two hours – if it goes in easily, the tongue is cooked. Eat it hot or cold.

PIG'S TROTTERS
(*Pieds de Porc*)

I once commented on the limited variety of prepared and cooked pork on sale in this country to an executive in a large pork factory. He recalled that in the early days of this century the Managing Director always had pig's trotters to start his important dinner parties, but that nowadays the housewife was ashamed to be seen coming out of the butcher's shop with a packet of trotters and tail. The French housewife has to pay the equivalent of 9*d* for half a pig's trotter, cooked it is true, but still a high price. There is usually a tray of them in most *charcuteries*, bread-crumbed (*pieds panés*), waiting to be taken home and grilled for an hors d'œuvre. As one is lucky enough to buy them so cheaply in England, I usually serve them in various ways for a main luncheon dish, accompanied by mashed potato. They have often spent forty-eight hours in brine, but this is not essential, though it certainly improves their flavour.

BASIC PREPARATION AND COOKING

4 pig's trotters
2 carrots, sliced
2 onions, stuck with 3 cloves each
2 leeks, sliced
2 sticks of celery, sliced
Bouquet garni (parsley, thyme, bay)
Some good bits of pork skin (*couenne*)
1 large wine-glass white wine
½ wine-glass wine vinegar

Singe, scrape and salt the trotters.

If you intend to breadcrumb and grill the trotters eventually, or if you intend to stuff them, you must tie the trotters one on each side of a small flat piece of wood about 2 inches wide and 8 inches long. Do this by bandaging them closely and firmly, so that they cannot lose their shape in the cooking.

(If you are going to serve the trotters straight from the cooking pot, with a vinaigrette or piquant sauce, you need not tie them up. But on the whole, I think it is worth the initial trouble. At least you are saved the final business of separating bits of trotter from bits of vegetable just before the meal, when there are better uses for your time.)

Bandaged or unbandaged, fit the trotters into a roomy pot. Add the rest of the ingredients and cover with plenty of water. Bring to the boil, cover tightly, and simmer for six hours. This is an ideal recipe for solid fuel cookers – leave the pot overnight on the simmering plate at the side.

Now you can deal with the trotters in many ways.

Pieds de Porc Vinaigrette

Untie the trotters, remove the bones but preserve the trotter shape, and lay them on a bed of mashed potato. Serve with a cold vinaigrette sauce (page 70), with additions to suit the family tastes – chopped raw shallot, parsley, chives, capers, chopped pickled gherkin or sweet-sour cucumber, chopped pickled walnuts, chopped fresh tarragon.

Pig's Trotters with Onion Sauce

Put two heaped tablespoons of chopped mild onion or shallot into a small pan, together with five tablespoons of wine vinegar, eight crushed juniper berries and six crushed peppercorns. Put over a good heat and cook until the vinegar has nearly evaporated. Add half a pint of liquor from the trotters. Simmer gently for 15 minutes. Fork a tablespoon of flour into a bare tablespoon of butter (beurre manié, see page 51), until they are well amalgamated; drop little bits into the simmering sauce, stirring gently until it is slightly thickened. Do not strain this sauce.

Pieds de Porc Panés

These are the crumbed trotters, all ready for grilling, that you can buy from the *charcuterie* in France. Like most recipes for pig's trotters, you can do the preparatory boiling one day, and the finishing the next.

Follow the basic preparation given on page 259, and unwrap the trotters when they are cool enough to handle. Cut them in half, making sure that the bones fall evenly. When they are quite cold, brush with melted butter and roll in toasted breadcrumbs (cornflake crumbs are heretical, but satisfactory – the point is that the crumbs must be crisp). You can now leave them until next day. All they will need is a gentle grilling to warm them through and crisp up the outside.

Serve a vinaigrette or piquant sauce, or *sauce Sainte-Ménéhould* (page 63).

Pieds de Porc à la Sainte-Ménéhould

The most famous of all the French ways of cooking pig's ears and pig's trotters, the Sainte-Ménéhould method, gives a crisp texture to gelatinous meat, which has been boiled, by rolling it in breadcrumbs, then grilling or frying – a method similar to that of the above recipe. But in Sainte-Ménéhould itself, in the Argonne where pigs once ran in the huge woods of the plateau (scene of much of the Verdun fighting in the First World War), pig's trotters with a difference can be bought for reheating. Spiced with *quatre-épices* and rolled, like *pieds panés*, in breadcrumbs, they have been cooked for so long – 48 hours – that they can be eaten bones and all. This gives three textures – crisp, gelatinous and the hard-soft biscuit of the edible bones. An extremely delicious combination. They are served in local hotels quite dry, without sauce, and you eat them with French mustard.

One *charcutière* told me that it's the addition of a certain vegetable or herb that causes the bones to soften, as well

as the prolonged slow cooking. Local sceptics tartly hint
at '*produits chimiques*'.

Pieds de Porc Farcis

> 4 pig's trotters
> Bouillon as in basic method
> ½ lb. pork, minced
> ½ lb. veal (or chicken), minced
> 1 onion, finely chopped
> 1 clove garlic, crushed
> 2 tablespoons parsley, chopped
> 2 egg yolks

Follow the basic method of preparing the trotters. While
they are cooking, make the stuffing with the pork, veal,
onion, garlic, parsley, and egg yolks. Season with salt and
pepper.

After five hours simmering, take the pot off the stove and
let it cool down. Remove the trotters when they are not too
hot to handle comfortably – do not let them get cold, as it
will be difficult to remove the bones then. Slit them carefully
lengthways, and take out the bones. This is a neat-fingered
operation which demands time and patience.

Stuff the trotters with the *farce* you've prepared, sew
them up, wrap them in cheese cloth and simmer them for
another hour in the bouillon. You can eat them hot; or
cold, sliced like a *saucisson*.

Pieds de Porc Truffés (or Farcis, if you can't afford truffles)

Ingredients as above, plus a tiny tin of truffles and some
pig's caul (*crépine*).

Follow the basic method, until the trotters are cooked
(five hours), and cool enough to handle. Make a stuffing as
in the recipe above. Run the caul under the hot tap (this
makes it easy and supple to handle), and cut it into 5-inch
squares. On each square lay a piece or two of truffle or
truffle peeling, then a layer of cooked trotter, a layer of

stuffing, a layer of cooked trotter, a layer of stuffing. Wrap
the caul round these layers to make a cutlet-shaped parcel.
Fry gently in butter or lard until golden brown, or grill.
Don't ruin their delicate flavour with a sauce.

PIGS' TAILS
(*Queues de Porc*)

If you live in a pig-producing county, Wiltshire for
instance, you often see a pile of pigs' tails in the butcher's
window. Like the other extremities, they are cheap and
delicious. In France, the *charcutier* uses them in his various
brawns — I have rarely seen them offered for sale as a
separate item. But on French farms, when the pig is killed,
its tail is well scalded and put into the brine tub for several
days.

BASIC METHOD

(If you have brine ready prepared (page 185), immerse 4
pigs' tails for two to three days.)

To cook, put the pigs' tails into a large pot with 2
onions, each stuck with 4 cloves, 1 sliced carrot and 2 sliced
leeks, 8 whole peppercorns, a *bouquet garni* and plenty of
water to cover. Simmer for 1½ to 2 hours. They are done
when the meat separates fairly easily from the bones —
though there is always some pleasurable picking to be done
at table, as the small vertebrae are complicated compared
with trotter bones.

Cut the tails into lengths and serve on a bed of mashed
potato, with a sprinkling of chopped parsley. The onion
sauce given on page 64 goes well with this dish, or else a
sauce made from the reduced and thickened boiling liquid.
(Keep any remaining liquid for soup.)

Queues de Porc aux Lentilles

Soak 1 lb. lentils overnight. A good hour before the pigs' tails are likely to be cooked, stew two large chopped onions in 3 oz. of butter. When they are golden and soft, add the soaked, drained lentils and cover with water. Season and simmer for an hour. Serve the pigs' tails on top of the lentils.

Queues de Porc Grillées

When the pigs' tails are cooked, remove them from the pot, cut them up and press under a light weight until they are cold. This can be done the day before they are required.

Half an hour before the meal, brush the pieces with melted butter and roll them firmly in toasted breadcrumbs. Grill gently.

Serve with mashed potatoes and a piquant sauce, or French mustard.

Queues de Porc Braisées

Dice an onion, a carrot, two sticks of celery and 4 oz. streaky bacon. Sweat them in 3 oz. butter in a heavy pan until they begin to brown. Add a tablespoon of flour and stir till it is cooked in with the fat – about two minutes. Gradually pour in $\frac{1}{4}$ pint of red wine and $\frac{1}{2}$ pint of stock, until you have a smooth sauce. Lay the pigs' tails on top of the vegetables, cover the pan tightly and simmer for two hours. Make a sauce by adding Madeira – or Vermouth – to the strained liquid, and serve the tails cut into short lengths, surrounded by buttered rice.

An attractive arrangement of vegetables – say, glazed onions, mushrooms, peas, or stuffed tomatoes – round the braised tails turns them into a dish for a special occasion.

Gelée de Cochon

Last of all, a recipe using the extremities – ears, trotters and tail, to make a clear soup or a jellied cold consommé.

A mixture of ears, tail, trotters and pork bones
1 large wine-glass of white wine (6 oz.)
1 large onion, chopped
1 bayleaf
2 cloves of garlic, crushed
Good pinch of *quatre-épices* or a mixture of spices
Juice of a lemon
Meat extract

Scald, scrape and singe ears, tail and trotters.

Put all the ingredients into a large pan, except for the lemon juice and meat extract. Barely cover with water and *add no salt*. Bring to the boil.

When the pot is bubbling hard, skim off any grey, bitty-looking froth as it rises. This helps to keep the jelly clear. Reduce the heat, cover the pan and simmer gently for six hours. This can be done either on top of the stove, or in the oven.

Strain off the liquid, through muslin, into a clean pan, and reduce it over a hard flame until you have about a pint left. Season with salt, lemon juice, and a little meat extract to improve colour and flavour, though the latter may not be necessary.

It can now be served hot (an excellent soup for people who are dieting), or left to cool into a jelly. To serve as cold consommé, break the jelly up with a fork and pile lightly into wide glasses. Chill.

In fact, this recipe gives you a sort of aspic jelly. Slightly unorthodox, perhaps, but quite delicious enough to make an hors d'œuvre or luncheon dish such as *œufs en gelée*.

For this you will need as many ramekins, or small soufflé-dishes, and as many eggs as you have visitors. Also a slice or two of ham, some unfrizzled parsley or stuffed olives – anything edible and decorative, to embellish the simple ingredients.

First of all poach the eggs, trim them neatly so that they will fit into the ramekins, and keep them in cold water until they are wanted.

Melt the jelly till it just runs, and set a thin layer of it in the bottom of the ramekins. Lay the parsley or olives on top, then another thin layer of jelly to hold them in place. The egg goes in next, with more jelly to fill up the surrounding gaps. Last of all the ham, and some jelly to hold it in place. Put the ramekins in a cool place, or the refrigerator, until they are set and ready to be turned out.

You can further improve the jelly by the addition of some sherry, or port, or Madeira, according to taste.

You will see from this that the *gelée de cochon* has many possible uses in the preparation of cold food – *chaudfroid* of chicken and game for instance (see page 53), or a cold ham mousse (see page 216).

The Insides

'Sowse us therefore, in the Powdering-
Tub of thy Mercy, that we may be Tripes fit for the
Heavenly Table.'

THE INTESTINES OR TRIPES

A FAVOURITE series for misericords and manuscript illumi-
nation in the Middle Ages was the Labours of the Months.
In both France and England, October is often given to the
grape harvest, and November to the acorn harvest or the
annual pig-killing (*le sacrifice du porc*). The pigs had fattened
on acorns, Christmas was coming, the weather was cool
and dry. The men sharpened their knives, and excited
children soon ran – as they had done since Neolithic times
and as they did in country villages until quite recently – to
the terrible dying squeal of the pigs. It wasn't horrified
sympathy that drew them, but the thought of bladder
balloons.

On many French farms still, to my own knowledge in the
Vendômois, pig-killing day is a festival. Of course with
modern feeding methods and the butcher's cold room in the
village, there is not the great pressure of excitement, the
heady feeling of survival and winter stores laid by. Neither
is it a set annual occasion any more; another pig is killed
whenever the last one is practically finished. Only a jar or
two left of *rillettes* and *rillons*, a few smoked sausages in the
coolest darkness of the cave-cellar, no more succulent
morsels of *confit du porc* to be speared by an exploratory fork
as the lard is slowly melted in the great pots.

So one convenient morning early, either a part-time
freelance *charcutier* or one of the men from the nearest

charcuterie, arrives at the farm. The pig is killed, scalded, scraped free of its fine silky hair, drained of its blood; and finally hung up on a tough sort of coat-hanger hooked onto a ladder against a shed, head down, back to the wall, still warm. The man makes a circular slit round the anus, and cuts right down the centre of the body to the snout, keeping the two sides apart with a wooden stick. Gradually the insides spill out – they musn't be split or burst by mistake – and the bladder is emptied, washed inside and out, and blown up. If the children don't get it, it's put to one side until the fat is all melted down together and the farmer's wife is presented with her bladder of lard.

Next comes the disentangling of the caul (*crépinette, toilette*) or peritoneum which enloses the guts in its fatty veil. This is treasured for *pieds farcis* and *crépinettes* (see pages 262 and 116). Then the mesentery (*fraise*), a frilly membrane which holds the intestines in position, has to be removed. This is used for lard-making, or most deliciously eaten on its own (see page 278). The intestines and stomach are put into a large basket, whilst the pluck and windpipe are pulled away and laid on the trestle table with the bladder and extra bits of fat that have come away.

Charcuterie handbooks now instruct you to 'take the basket of intestines to the nearest river or stream where they can be washed in plenty of water'. Lucky the farmer's wife who has a bath, because this process is heavy and boring. You start with the stomach and large intestine (*gros boyau,* consisting of the rectum and colon), cleaning, scraping, outside and inside, removing the inner mucous lining. The small intestine is trickier (*le menu*) – it needs a small piece of wood to turn it inside out. Divide it into lengths first, it's much easier, then scrape and wash it until it's transparent. If you have taps, you can fit the lengths on like hosepipes to wash them thoroughly. Knot one end of each piece of small intestine, in preparation for sausage making, then leave everything covered with salt until you need it.

It is easy to see why more and more people in France

prefer to patronise the *charcutier*. On the other hand it is much cheaper to rear your own pig and have your own *charcuterie*. You also have the comfortable knowledge that the pig has been well fed. 'Everything's raised on powder these days,' the country housewives grumble. 'Chickens, pork, all collapse to mush when you cook them. Even the peasants use powder' – but not for the pigs they eat themselves. That's the story you hear. Perhaps it is true. But I am sure that those medieval pigs hanging headless on misericords, or strung up by their feet, were fairly tough by today's standards. Though this is probably a matter of improved breeding, rather than improved modern feeding stuffs.

TRIPE OR CHITTERLING SAUSAGES
(*Andouilles, Andouillettes*)

Andouilles are large, invariably salted and smoked, sold in slices by weight, like salami, and eaten cold. *Andouillettes* are smaller, the size of a large sausage or a little bigger, occasionally smoked or salted, and eaten hot after a gentle grilling.*

If the *charcutier* orders his *andouilles* from Vire in Normandy, the capital of the *andouille*, they will be hanging up among the other *saucissons secs*. They are easily distinguishable on account of their black skins and their mottled greyish-brown section, with the pieces of tripe looking like the fossilized coral in Frosterley marble, or else graded by size and drawn into each other, so that the slices look like regular growth rings across a tree-stump. If the *charcutier* makes his own, they may well be a lot smaller, about the size of a man's clenched fist and about as knobbly. Their skins are

* *Andouille*, which sounds unusual, is in fact most appropriately derived from a Late Latin adjective, *inductibilis*, 'that may be drawn over something'. When you come to the method of filling the skins, you will understand how nice the derivation is. In Palsgrave's *Lesclaircissement de la langue francoise*, 1530, he gives 'Chyterlyng, Endoile', a good halfway name between *inductibilis* and *andouille*.

probably more succulent and wrinkled black, and when you go near to choose one your mouth waters with their sharp smell of a white wine marinade.

Andouille, *andouillettes* and tripe

Andouillettes are about the same size as *boudins blancs*, but craggier with the pieces of tripe. Some *charcutiers*, however, mould them into squared prisms cut off into exactly similar lengths, and pile them up quite architecturally into a pyramid. Or they may be wrapped up, each one, in a roll of greaseproof paper. It may be pure coincidence, but the nicest *andouillettes* we've ever eaten belonged to the more rugged, tied-at-each-end school, and we bought them in the Dordogne at Montignac, after an unusually solitary hour in the Lascaux caves. They were fried too quickly over a picnic stove from Woolworth's, but no other *andouillettes* have ever tasted so good.

Andouilles and *andouillettes* are quite easy to make at home, the most difficult part is acquiring the large intestine and belly of the pig. Chain butchers are no help in this, you need to find a butcher who chooses his own meat at the local slaughter house. Pig factories are sometimes obliging. If you have to clean the tripes yourself, the bath is the best place because, as well as having plenty of room, you can fix the ends of the intestines over the cold tap and run plenty of water through. When it comes to the manufacture, a relay of unsqueamish helpers with neat fingers is an advantage.

The basic mixture is the same for both *andouilles* and *andouillettes*, apart from local variations. It's the size that distinguishes them as far as the home cook is concerned.

BASIC METHOD

Large intestine and belly of the pig (or part)
Fat bacon ($\frac{1}{3}$ of above weight)
Spices

BOUILLON

Half-and-half milk and water to cover, 2 or 3 onions stuck with 4 cloves each, 3 medium carrots, salt, pepper, *bouquet garni*, spices

(If the intestines, etc., have not been cleaned, soak in cold water for twenty-four hours in a cool place. Overnight only in warm, humid weather. Then clean and scrape them. Simmer for an hour in water.)

Set aside enough intestine for the casings – thinner pieces for *andouillettes*, fatter for *andouilles* – and cut them into suitable lengths. Sprinkle with salt and store in the refrigerator, or the coolest part of the larder.

Slice up, with scissors or a sharp knife, the rest of the intestine and the belly, into strips $\frac{1}{3}$ to a $\frac{1}{2}$ inch wide and a little shorter than your lengths of casing. Put them in a bowl and sprinkle with plenty of salt, freshly ground black pepper and a mixture of spices such as *quatre-épices* (page 40). Remember that *andouillettes* and *andouilles* need a strong spice contrast to the slightly rubbery smoothness of the tripe filling. Let the strips macerate in the seasonings for twenty-four hours, in a cool dry place.

Next day, cut the bacon fat into pieces about the width and length of the tripe pieces. If you refrigerate the fat first, this job becomes quite easy. Divide the tripe and bacon strips into bundles and tie each one, at one end, with a length of button thread.

Wash the salt off the casings, and draw the bundles in,

by means of the button thread (this is where the neat-fingered are at a premium). Cut away the thread and tie the *andouilles* or *andouillettes* at each end.

(If this process appals you, you can, more simply, chop the tripe and bacon fat rather than slice it into regular lengths. If you have a sausage-making attachment to an electric mixer, you can treat the mixture like sausage-meat and fill the skins that way – but use the very large-holed plate as the final result should not be too smooth or solid in texture.)

If the knobbliness of your *andouilles* and *andouillettes* seems excessively exaggerated, roll them backwards and forwards with the palm of your hand on a smooth surface (formica, marble slab).

COOKING ANDOUILLETTES

Prick them with a darning needle and arrange evenly in a large saucepan. Cover with milk and water in equal quantities, add the other bouillon ingredients and bring to the boil. Simmer gently for three hours. Leave them to cool down in the liquid until tepid, then lay them side by side closely in a shallow dish and put a lightly weighted board on top. This gives a handsome squared-off appearance, which is not strictly necessary but gratifying. In France they are often glazed with a mixture of lard and veal fat in equal quantities, or – when the weather gets warmer – with one-fifth mutton fat and four-fifths veal fat.

Now they can be fried, or else slashed across in three or four places and grilled. Serve them on their own, as a starting course, with French mustard; or with mashed potato as a main luncheon dish. Well-spiced *andouillettes* are a great treat, and worth the trouble of making them.

COOKING ANDOUILLES

The *andouillettes* cooking programme can be followed entirely – or when the *andouilles* have quite cooled under a light weight, they can be sliced and served as part of an hors d'œuvre.

It is better to salt, or salt and smoke, them first. Four days in brine (page 185) is a great improver, two days in brine and three days smoking is better still. Smoking produces a wrinkly, brownish-black exterior, which is most appetizing.

Substitute white wine for milk in the bouillon recipe.

Although, as I have said above, *andouilles* can be eaten hot like *andouillettes,* they are at their best salted, smoked and smelling of white wine, and served cold in thin slices.

Although *andouilles* are served like *saucissons secs,* they are not when domestically produced a keeping sausage. When salted and smoked they keep good longer than *andouillettes,* which should be eaten within two days of manufacture, but it is wise to eat them within the week.

Andouilles de Campagne

Follow the Basic Method. Salt for four days in brine (page 185), before hanging up in a cool airy place to dry out thoroughly. Poach for three hours in the milk and water bouillon, cool and grill.

Andouillettes Fines de Porc

A delectable recipe from *Larousse Gastronomique.*

> Mudgeon, mesentery (*fraise*), cut in squares
> Half its weight in lean bacon, cut in squares
> Enough meat stock to cover
> Onion stuck with cloves
> Thyme, parsley and bay leaf
> Salt and pepper
> Enough intestines to contain the meat, soaking in cold water

Put everything, except the intestine skins, into a large pan and bring it slowly to the boil. Keep well covered and simmer gently for $1\frac{1}{2}$ to 2 hours.

Pour off the liquid, chop the meat coarsely and mix in 4 oz. mushrooms which have been lightly fried in butter with chopped onions and parsley. Do not let the onion brown. Add 2 oz. of well-flavoured meat stock, and six raw egg yolks.

As with all sausage-making when chopped or minced meats are used, your task is virtually impossible without an electric mixer with a sausage-making attachment. If you don't have such a thing, it will be a good deal quicker to take your mixture in to the butcher's shop and ask them to put it into skins, than to laboriously push it down yourself.

Assuming that you have filled the skins one way or another, you should tie them every five inches, prick each *andouillette* several times with a needle, and poach in a milk-and-water bouillon as described in the Basic Method. Drain, press, glaze and grill as described.

Andouillettes de Nancy (Lorraine)

Nancy, like Troyes, Tours and Strasbourg, is famous for its *andouillettes*. There are several variants, but this is the most exotic of the recipes.

  2 lb. calf's mesentery (*fraise*)
  2 lb. all-fat pork (*panne*)
  As many truffles as you can afford, up to 6 oz.
  5 oz. Madeira
  Salt, freshly-ground black pepper, spices according to taste

Soak the mesentery well in plenty of cold water for at least two hours. Then blanch it in boiling, salted water for another two hours. Whilst it is draining and cooling down, chop the fat pork (excluding the rind, *couenne*) into fairly small pieces. Do not mince. Mix it in a large bowl with the wine and truffles and seasonings. Then chop the mudgeon into small strips – much smaller than the basic method, more like shreds. Add this to the bowl, and stir everything together well. Cover and leave in a cool place for twenty-four hours.

Wash the intestine-skins well, and fill them with the mixture. Tie every five inches, finish as in the basic method.

You can salt these (three days in brine), but they are much nicer eaten fresh. Don't smoke them as this would be too much for the delicate flavour of truffles and Madeira.

Andouillettes de Troyes (Aube district of Champagne)

2 lb. calf's udder – young heifer, not old cow (*tétine*)
2 lb. calf's mudgeon (*fraise*)
½ lb. mushrooms
2 oz. chopped mild onion, or shallots
1 tablespoon, heaped, chopped parsley
3 oz. butter
1 wineglass white wine
4 egg yolks
Salt, freshly-ground black pepper, ground nutmeg

Soak both udder and mudgeon well in plenty of cold water for two hours. Blanch them in boiling, salted water for an hour. Cut them into small strips. Sauté mushrooms, onion and parsley in the butter until the onions are golden, *but not browned*. Add pepper, nutmeg, and wine. Bubble for a moment, salt well and put into a big bowl. Add the meat and bind with the egg yolks. Fill the skins, simmer in half white wine and half water bouillon for three-quarters of an hour – in other words, follow the Basic Method, apart from the cooking time.

Omelette à l'Andouillette

Andouillettes are expensive in the *charcuterie* – this is an excellent way of stretching them with the more economical addition of eggs. Or if you have an *andouillette* or two left from a previous meal, this is the best way to use them up. The amount of *andouillette* can be less, but here are the usual quantity of ingredients for four people:

2 *andouillettes,* cooked or uncooked
8 eggs
Salt, pepper, chopped parsley
Butter for greasing the pan

If the *andouillettes* are uncooked, fry them in lard or butter first. Skin the *andouillettes* and crumble the inside. Grease the omelette pan – a large one – and put the pieces of *andouillettes* in to heat through thoroughly. Beat the eggs, season with salt, a very little pepper because the *andouillettes* will be spicy, and parsley, pour over the pieces in the omelette pan and finish as for an ordinary omelette. Keep the inside a little runny. Serve on a hot dish, with hot plates, red wine, bread and unsalted butter.

Andouilles de Vire

The old granite town of Vire, in the Normandy department of Calvados, has been rebuilt with rather cheerless efficiency after its wartime desolation. Almost every other shop sign in this cross-roads town proclaims the famous *andouilles*: but they are good all the same, and here is one of the many recipes:

> 2 lb. large intestine, stomach, and mesentery, *or* 2 lb. calf's mesentery
> 5 oz. white wine
> 1 small red pepper (*piment doux*)
> 1 dessertspoon mustard powder
> Salt, freshly ground black pepper
> Length of large intestine for the *andouille* skin

Clean the meat, leave it to soak in cold water for 24 hours. Then wash in hot water, drain and dry thoroughly. Cut the meat into strips the length of the *andouilles*, and about half an inch wide – the strips from the mesentery will be shorter, as they should be cut straight across the frill, rather than lengthways.

Mix the white wine, mustard, salt and pepper and the red pepper, freed of its seeds and stalk and crushed to a pulp. This can all be done in the liquidizer goblet of an electric mixer.

Marinade the strips in the white wine and pepper liquid for two days, covered. Then insert them into the skin(s) and tie both ends. Now you should smoke them for three days (see page 194), then simmer them for three hours in a white wine and water bouillon (50/50). Some recipes suggest leaving the *andouilles* in brine for two days before the smoking – see brine recipe, page 185.

Alternatively you can omit the salting and smoking processes, and proceed with the cooking. They won't be exactly *andouilles de Vire*, but they will be good.

CHITTERLINGS

Here is the English way of dealing with the large intestine of the pig. The unforgettable name is of unknown derivation, but appears in the thirteenth century in dog-latin form in a description of women washing 'chitterlingis' down by the waterside. Which brings us right up to modern French handbooks, 'take the stomach and intestines to the nearest stream or river'.

In the West Country you often see these opaque white plaited objects in the windows of pork butchers' shops. They have been all prepared and are ready to be grilled. If you can get some suitable intestine for skins, you can make *andouillettes de Nancy* and *Troyes* with these chitterlings. Naturally you omit the first cooking, the preparatory blanching in boiling water.

But supposing you are starting from scratch, this is what you do. Use the stomach and large intestine, which should be freed of its fat. Separate them, and clean the intestine thoroughly by turning it inside out with the aid of a piece of wood. There you will find a mucous skin which must be got rid of – the same thing applies to the stomach. Wash thoroughly in cold water, leave to soak in freshly-drawn salted water until you need them. Simmer in a milk-and-water bouillon, half-and-half, seasoned with salt, pepper, spices onion stuck with cloves, carrots, spices and a *bouquet garni*, for about two hours or until they are cooked. Let them cool in the liquid; then drain and dry before grilling. It is usual, in Wiltshire at any rate, to plait the intestines after their soak in cold, salted water. They certainly look more attractive. *Serve with* mashed potatoes, and an oil-and-lemon-juice vinaigrette sauce and French mustard.

MESENTERY, FRILL OR CROW
(*fraise*)

The mesentery is a fatty membrane, 'a pellycle or a skyn the whiche doth tye the guttes together'. It's a beautiful frilly object like a creamy ruff, but you won't see it offered for sale, as a general rule, in England or France. *Charcutiers* incorporate it into their *andouilles* and *andouillettes* (pages 269-77), English pig factories use it exclusively in the making of lard (page 314).

We did once buy some in a seaside *charcuterie* at Préfailles near Pornic, south of Nantes. These attractive, crisply browned morsels, like paper frills, were sold under the name of *grillons*. They didn't at all resemble the *grillons* or *grattons*, which remain when all the fatty parts of the pig have been melted down for lard (*saindoux*) – these are usually a soft hash, like poor-quality *rillettes* (page 316).

BASIC METHOD

Soak the mesentery in cold water, salted, for two hours after it has been cleaned under a cold running tap. If you ask your butcher to order you some from the slaughter house, specify a certain quantity (bearing in mind that it shrinks in cooking, but that it is also very rich and to be eaten in small quantities) or you will end up, as I did the first time, with a plastic bucketful.

Drain, dry and cut into 6-inch lengths.

Either

Put a tablespoon of lard into a heavy frying pan, set on the stove, and when it is smoking put the bits of mesentery in to fry until they are crisp and browned at the edges. Eat hot or cold; with mashed potato if hot, and a lemon juice and oil vinaigrette.

Or

Poach for two hours in a milk and water bouillon, with the usual seasonings. Alternatively, in a white bouillon, which is 2 pints of water very slightly thickened with flour, and seasoned in the usual way plus a dash of wine vinegar.

When it is cooked, serve with mashed potatoes, and a lemon-juice and oil vinaigrette, sharpened with chopped gherkins, capers and chopped, raw onion.

Or else, cut the pieces in half, drain them well, and fry them in foaming butter as they are, *or* dipped in batter, *or* egg-and-breadcrumbed.

TRIPE RECIPES

In France, large towns will have their own *triperies*, where cooked tripe is sold as well as offal. It is, of course, calf's tripe, but in small towns and villages the *charcutier* sells it regularly in jellied hunks, starred with brilliant rounds of carrot. It is an excellent thing to warm through for a cold day's picnic, particularly if you can improve it with tomatoes stewed in a little wine, or Normandy cider, with a spoonful or two of Calvados as well. There is no denying that tripe is best cooked in large quantities for a long, slow time, which is why most French housewives like to buy it ready prepared. Ideally, too, it should go to the oven in the beautiful honey-golden *tripières*, that can sometimes be bought in large kitchen-ware shops in France. They are bulbous round pots, with two small handles or lugs; and a small round opening in the top, with a well-fitting lid which should be fastened securely onto the pot with a flour-and-water paste, so that none of the juice evaporates.

As a hard-up student in Florence, I alternated my daily diet of eggs cooked in oil in the oven, with *trippa alla fiorentina* – a delicious confection of tripe, tomatoes and parmesan cheese. But I must confess that for a deep midday sense of internal peace, there is nothing to beat *tripes à la mode de Caen*, eaten in a small restaurant in Caen, with good Normandy cider to bear it company, and a glass of Calvados, a *trou Normand*, to follow. Tripes fit, indeed, for the Heavenly Table.

Tripière and tripe

Many English people have been put off tripe by the insipid flavour of tripe and onions, in the Lancashire style. Tripe needs to be raised from its visceral connexions with a more seasoned form of preparation, and I make no excuse for including the Italian, or rather Florentine, manner of preparing tripe. If you have to convert a reluctant family, start with *Trippa alla Fiorentina;* if you have a number of friends who like tripe, cook *tripes à la mode de Caen* in vast quantity and invite them all. *Tripes à la Lyonnaise*, a slightly unorthodox version, is for the true *amateur*. First the classic:

Tripes à la Mode de Caen

NOTE: Ask your butcher to try and get you calf's tripe. I doubt you'll be successful, but it's worth asking. The one usually on sale is ox-tripe. Include 1 lb. of mesentery, if possible.

3 lb. tripe, cut in squares, if it's already blanched
2 calves feet } or 4 pig's trotters, chopped into pieces by the
1 cow-heel } butcher
4 leeks, halved lengthways

3 carrots, quartered lengthways

5 large onions, stuck with 2 cloves each

2 cloves garlic

Bouquet garni – bay-leaf, thyme, parsley, tied together

2 sticks celery

Enough dry cider to cover (not a sweet, cheap, commercially ruined cider)

Cocktail glass of Calvados preferably, otherwise brandy

4 oz. pig's skin (*couenne*)

Tripe has usually been cleaned, washed and blanched, whether you buy it in France or England. But if it hasn't been prepared, you must scrape it under a cold running tap and blanch it for half an hour in boiling water. Drain and dry it thoroughly.

Do not omit the feet, calf's, pig's or cow-heel. They are absolutely essential for a gelantinous smoothness. The butcher will split and divide them into pieces.

Find a large, thick pot with a good lid. Lay the pig's skin, cut in strips, on the bottom; next a mixed layer of tripe, feet and vegetables, put the *bouquet garni* in the centre and some salt pork if you have it to hand (inessential, but pleasant), then the rest of the meat and vegetables. Season with salt, freshly-ground black pepper, Cayenne pepper – or a dash of Tabasco sauce.

Pour in dry cider to the height of the ingredients, and the glass of Calvados or brandy. Do not be tempted to use the sweet, gaseous liquid sometimes sold as cider – as a green cook I once did so, and the results were too horrible to describe. A dry white wine is the best alternative. If you cannot afford the alcohol, switch quickly to the Italian style of cooking tripe, described on page 283.

Make a slightly tacky flour-and-water dough. Put a ring of it round the edge of the pot, slap the lid on and bend the dough up over it. If you aren't used to doing this, allow yourself plenty of time and plenty of dough.

Put the pot into a slow oven (Mark 2, 310°–320°F.), and go out for the day or go to bed. Anyway leave it alone for 10 hours – a gruelling test of will-power.

Next day, assuming you have left it to cook all night, remove the lid with the aid of a knife. Take out the vegetables and bones and *bouquet garni,* and pour off the sauce into a clean pan. You will have to skim off the fat first of all, then taste it. If the flavour leaves something to be desired, boil the sauce down hard and reach for the pepper mill. Some cooks add a knob of *beurre manié* (1 tablespoon of flour kneaded into one tablespoon of butter), which slightly thickens the sauce, but the feet and skin should give enough thick smoothness without the addition of flour.

Bring the sauce to the boil again when you have poured it back onto the tripe, let it bubble gently for 10 minutes. Serve very hot with a good sprinkling of parsley, and have well-heated soup plates. You will also need plenty of crusty bread, cut very thick, to mop up the sauce; cider or white wine to drink; and if possible a glass of Calvados or brandy afterwards. This is a great aid to digestion, and should certainly not be overlooked if you intend to eat anything else afterwards.

Tripes à la Lyonnaise
A more lively version of Tripe-and-Onions.

> Equal weight of tripe and onions
> Water to cover the tripe
> Extra onion stuck with 4 cloves
> Carrots
> Celery
> Leeks
> *Bouquet garni*
> Pepper and salt
> Beaten egg
> Breadcrumbs
> Butter

Buy your tripe ready blanched; if not, you will have to scald it, scrape it and soak it for three hours in cold water with a dash of vinegar. Then blanch it for a good half-hour in boiling, salted water.

Cook it for two hours in the water flavoured with vegetables, seasoning and herbs. Peel and slice the onions (except the onion stuck with cloves, which is used in the bouillon), and sauté them gently in the butter until they are cooked and golden. Keep them warm. Do not cook the onions until the tripe is ready and drained. Cut the tripe into squares, dip them in the beaten egg, then in the breadcrumbs and fry in butter until they are crisp. This can be done in the butter left from frying the onions. Put the tripe pieces on top of the onions, swill the buttery pan round with some wine vinegar and pour it over the tripe. Sprinkle the top with chopped parsley and serve the dish very hot, with very hot plates.

Tripes à l'Italienne (*Trippa alla Fiorentina*)

2 lb. tripe
Bouillon as above, with the addition of some white wine
Well-flavoured tomato sauce:
1 onion, garlic
1 carrot
olive oil
1½ lb. tomatoes
tablespoon flour
Some red wine and spices
Pinch of bicarbonate of soda
Bouquet garni
An extra onion, and butter

Cook the tripe as in *Tripes à la Lyonnaise,* but for 1 hour only Let it cool down completely and dry.

Start the tomato sauce as soon as you have set the tripe on to simmer in the bouillon. Fry the onion and carrot chopped in a little olive oil, with one or two crushed cloves of garlic. Peel the tomatoes. Alternatively, open a tin of Italian tomatoes; they are likely to have a much better flavour than any bought fresh in this country. Sprinkle the flour onto the onion when it is golden, and add a glass of red wine and the tomatoes. You can season it with newly ground black pepper, a spoonful of sugar according to taste, and some allspice. Don't add any salt at this stage, because the sauce should reduce to a delicious thick state and you don't want it to get too salty in this process. Let the sauce bubble gently on a corner of the stove, or in the oven with the tripe.

Whilst the tripe is cooling down, keep the sauce bubbling. Add more red wine if it is too thick, and finally a pinch of bicarbonate of soda, some salt and seasonings. If after the addition of extra sugar and pepper, the sauce still seems slightly insipid add some tomato concentrate (in tins and tubes from Italy, sold by most grocers); even bottled tomato ketchup will give it a lift.

Add some fresh basil if you are lucky enough to have some, dried if you haven't; wild marjoram, the Italian *origano*, can be found in England quite easily, and that or the sweet marjoram of the herb gardens, can also be used. Then put in the pieces of tripe, and simmer for an hour.

Serve in well-heated earthenware pots or bowls, with grated Parmesan cheese to sprinkle on top. Good, thick hunks of crusty bread, and red wine are most satisfactory accompaniments.

Tripes Frites

Prepare and cook the tripe in a bouillon, as in the recipe for *Tripes à la Lyonnaise*.

Whilst it is cooking, make a light frying batter, in which you add the beaten white of egg at the end.

Decide on which spicy, piquant sauce you intend to serve with the tripe, and make it. The tomato sauce, (page 65), is a good one; a piquant sauce such as *sauce diable* (page 55), or a *sauce Robert* (page 62), do very well too. If you are pressed for time, grill some halves of tomato, sprinkled with chopped garlic and salt and melted butter, and serve them round the tripe fritters with lemon quarters and a dressing of chopped parsley.

When the tripe is cooked, drain it well and dry it. Cut it into squares, and dip them in the batter, to which you have just previously added the beaten white of egg. Fry in deep smoking oil.

Tripes à l'Espagnole

3 lb. tripe
1½ pints each water and white wine (dry)
2 large onions stuck with cloves
3 medium carrots, quartered
2 sticks celery
Salt, pepper, spices

FOR THE SAUCE
Olive oil
½–¾ pint of tomato sauce as described on page 65, but made with dry white wine, not red
¼ teaspoon ground mace
Lemon juice
Extra clove of garlic
¼ lb. black olives
Parsley

Prepare and cook the tripe in the bouillon ingredients, along the lines for *tripes à la lyonnaise*, for at least two hours.

Drain and dry it well, cut it into small squares. Heat the olive oil in a large heavy frying pan, and put in the pieces of tripe. Fry them for ten minutes, then add the tomato sauce, the mace and some parsley, rather than the basil or marjoram mentioned for *tripes à la lyonnaise*. Correct the seasoning, transfer everything to an oven dish that can be sent to table, and simmer in a low oven for half an hour. Ten minutes before the end add the black olives and lemon juice to taste. Serve sprinkled with more parsley, and plenty of bread in crusty slices.

NOTE: The prolonged cooking of the tripe, as in recipes (pages 282 to 284), can be quite well done in advance of the final preparation of the dishes.

Tripe can, of course, be cooked in a *blanquette* or other bland, creamy sauce; the flavour is delicate, but the only word to describe the texture of tripe under these circumstances is slithy.

THE ORGANS OR OFFAL OR VARIETY MEATS
(Abats)

Organs, offal in other words, or variety meats if you live in
the United States, can be a point of prejudice. Before the
war I remember hearing 'Ai never eat Offal', spoken with
emphasis and pride, a brave flicker of light in a crude waste
of offal-gobblers, yet another pea felt through twenty
mattresses. War shortages taught better sense. Nutritive
values were proclaimed and prejudices fell, at least as far as
kidneys, liver and hearts went. Lungs and spleen make no
grand public appearance in this country, any more than
they do in France. Unknowingly we buy them in faggots,
sausages and pâtés. Knowingly we may buy them to feed
our cats and dogs.

But I suggest that next time you buy some pig's pluck,
you prepare it for the family in the various French ways
I've listed at the end of this section. But first –

THE KIDNEYS

Along with all the other parts of the pig, you can buy kidneys at the *charcuterie*. They are usually sold raw – and very
fresh, which is how they should be. If you can, order them
in advance, with some surrounding flare fat. To my mind,
the most delicious way to cook kidneys is to pop them into a
moderately hot oven, encased in flare fat, and roast them
for an hour. This applies to lambs' and calves' kidneys as
well. And you will have a basin of beautiful fat, superb for
pastry-making. The next most simple way is to grill them.

Rognons–Brochette Grillés

Skin the kidneys; then slit them in two so that they are
not completely separated into two halves, but can be laid
out flat. Remove the small hard white part. If you have

some very fine skewers, you could skewer them crosswise in the French style, otherwise use two skewers for each kidney side by side across the two halves.

Brush the cut side with melted butter, and season with salt, freshly ground black pepper, and perhaps some ground sage – be discreet about this. Set the kidneys, cut side up, of course, under the grill for several minutes at a moderate heat. Then turn them over, brush with melted butter, and grill the outside.

The usual garnish is butter, pounded with chopped parsley and some lemon juice. In other words, *à la maître d'hôtel*.

Skewered kidneys

VARIATIONS

1. When you have brushed the kidneys with melted butter, sprinkle them with breadcrumbs.

2. With *Beurre Colbert*, butter, pounded with tarragon, and salt and pepper.

3. With *Beurre de Ciboulette*, butter, pounded with chopped chives, salt and pepper.

4. With *Beurre de Moutarde*, butter, blended with mustard (French).

5. With *Beurre d'Échalote*: shallots, chopped, then blanched for three minutes in boiling water, and pounded to a mash. Add butter.

SERVE

1. With a nice arrangement of bacon, boiled or mashed potatoes, and watercress (*à l'anglaise*), with the addition of one of the butters suggested above, served in little pats, one on each half of each kidney.

2. On a bed of risotto.

3. Encircled by crisp fried potatoes, whether as straws, or crisps, or fluted crisps. Add pats of butter, and a sprinkling of chopped parsley or tarragon or sage, as appropriate.

Here is another simple but delicious way of cooking kidneys:

Kidney Kebabs (*Rognons en Brochette*)

Skin the kidneys, cut them into suitable sized pieces of a uniform thickness. Alternate them on the skewers with squares of streaky bacon and small mushroom caps. Brush with melted butter, roll them in breadcrumbs, and grill. Turn them every few minutes, so that they are cooked all round.

Serve them on a bed of mashed potato, laid side by side, with the juices from the grill pan poured over them. Sprinkle them with chopped chives, or parsley, or sage.

This recipe can be varied in all kinds of ways. The main thing is to alternate lean, dry ingredients with fat or juicy ones. I learnt this at open-air lunch-parties, organized, *en brochette*, by an Anglo-French friend years before the barbecue became fashionable. The day before, he would go down to the butcher's shop, and return with a load of kidneys, liver, belly of pork, heart and smoked bacon, conveniently cut up into rough cubes. Then he prepared a fearsome marinade in his cave-house kitchen – oil, red wine, herbs, garlic, spices, and raw onion – and soaked the meat in it overnight.

Next day he left his women guests, soon oil to the elbow, to string the meat onto long thin, almost bodkin-thin, fencing foils, which he'd picked up in a Paris flea-market. Tomato-chunk, lean meat, onion, fat meat, lean meat, mushroom cap, bacon, tomato-chunk ... while he built his brick fireplace and got the charcoal to the right temperature. Food never tasted so delicious – or was judgement seduced by the strong full wine of Mesland, the cave-encircled courtyard, and the golden, harmonious view of Touraine?

Rognons de Porc Sautés (1)

Skin the kidneys, remove the hard white core, and slice thinly. Melt some butter to a froth in a heavy frying pan, add the kidney slices and sprinkle with salt and freshly-ground black pepper. Cook quickly on both sides. Serve with lemon quarters.

Rognons de Porc Sautés en Pilaff

Soften a medium, chopped onion in 3 oz. of butter until it is golden. Add half a pound of rice and stir in the melted butter until it is transparent. Pour in a pint of hot water and boil until the rice is cooked. Meanwhile blanch and fry two ounces of almonds. Cook four pig's kidneys as in the above recipe. Drain the rice, arrange on a serving dish in a ring, put the kidneys in the centre and garnish with the fried almonds. Make a little sauce by swilling a quarter of a pint of good stock round the kidney pan, and quickly reducing it – pour over the kidneys and serve.

Rognons Sautés aux Champignons

You need $\frac{1}{4}$ lb. mushrooms to each kidney for this recipe. And for four kidneys, 6 oz. fortified wine (sherry, Marsala, Madeira, sweet vermouth), 6 oz. good meat stock and 3-4 oz. sour cream. Cook the sliced mushrooms and sliced kidneys in two separate pans, in butter as for *Rognons*

Sautés above. Put onto the serving dish and keep hot while you make the sauce. Raise the heat under the kidney pan and pour in the wine and stock. Bubble fiercely until you have a rich, well-flavoured liquid. Stir in the cream, taste, correct seasoning and pour over the kidneys and mushrooms. Serve with triangles of toast, or baked bread slices.

Rognons de Porc Sautés (2)

This is a good way to cook kidneys, if they have a 'goût très prononcé d'urine si désagréable', as one book firmly puts it.

Skin the kidneys, remove the hard white centre bit, and slit in two. Put some lard into a heavy frying pan and sauté the pieces of kidney on each side; a minute a side is enough. Remove the kidneys, drain them well. Throw away the fat and juice from the pan, wash it out and put it back on the stove with some butter in it. When the butter foams, put the kidneys in and fry till they are done.

If at the same time you fry some croutons of bread in butter, cut to the same size as the pieces of kidney, and serve the kidneys on top, sprinkled with salt, pepper, parsley, and *chopped garlic* (not crushed) which has been simmered for a moment or two in the pan juices, you will have *rognons sautés à l'ail*. A deliciously hearty dish.

Rognons au Vin Blanc

Another homely and excellent recipe from the same source (*La Charcuterie à la Campagne*, Henriette Babet-Charton). Prepare the kidneys as in the previous recipe, then instead of frying them in lard, put them into a pan of boiling water for three minutes, removed from the heat immediately the kidneys go in. Drain and dry them. Melt some butter in a frying pan, add the kidneys when it is frothing. As soon as they begin to turn golden, sprinkle them with a little flour and continue to cook until they are a yellowish-brown. Add enough white wine to make a little sauce, salt and pepper. Let it bubble away for a few minutes, and turn it all into a serving dish; keep warm in a low oven whilst you make some triangular croutons, enough to go round the edge of the kidneys in the dish.

Rognons de Porc en Casserole

To each kidney, you will need 2 oz. of bacon, 4 tiny onions, ¼ lb. small new potatoes, nearly cooked, half a small clove of garlic, 2 oz. of good stock.

Use a casserole that will go on top of the stove, as well as in the oven. Enamelled cast iron is best. Otherwise use a frying pan for the preparatory cooking, then transfer the ingredients to an earthenware or pyrex dish.

Put some butter into the casserole, fry the bacon diced and the onions whole. When they are golden, the bacon transparent, remove and keep on one side whilst you sauté the kidneys, skinned but whole, both sides. When they have changed colour, put the onions and bacon back into the pot, and surround the kidneys with the small new potatoes. Add a little more butter, salt, pepper and garlic. Put the pot into the oven, *without covering it,* at a medium heat, and leave to finish cooking. About twenty-five minutes. Five minutes before the end pour in the stock, which should be enough to moisten the ingredients, rather than drown them. Serve in the cooking dish.

Rognons de Porc à la Liégeoise

This is a delicious recipe if you have some fresh juniper berries. The number you require depends on the number of kidneys you are using. Follow the recipe above except that you omit the vegetables and bacon. Five minutes before the kidneys have finished cooking in the oven, pour on a little stock, add the juniper berries (crushed – about 2 or 3 per kidney), and a measure of gin which has been warmed and set alight.

Rognons de Porc Clémentine

Follow the above recipe, omitting the vegetables and bacon. Five minutes before the end add half a pound of small mushroom caps (per two kidneys), which have been sautéed in butter for five minutes first, pour on four table-spoons of port (or other fortified wine like Marsala, Madeira, or sherry), and let this bubble down to a good sauce. Season with a teaspoon of French mustard, and put the casserole back in the oven for five minutes.

Omelette aux Rognons

Mince (or chop finely) a pig's kidney into a small saucepan. Pour on enough boiling water to cover. Leave for two minutes. Strain and sauté the kidney in hot, frothing butter until it is cooked. Beat two eggs lightly in a basin, tip in the cooked kidney and season. Run a small knob of butter round a heated 8-inch omelette pan until it is coated. Pour in the mixture and draw the cooked part up, away from the heat, tilting the pan slightly. Use a palette knife or a small fish slice to do this, and let the runny part flow down. Don't overcook – omelettes are best when they are firm outside and almost liquid in the centre. Fold in half, slide onto a very hot plate, top with a knob of butter and a little chopped parsley and rush to the table.

This is enough for one person. If you have a number to feed, it is advisable to make one large omelette in a huge pan, rather than a lot of small ones.

Pithiviers aux Rognons

This is an old, exotic version of the un-kidneyed Pithiviers cakes which are sold in many northern French pâtisseries. Nobody will be able to guess what gives the delicious almond filling its interesting, nutty texture. Serve it warm, with single cream, as a pudding in the traditional French Sunday-lunch way. This recipe is slightly adapted from

Carême's (part VIII of *French Cookery*, the translation by William Hall, published in 1836). You can, of course, leave out the kidney – but don't.

The rose-shape is traditional to the *gâteau de Pithiviers feuilleté* – Pithiviers is a small town in the Loiret, south of Paris, where the cake was, by tradition, first made. You can make a good stop at the small modern restaurant, Au Péché Mignon on the outskirts of the town; start with the other great speciality, lark pâté, and drink Quincy, a beautiful Loire wine.

Buy or make 1 lb. puff pastry.

FILLING

    1 pig's kidney, baked for 10 minutes in a hot oven, then minced
    ¼ lb. ground almonds
    3 oz. softened butter
    3 oz. caster sugar
    1 oz. crushed macaroons or ratafias (optional)
    Finely grated rind of a lemon
    2 egg yolks
    2 tablespoons thick cream
    Beaten up egg and tablespoon water to glaze
    Icing sugar for final glaze

Pithiviers cake

Mix all the ingredients together for the filling. An electric blender is the best solution. It should result in a smooth yellow cream with little flecks of kidney.

Line a 9½-inch diameter pie plate (shallow, like a dinner

plate with an inch rim) with half the puff pastry. Put on the filling, but keep the raised edge clear. If you have too much, keep it to make small tarts with the pastry trimmings. Brush the pastry edge with the beaten egg, and lay on a lid of pastry.

Now the fun begins. Make eight small nicks at regular intervals round the edge, then press up the pastry in and up on either side of each nick to form eight petals. Pierce a small hole in the centre. Brush the lid with the egg glaze and score it, with a sharp pointed knife, with curvy lines – be careful not to go through to the filling – for a flower effect. The illustration will give you a good idea of how this is usually done, the Pithiviers trademark so to say.

Put into a hot oven (430°F., Mark 7) for ten minutes to puff up the pastry well. But watch it, and lower the heat to Mark 3, 350°F., so that it can cook steadily for another half an hour. Lay a sheet of greaseproof paper on top if it shows signs of catching too much. You will observe that the pastry parts along the scored lines now appear white against the rich golden brown of the rest of the lid. Take it out of the oven, turn the oven up to Mark 8, and sprinkle the Pithiviers evenly with sifted icing sugar before putting it back to glaze. Once again, watch it – charring at this stage would be a tragedy – and remove the moment it is shiny and gold.

THE LIVER

Pig's liver can be bought at the *charcuterie*, but makes its usual appearance in *pâté de foie*, page 79. It must be confessed that pig's liver is neither so delicate in flavour nor so tender as the fine calf's liver to be bought at a high price in France (English calf's liver cannot be compared with it – I imagine this is due to methods of rearing or a more lax definition of the word 'calf'). Nonetheless, pig's liver is nutritious and inexpensive, and can be turned into dishes that are well worth eating, apart from the delicious pâtés.

Foie de Porc en Brochette

Slice the liver, and divide the slices into uniform-sized pieces. An overnight soak in a well-seasoned marinade (herbs, spices, as well as oil and some red wine) is an improvement, but not essential. Cut some fat pork into the same number of pieces, and string them alternately with the liver onto skewers. Mushrooms, tomatoes, onions, can be used as well. Very fat bacon is also suitable, the kind you buy for a few coppers with hardly any lean at all. Brush with melted butter, roll in breadcrumbs and grill gently until crisp and brown. Turn the skewers from time to time. Serve on a bed of mashed potatoes, surrounded with watercress, or mushrooms, tomatoes, and glazed onions.

Foie de Porc à l'Anglaise

In other words liver and bacon.

Slice the liver thinly, turn it over in seasoned flour.

Prepare the bacon, as many rashers as slices of liver, and fry it in butter, arranging it nicely on an oven dish. Have some scrubbed, unpeeled potatoes boiling at the same time, so that they will be cooked when the liver is finished. Pour off and keep the bacon fat.

Keep the bacon hot in a low oven, and fry the liver very quickly in a fresh lot of butter. Two minutes a side should be ample, unless your slices are rather thick. Time this carefully – the liver should only just be cooked to a point of juicy succulence. Nothing is worse than leathery liver. Remove to the serving dish which already contains the bacon.

Add the bacon fat to the liver fat and juices, add some lemon juice, and pour over the dish. Sprinkle with chopped parsley.

Drain the potatoes, cut them to a convenient size, take off the skins, and finish them with butter and parsley.

A simple dish, but very much better for taking care with its preparation.

Foie de Porc au Beurre Bercy

Sauté slices of pig's liver and serve *beurre Bercy*.

Put a tablespoon of chopped onion into a small pan with ¼ pint of white wine (5 oz.). Bring to the boil, and leave it to bubble away until it's reduced to half the original quantity. Let the mixture cool, then mix it up with 6 oz. of butter. Add chopped parsley and lemon juice to taste. Ideally you should also add 8 to 10 oz. of cooked beef marrow. You can serve it chilled, in pats; or else make a sauce, by adding the onion and wine mixture to half a pint of *velouté* sauce (page 66). Simmer it for five minutes, and just before serving stir in 3 oz. of butter cut into pieces, and some chopped parsley.

Foie de Porc à l'Espagnole

Spicy combinations of onion and tomato go well with liver. For *foie de porc à l'espagnole*, serve the fried liver on a bed of tomatoes cooked to a pulp, and flavoured with a little tarragon (sauté chopped onion in butter till golden and transparent, add a crushed clove of onion and half a pound of peeled tomatoes cut in quarters. Cover closely and let it bubble down to a good flavoury mass, season with salt, pepper and the tarragon). Garnish with onion rings, soaked in milk for an hour, tossed in seasoned flour and fried in deep oil. Scatter some chopped parsley on top.

Foie de Porc à la Lyonnaise

Onions alone are a delicious accompaniment. Cover the slices of fried liver with a scatter of onion rings fried gently in butter (not overdone to a burnt frizzle). Add 2 tablespoons wine vinegar or lemon juice to the pan juices, and ½ pint good stock. Bubble it down to a small amount of good sauce, and pour it over the liver and onions. Chopped parsley is the usual finish, but try chopped sage and a dash or two of cayenne pepper.

Foie de Porc Braisé

Buy a large piece of pig's liver, say 2 lb., and half a pound
of very fat bacon. Cut the bacon into strips and lard the liver,
using a larding needle. More messily, if you don't possess a
larding needle, make incisions in the liver with a sharp
pointed knife and push short strips of the bacon in.

Season the liver with salt, black pepper and parsley,
wrap it up in a piece of caul (softened in tepid water), and
lay it on some strips of pig's skin (*couenne*), or the left-over
pieces of fat bacon.

Pour over it a measure of brandy, surround with three
carrots, cut into round sections, three small onions stuck
with two cloves each, a *bouquet garni* (parsley, thyme, bay),
a large clove of garlic crushed and some black peppercorns.

Add enough white wine, or white wine and stock, to
come just below the top of the liver. Put the lid on the dish,
jamming it tight with silver foil. Simmer it for an hour.

To make the sauce, drain the liquid, skim off the fat, and
reduce it by boiling hard.

The two essentials in this recipe are the preliminary
larding, and the brandy and white wine.

If you substitute very small onions, the kind sold for
pickling, and omit the cloves, you can serve the liver
surrounded by carrots and onions, with the sauce poured
over and a sprinkling of parsley, as *foie de porc à la bourgeoise*.

Foie de Porc Rôti aux Truffes

This is a magnificent recipe, accompanied by a magnificent
sauce, *sauce Périgueux*; Périgueux is the capital of the
Dordogne, the most important truffle area, and any dish
described as *Périgueux* means that it's been prepared with
truffles.

1 large piece of pig's liver, 2–3 lb.
1 large piece of caul, enough to wrap easily round the liver
4–5 oz. truffles
4 oz. very fat pork

2 wineglasses olive oil
1 wineglass of Madeira
Salt, pepper, spices
A little good brown jelly from roast meat or poultry to glaze at
the end

First prepare the liver. Lard it with small strips of the fat pork, make small incisions with the point of a sharp knife and push in tiny pieces of truffle so that they are well distributed. Leave the liver for twenty-four hours in a marinade of the oil, wine and seasonings.

When you are ready to cook, assemble two sheets of greaseproof, plenty of silver foil and a shallow oven dish, or baking sheet with raised edges, in case the juices from the meat leak out.

Oil the greaseproof paper on one side only, and put one piece, un-oiled side down, on top of the other piece, oiled side up. Wrap the liver in the caul (run under a warm tap for a moment to make it pliable), and lay it, with the juices from the marinade, on the greaseproof paper. Wrap the liver up, lay it on a sheet of silver foil and crinkle the edges together to make a loose, but firmly sealed parcel. Lay this in the oven dish, or baking sheet, and put in a medium oven for an hour and a half.

Just before taking the meat out of the oven, melt down a little jelly from a roast. This you will pour over the caul-wrapped liver, when the greaseproof and foil have been removed, and return it to the oven for a moment or two to glaze, whilst you finish off the *sauce Périgueux*.

Sauce Périgueux (page 60), might just as well be made from a *good sauce espagnole*, since the truffles cost so much, rather than the remains of the gravy from a roast or stew. Do the hard work the previous day, and add the Madeira and truffles just before the liver is ready to serve. *Remember that the sauce must not boil* after the truffles and Madeira have been added.

HEART, LUNGS AND SPLEEN

The heart, lungs and spleen do not make an appearance in the *charcutier*'s shop, any more than they do (except for the heart sometimes) in an English butcher's. But they aren't wasted, disappearing discreetly but nutritiously into pâtés, *gayettes*, sausages and faggots according to nationality. Here is a recipe for all three of them together.

Fressure de Porc à l'Anglaise

  Pig's heart, lungs, spleen
  Clarified butter (or butter and oil)
  Plain flour
  Salt and pepper
  Wineglass Madeira, Marsala or equivalent
  ¼ pint beef stock
  Dash Worcester sauce
  Parsley

Set a pan of water, salted, on to boil. Put the lungs and spleen in when it is bubbling. The lungs will float, as they are full of air, so they must be held down. The other alternative is to beat the air out of them first. Keep the water bubbling away for 15 minutes. Cut the heart into thin slices, then the lungs and spleen when they have finished blanching. Dredge the slices with flour, salt and pepper.

Melt the clarified butter in a large, heavy frying pan, and brown the meat gently. It should be an appetizing golden colour, not frizzled.

Arrange the pieces on an ovenproof dish attractively – remember that you have a certain amount of prejudice to overcome. Keep warm in a low oven whilst you make the sauce.

Stir a tablespoon of flour into the pan juices, to make a medium-brown *roux*. Next moisten with the wine and beef stock. Add more stock if you require a runnier sauce.

Finally flavour with salt and pepper, if necessary, Worcester sauce or a dash of lemon juice, pour it over the meat and sprinkle with chopped parsley. It is absolutely essential to serve this with crisply fried, golden brown croutons. Cut the bread into triangles, fry them in butter-and-oil; then dip one corner in sauce, then in more chopped parsley and stick the opposite corner into the dish.

Cœur de Porc à l'Orange

The heart can be cooked to provide a most delicious dish – to my mind, greatly preferable to the *fressure à l'anglaise*. One heart per person is ample – and four would do for five people.

    4 pigs' hearts
    2–3 oz. butter-and-oil
    ½ lb. onions
    Rasher or two bacon
    1 heaped tablespoon flour
    ¾–1 pint stock
    6 oz. wineglass of wine, red or white
    Marmalade
    1 orange
    Orange liqueur – miniature bottle
    1 clove garlic
    Salt and pepper

Cut the surplus fat off the hearts, brown them with chopped onion and bacon rashers in a large heavy frying pan, in the butter-and-oil. Remove the meat and vegetables to the casserole, stir enough flour into the pan juices to make a brown *roux*, and add stock and wine enough to make a sauce. Add the garlic, salt and pepper to taste, and a tablespoon or two of marmalade (the bitter chunky kind). Pour this into the casserole, and simmer gently until the hearts are done – about 1½ hours.

Remove the hearts, slice them thinly and arrange in a shallow oven-proof dish. Skim fat off the sauce, and taste it. If it is a bit tasteless, boil it down hard until it improves. Flavour finally with orange juice, orange peel and liqueur.

Barely cover the hearts with this sauce, putting the rest into a sauceboat to hand separately. Warm through in the oven, and sprinkle with chopped parsley. Serve with boiled potatoes, and an orange and tomato salad.

Another way to finish the hearts is to spread a layer of breadcrumbs, quarter of an inch thick, on top of the hearts and sauce, and put the dish into a hot oven for the crumbs to brown. You could dot them with tiny bits of butter, but don't make them too fatty.

Cœur et Rognons en Brochette

In other words heart and kidney kebabs. Amounts depend on the number of people who are eating – I allow 6 oz. of meat per head. So for four people you would need 8 oz. of heart, 8 oz. of kidneys, and 8 oz. of very fat belly of pork, fresh or salted. Cut them all up into cubes.

Marinade them overnight in a spicy and herby mixture of half a pint of oil, quarter of a pint of red wine or wine vinegar, 2 medium onions cut up roughly, 2 sprigs of thyme, 2 bay leaves, plenty of ground pepper, salt, 3 cloves of garlic crushed, a teaspoon of *quatre-épices* or of any mixture of spices that you like. You can of course add orange peel, lemon peel and juice – anything that imagination and experience suggests. Give everything a good stir up before you go to bed, and again first thing in the morning. Incidentally marinade is the poor man's refrigerator – you can keep meat in it for four or five days in cold weather. Anything that can't really go into the brine tub can soak in a marinade. Prepare the kebabs by stringing the meat onto the skewers – fat pork, kidney, heart, fat pork, kidney, heart, fat pork . . . . Grill gently, turning them over from time to time and basting with the marinade. This gives some good flavoury juice in the grill pan.

Serve the kebabs, sprinkled with parsley, on a bed of rice or mashed potato, with the juices poured over them. A cool green salad is all that's required by way of a second vegetable.

THE LIGHTS

Lights have no great nutritional value, whether for humans, cats or dogs. They can be delicious, however, which is another thing. The trouble is that most people cheerfully beat out some veal or steak, but baulk at beating the air out of lungs. I suspect that this is the main reason why they are not usually displayed for sale either in France or England, rather than their lack of food value. But take courage. The way to cook them is to stew them – here is the basic method, with variations:

Civet de Mou de Porc

Beat the lungs to expel the air – an all-wooden rolling pin is ideal for this. Cut them into small pieces, discarding the larger tubes and windpipe. Season with salt and pepper.

Set a heavy frying-pan on a medium heat, with clarified butter, butter-and-oil, or lard in it. It is important to keep flavours clear when frying, particularly in the preparation of slightly off-beat food, so never use a muddle-up of weeks of dripping. This dish would be ruined if the preliminary cooking were done in a tired combination of mutton and beef fat – in fact, I can think of no dish that would be improved by it, and few that could stand it. If you have no clarified butter to hand, the addition of oil to ordinary butter will prevent it from browning rapidly. Pure fat from cooking bacon would, of course, do instead of lard.

Brown the pieces of lung evenly, then add 2 tablespoons of flour.

Let it colour to a coffee shade, before adding stock (chicken cube stock, or veal stock) and red wine in the proportion of two to one. Stir until everything bubbles away gently, with the meat bathed in a smooth sauce. Turn into a casserole with a well-fitting lid. This is the time to add embellishments – a clove or two of garlic crushed, celery sticks, cut into two lengthways, leeks cut into two lengthways, a large onion quartered, carrots quartered, a *bouquet garni* tied together. The point being that all these things, apart from the garlic, will have eventually to be removed, so keep them large.

Cover closely and put into a gentle, simmering oven for an hour and a half.

Take out the vegetables and *bouquet*, put the meat into another oven-worthy serving dish. Add finely grated lemon peel to the sauce, and some lemon juice to taste, then pour enough over the pieces of meat to keep them moist, without drowning them. Lid on (or silver foil), and into the oven for another 30 minutes simmering.

Serve with a sprinkling of chopped parsley on top, and an accompanying dish of plainly boiled *pasta* – spaghetti, noodles, bows, shells, what you will. Devotees always of crispness, we like triangles of toast or fried bread; in early summer, green beans just cooked until they still retain a hint of crispness (*al dente*) and not a second longer.

Mou à la Bourgeoise

When the meat is transferred to the second casserole for its final cooking, add tiny pickling onions cooked in a small amount of red wine and a tablespoon of brown sugar and a tablespoon of butter (shake them often to make sure they don't catch, and don't use a small pan – one layer of onions is the most satisfactory), glazed carrots (cut in rings, cooked in a tight-lidded pan with a tablespoon each of water and butter and white sugar), and sautéed cubes of bacon.

Mou à la Bonne Femme

Add mushrooms instead of the carrots in *Mou à la Bourgeoise*, and small new potatoes.

Mou à la Provençale

Essentially garlic in the first instance, when you fry the meat. Then no flour but white wine – boil hard to reduce to a good flavour. Then add chicken stock and tomato sauce or tomatoes (if fresh, peeled and quartered). Half a pepper is a good addition – cut into strips, and no seeds. When this is all bubbling away, pour some of the liquid onto two or three tablespoons of flour in a bowl. Stir so that there are no lumps, and return to the pan. Cook in a covered casserole for an hour and a half, then transfer the pieces of meat to a second casserole, arrange black olives around them (2-4 oz., according to taste and the amount of lung), and some of the sauce, and simmer for half an hour.

Initially it is best to fry the meat in olive oil. If you haven't got any, soak the black olives in some plain vegetable oil for a few days. I normally keep black olives in a jar of this oil in the store cupboard, and use it for dishes *à la provençale*.

Mou en Blanquette

Cook as in the first recipe, but use white wine instead of red, and add mushrooms, leeks and onions only. Add an extra chicken cube. Of course if you have some good chicken stock, this is the ideal. After the hour and a half, remove the meat to the second casserole and keep it warm whilst the liquid reduces by boiling hard. Keep tasting.

For a pint of sauce mix two egg yolks and four tablespoons of cream together in a bowl. Just before you are ready to serve, pour the sauce onto the yolks and cream, stirring briskly. Return this to the pan and cook gently over a very low heat until it is thick and bland. *It absolutely must not boil.* If you feel nervous about this, don't return the sauce to the pan, but set the bowl over a pan of simmering water and stir it with attention. This should certainly be safe from curdling. For the second process allow yourself ten minutes, and clear the kitchen. Finally add some unsalted butter, lemon juice to taste and chopped parsley. Pour this over the meat and serve.

Wienerbeuscherl

Austrian *Wienerbeuscherl* is a variation of these recipes, using the heart as well as the lungs. Do not fry them to begin with, but cook for as long as necessary in the *court-bouillon*. Melt some butter in a medium-sized saucepan, and cook two tablespoonfuls of flour in it until you have a golden *roux*. Leave this to one side whilst you cut the meat into small strips. Make a lightly-thickened sauce, by returning the *roux* to the fire and pouring on some of the strained *bouillon* in which the lung and heart cooked. When this is ready, add the chopped meat, warm it through and give a final flavouring of lemon peel, finely grated, and some lemon juice. The sauce should taste pleasantly sharp. Let it simmer for five minutes very gently. Serve it in a sturdy dish, and accompany with *pasta*, or potato dumplings.

THE SPLEEN

The spleen (*rate*) is a long flat oval of dark reddish brown meat, with a line of white fat running from end to end. It usually disappears – in England, as in France – with the rest of the pluck into faggots, sausages and pâtés. In the

Spleen

charcuterie, however, you do see small succulent rolls of an appetizing brown on occasion; these are the spleen, cut in half, rolled up round the line of fat, speared with a tooth-pick and cooked in with the *rillons* (page 320), which provide necessary extra fat. They are eaten cold, with plenty of French mustard, and bread.

Cut 1 lb. fat belly of pork into 2-inch cubes. Remove the skin and keep it to enrich a beef stew. Cut two spleens in half, roll up each half with the line of fat turned inwards and spear them through with a toothpick or sharpened matchstick. Set a heavy pan to heat with a ladle of water. Put in the cubes of belly of pork and the spleen rolls. Cover and set in a slow oven for an hour. Remove the spleen rolls. Leave off the lid and give the pork *rillons* another hour to brown all over.

Rolled spleen

Country people in Wiltshire make a good sage and onion stuffing, spread the spleen thickly with it and sew it up. Wrapped in a large piece of caul, softened to pliability in tepid water and tied with string, it is then roasted in a medium oven for an hour.

THE TESTICLES

Unless you breed and rear your own pigs, the testicles are a delicacy unlikely to come your way – whether in England or France. Most male pigs are castrated soon after they are born, so even the most co-operative butcher will not be able to help you. I have eaten calf's *animelles* in Italy, as part of the *financière* garnish: they are delicate in flavour and quite delicious. Far superior, for instance, to heart, lungs, brains and spleen. *Larousse Gastronomique* concurs in this opinion, saying also that in the past they were much favoured in Italy, Spain and France. I should like to know whether this was really because of their flavour, or because of a belief in sympathetic magic. Even the best reference books can be most tantalizing – but at least Prosper Montagne gives several recipes for sheep's *animelles*, which would be quite suitable for the pig's too. Here is a summary of them:

PREPARATION

First the *animelles* must be skinned by scalding, then soaked in cold, salted water, for between two and three hours. Slice them. After this they can be fried in butter, dipped in batter and fried in butter, marinaded and fried in butter, simmered in a *court-bouillon* and served with a bland cream sauce or a sharp vinaigrette.

Animelles de Porc Frites

Prepare and slice.

Marinade for at least an hour, or until you are ready to start cooking, in a small amount of oil, vinegar, spices and herbs. Dry them well, then sprinkle with seasoned flour or dip in batter, and fry in foaming butter.

Serve them with fried mushrooms (*aux champignons*), or fried parsley. I can never bring myself to fry parsley – to me the idea has bituminous, mummified overtones, ever since I read that Richard Wilson compared Gainsborough's trees to fried parsley. But I pass on the suggestion.

Animelles de Porc à la Crème

Prepare and slice, but don't marinade. Fry in butter until they are cooked.

At the same time have half a pint of unsalted *Béchamel* sauce (butter, flour and milk) reducing. If you have cream to spare, enrich the sauce with this and a tablespoonful of butter just before adding the fried *animelles*. Season with salt.

After this point do not let the sauce boil again, or you risk curdling. Keep it just under the simmer for about ten minutes. If you feel nervous about this, do it in a double saucepan or a bowl over a pan of barely simmering water. Don't take any risks.

If you want to stretch the quantity to a more substantial dish, serve the creamed *animelles* in a pre-baked puff pastry case or in small vol-au-vent cases.

Instead of frying the slices of *animelle*, simmer them in a *court-bouillon* of a light kind – white wine, for instance, not red. Then drain them and add to the cream sauce I've just described, or serve them with a lemon juice and oil vinaigrette.

The Fat of the Pig

PORK FAT

FROM early times, one of the pig's most valuable assets was the high proportion of fat his carcass provided. Apart from being important to the human body's welfare, fat makes a good preservative of lean meat, particularly neutral-tasting pork fat. Even nowadays, with refrigeration, many farmer's wives in France like to preserve pork, goose, turkey, rabbit and duck in lard. These *confits*, as they are called, may be used gradually. One has only to melt the huge crock of meat and lard very gently, take out enough pieces for the occasion, then return the crock to a cool larder for the fat to solidify again. This can be repeated a time or two, so long as the remaining pieces of meat do not come in contact with the air, but stay covered by the lard. Goose is preserved in its own fat, eked out with lard; joints of it go into the famous *cassoulet* of Languedoc (page 163), and the fat imparts a delicious flavour to potatoes and bread fried in it.

But the *confits* are really farmhouse preparations, for the protracted convenience of a single, often isolated, family. In the *charcuteries*, the fatness of the pig is delectably presented in three other ways. Firstly, in great white earthenware pots of whipped and whirled lard; secondly in large and small bowls and mugs of *rillettes*, a kind of potted pork; and thirdly, in golden-brown cubes called *rillons*, belly of pork cut up and cooked in its own fat until crisp outside and moist within.

If, as often happens in small towns and villages, the *charcutier* is also the butcher, you will see how beautifully he prepares joints of beef for roasting. By English standards, or lack of standards, they are hardly recognizable, these elegantly tied, sausage-shaped pieces of beef, with wide strips or bards of pork fat along the sides to keep the meat basted while it roasts. For a dinner party, you may find that the joint you ordered has been further embellished by flowers or geometric shapes cut in pork fat, at once decorative and practical.

Should you wish to lard your own fillet steak, or hare saddle, or pigeon, you can always buy small chunks of pork fat for the purpose (page 313). I find larding one of the most satisfactory of the quieter kitchen occupations. It is a soothing and unhurried performance; and I like being reminded, too, of Perrault's Princess, in *Riquet à la Houppe*, who saw the ground open before her, and a number of roasting cooks emerge, who promptly set to work with their larding needles on joints of meat, set on a trestle table

Storage and Preserving Jars

beneath the high trees of the wood. Only a French fairy story would pay such nice attention to cooking!

Rillettes and *rillons*, the former often sold in brown-glazed stoneware mugs of various sizes, are on sale throughout France, but I look in vain, even in Tours itself, for a *quiche tourangelle*. I always end up buying the *rillettes* and *rillons*, and making one myself (page 324). In England, of course, you have to make everything yourself – unless you are in easy distance of Soho. It's worth doing this in large quantity. *Rillettes* and potted *rillons* can be kept for months, so you have a ready-to-hand hors d'œuvre, or the basic materials for a *quiche tourangelle*, which most people would find adequate as a main dish.

In France, don't make the mistake of asking for *lard* if you want lard. *Lard* is the French for bacon, and very expensive it is too. Where we might use it in pâtés or *daubes*, the French housewife would use thin strips of pork fat, or salt pork, or a slice of fresh belly of pork. This is worth following, the result is blander and less aggressive. If you intend to make your own fat pork dishes, it is worth searching for stoneware pots (*pots de grès*) in which to preserve them. Not earthenware. Its coarser clay and glaze need firing at a low temperature, which means that the glaze chips easily, and the body is frequently porous and easily cracked, making sterilization impossible. Wide-mouthed French preserving jars (*bocal*, pl. *bocaux*) are excellent (Kilner jars are quite all right though the narrower openings are not so convenient). French *bazaars* are the best places to get suitable preserving containers – they cost very little, and there are many attractive shapes to choose from. A *bazaar* is not a few stalls and a bran tub opened by the squire's wife, but a most useful emporium where you may buy a wide range of things from hair-grips to saucepans, toys, and household china both useful (storage jars, casseroles) and frivolous (wild duck plaques, of a garishness only the French could achieve).

The different sorts of pork fat are:

La panne (flair, flare, flay, flead, flick, leaf fat), a sheet or layer of fat forming an interior covering to the loin, and enveloping the kidneys. Best taken from bacon pigs, and used for the best lard, *boudins blancs* (page 144), and fine pâtés.

Lard de poitrine – the fat belly-cut, which includes the hard fat lying under the skin, the lean meat and the softer fat. When cured, or cured and smoked, this gives green or smoked streaky bacon. In France this self-basting cut is used for *rillons, rillettes* (pages 320 to 323), and *petit salé* (salt belly of pork, page 176) by the *charcutier*, and as an enriching ingredient in beef stews by the housewife.

Gras dur (back fat, speck), the hard layer of fat under the skin (*couenne*), can be salted for keeping, melted for good-quality lard, or used fresh in sausages, stuffings, pâtés and for larding. Expertly-cut slices of this hard fat are tied neatly round lean joints of beef for roasting, or poultry, or game, to keep them moist.

Gras mou or *fondant* includes the poorer quality fat immediately touching the lean pork, and all the scrapings (*les ratis*) of fat which surround the intestines and the mesentery (mudgeon, gut fat, crow or frill, page 278) which holds the intestines in place. This fat provides an inferior lard, which should not be mixed in with the fine lard coming from the flair and hard back fat.

Crépine (caul, veil, kell) is a veil of fat surrounding the stomach. Made pliable in tepid water, it is wrapped round lean meat for roasting, or pâtés, faggots and *gayettes*, to provide a permanent basting layer.

Caul fat

Grillons, or *grattons* (skretchings, cracklings, scribbings, graves, greaves) are solid scraps remaining after the fat parts have been melted down for lard, and the liquid poured off. They can be potted and eaten like *rillettes* (page 320), or, in the case of the mesentery, eaten immediately as an hors d'œuvre.

LARDING

Larding is the introduction of small strips of pork fat known as lardoons (*lardons*) into very lean meat such as fillet steak, pigeons, saddle of hare, which might otherwise be too dry when cooked. For this pleasant little job you need, like the roasting cooks in Perrault's *Riquet à la Houppe*, a larding needle (*lardoire*), which is shaped like a very elongated, sharp-pointed cornet (page 28).

You can cut bacon fat into strips (*lardonner*) but the ideal is a nice slab of hard back fat, cut from under the skin of the loin. Chill it if possible, then cut into slices downwards and then across – see the illustration. Push each little *lardon* into the open end of the needle.

As one nineteenth-century cookery book says, seat yourself comfortably, lay a clean linen cloth on your left knee, then put the joint to be larded on top of the cloth. Take a stitch in the joint from right to left and pull the needle

Larding process

through, whilst releasing the *lardon*. It should project neatly at each end, like the second illustration.

This operation is great fun to do, and most soothing. It adds to the tenderness and flavour of the meat, and looks sensational: What more could one ask?

LARD

(*Saindoux*)

When the pig has been split in two, after the insides have all
been removed, a sheet of fat can be seen lying on the inside
of the ribs. It's easy to rip off, and from it and the hard fat
underneath the skin the best lard is made. At the bacon
factory, other fat parts are included in the final lard, the
mesentery is one of them. But if you have a good fat bacon
pig, keep this flay fat (*panne*) apart from the rest. For one
thing it melts at a different rate, and if it catches, it is
spoilt. Of course you can, if you wish, amalgamate the two
kinds of lard once they have been melted and are off the
fire, but not set.

If you want to have a bladder of lard to hang up in the
larder, you will have to soak the cleaned bladder in water
until it is soft. Don't pour in the lard (best quality only)
before it is half-set. Tie the bladder up so that there is no
air space between the lard and the string, and leave it to
cool off completely in cold water. Keep it hung up in a cool
dry place.

Preparation of Lard

NOTE: Do not add salt (it merely falls to the bottom of the
melting-pot), or herbs and spices (you may wish to use the
lard for recipes where such flavours would be inappropriate).

Panne, or flay in English. Remove fibres and any blood-
stained part of the fat. Cut into suitable sizes for passing
through a mincing machine – an electric one saves a lot of
time and strength – then soak it for five hours in cold water,
$\frac{1}{4}$ pint water to 1 lb. fat.

You can omit the soaking, and put the minced fat into a
heavy pan (cast-iron or enamelled cast-iron) with about
quarter of an inch of water in the bottom to stop the fat
sticking.

If you've soaked the fat, you will need hardly any water in the pan. Just a little to start it off.

Now set the pan on a very low, steady heat. Do not hurry this part of the process, or you will end up with a grimy-looking grease instead of beautifully snowy lard.

Pour off the fat as it melts to a milky liquid, through a strainer straight into sterilized glass jars. Even stoneware pots are too porous for the long-term storage of lard, and I do not suppose that most households have suitable metal containers, such as *charcuterie* handbooks recommend. In any event fill the jars right to the brim; the fat contracts as it hardens. Do not cover for forty-eight hours, then use jam-pot covers, with a final cover of silver-foil tied on tightly with fine string.

Lard Gras Dur. It is easy to see in a piece of loin or belly of pork, how the fat between the skin and the first bit of lean meat divides into two layers quite noticeably. The outer layer is easily pulled off, and makes excellent lard.

Skin it, and mince it as for the *panne* above. Then leave it to soak for five hours in cold water: if you have a pound of fat, soak it in a quarter of a pint of water.

You will find that this melts much more slowly than the *panne* fat. Whatever you do, don't hurry it along. If you doubt the thickness of your pot, use an asbestos mat to be absolutely sure. The little hard bits, the *grillons* as they are called, may take on a light brown colour, but this is all right. Just keep pouring off the liquid lard through a strainer, into jars, or into a large bowl if you intend to use it fairly soon. It can be mixed with melted lard from the *panne*, or flay, at this stage. *Charcutiers* whip the fat electrically as it cools. If you have an electric beater you could do the same. It makes a very light and delicate substance.

Soft fat, and scraps of fatty meat, the mesentery, can all be used to extract fat for quick consumption. Cut it into rough pieces, skin and all, except for the mesentery which should be cut into six-inch lengths. Soak the pieces for five hours in cold water as in recipe above, and use the same method of cooking. With the golden-brown pieces left in the strainer you can make:

GRATTONS, OR GRILLONS

The simplest way is to salt and pepper these bits, and eat them hot with mashed potatoes, or cold on bread as an hors d'œuvre. You can keep them too, by packing them closely into sterilized stoneware pots or glass jars, and covering them with half an inch of melted lard. If you're not going to eat the frilly mesentery separately (see page 278), chop the pieces to a uniform size with the other *grillons*. A moment or two in an electric blender produces quite a satisfactory result, somewhere between a laboriously-acquired chop and an unsatisfactory mush of mince.

VARIATIONS

Leave the remains to cool down properly. Chop them small (or whirl them in an electric blender, dropping them through the hole in the lid onto the fast-spinning blades – but don't overdo it to a purée), and season with salt, freshly-ground black pepper, *quatre-épices* or other spices, some chopped mild onion and crushed garlic and thyme. Put a glass of white wine in a heavy pan or casserole, add the meat mixture and let it simmer gently but steadily for an hour and a half. Be sure it doesn't catch. The best way to do this is to stir it often with a wooden spoon, and put the pan on an asbestos mat if you are using gas.

Unless you have had a marathon lard-making, there will not be enough *grillons* to keep. But you can always pot it in sterilized jars, and cover it hermetically with half an inch of melted lard.

Grillons Fines

These are really a sort of *rillettes* (page 320), because you don't just make them from remains as in the other two recipes above, but from fresh meat. But as they are known as *grillons,* I give the recipe here.

You need equal quantities of lean pork and the hard fat beneath the skin. Chop them roughly and leave them overnight in a mixture of salt, pepper and *quatre-épices* (or your own mixture of spices). The proportion of salt should be 2 oz. to 3 lb. of meat and fat together, with pepper and spices according to your own tastes but about one-eighth of the amount of salt.

Next day put a wineglass (4-5 oz.) of dry white wine in the cooking pot – proportionately more if you have over 3 lb. of meat. Add the meat, after washing it in a colander under the tap, and leave to cook very slowly for three hours, giving it an occasional stir with a wooden spoon to make sure it isn't sticking. About an hour before the end of the cooking time, correct the seasoning. Add more spices, and some chopped mild onion and garlic.

When they are cooked, strain off the fat, pack the *grillons* into sterilized stoneware pots or glass jars. When they are cold, melt the fat again which you strained off and cover the *grillons* to about half an inch deep, at least, better three-quarters of an inch. When the fat has hardened, cover with a close layer of silver foil and keep in a cool, dry place. This way they will last for months.

Grattons, or *Gratterons*

Larousse Gastronomique gives this recipe for *Grattons,* or *Gratterons,* from the Île de la Réunion. It is a huge success with children, and anyone who likes crackling.

Ask the butcher for a sheet of pig's skin with about three-quarters of an inch of fat attached. In other words the skin and layer of hard fat I was talking about, that can be separated quite easily. Ask him not to score it for crackling. Stress this: most butchers do it quite automatically.

Cut the skin and fat into 3-inch squares, and score the fat side only into smallish diamonds.

Now set a heavy pan on a gentle heat, and melt 2 oz. of

lard. Add the pork, fat side downwards, and transfer to a
gentle oven for about 4 hours. The skin will look quite
transparent. Now turn the heat up and leave the skin for
another half an hour, watching that it doesn't burn. The
idea is that it should swell into golden, crisp bubbles – a
crackling *de luxe*.

When they are done put them in a dish, well-drained of
fat, sprinkle with salt and serve.

As this dish can quite well be cooked on top of the oven –
remembering not to cover the pan at any stage of the
cooking whether you do it in the oven, or on top – I often
serve it as an accompaniment to a piece of roast pork.

PRESERVED PORK, GOOSE, TURKEY, DUCK AND RABBIT
(*Confits de Porc, d'Oie, de Dinde, de Canard, et de Lapin*)

Nowadays *confits d'oie* are particularly associated with the
south-west of France, but the goose is traditionally under
the protection of St Martin of Tours (? 315–97), that most
untypical Roman soldier who halved his cloak with a
beggar one freezing night, and who was loved and com-
memorated in churches all over Europe from his lifetime
onwards (even in far-off Galloway, St Ninian built a church
dedicated to him in about A D 400).

Back in not-so-far-off England after a good vintage in our
small Loir village, I like to make *confits d'oie et de porc* for the
winter ahead, soon after his feast day on November 11th
in the golden days of St Martin's Summer. Even in the
time of St Martin and St Ninian, Gaul had long been
celebrated for its hams. Did these great ascetics occasionally
profit by Touraine's tradition of *charcuterie*? I hope so; and I
am sure that later pilgrims did, who stopped at Tours on
their way to St James at Compostella. Without doubt they
ate *confits* and drank Loire wines on freezing nights, *in
memoriam Sancti Martini,* as a shield against the weather
outside.

BASIC METHOD FOR ALL CONFITS

Use boned pork from the hind loin. Cut it into large pieces and tie them with button thread so that they will not lose their shape in cooking.

Joint the birds and rabbit. Do not bone.

Leave the meat to salt for 24 hours, in the proportions of 2 lb. meat (boned pork, unboned birds and rabbit) to a mixture of 1½ oz. salt, a good pinch of saltpetre, half a teaspoon of thyme and half a bay leaf, and quarter of a teaspoon of freshly-ground black pepper. Rub the salt mixture into the meat, then leave it. Meanwhile assemble your pots: stoneware (*not earthenware*, it's too porous) or porcelain or wide-mouthed glass preserving jars. Wash them with boiling soda water to make sure they are absolutely clean, then sterilize them when the meat is nearly cooked and ready to be potted. Also prepare some wooden sticks by boiling. You need to lay two crosswise in each pot, so that the fat is able to encircle the meat completely.

Although one can in theory use large jars, and remove the preserved meat over a period of time at intervals, I have never pushed this too far. I use lidded stoneware storage jars of the kind sold widely in household *bazaars* in France, of a size to hold about six or seven pieces of meat, or even less (page 310).

Set a heavy cast-iron pan or large casserole on a gentle heat and melt in it half the amount of best lard (see page 314) that you have of meat. If you are lucky enough to be making *confits d'oie*, use the fat from the goose, and make it up to half the weight of meat with lard if necessary.

When the fat is hot, add the pieces of meat and cook them gently for between 1¼ and 2 hours. The way to judge when they are cooked is to pierce them with a knitting needle. If no liquid comes out, they are cooked; try the pieces at 1¼ hours, then at 15-minute intervals, because you do not want to overcook them. They will look pinkish because of the saltpetre, so don't be put off by that.

Put some strained fat into the jars you intend to use, up

to the top of the cross of sticks. Then pack in the pieces of meat, leaving 2 inches at the top of the jar. Pour over the strained fat right up to the brim, remembering that it will contract as it cools.

When the contents are quite cold, cover the jars with silver foil, pressing it right down onto the lard. Untouched the meat will keep for six months to a year.

To remove some meat from the jar, stand it at the side of the stove when it is warm, until the lard melts enough for you to spear the pieces. Put the jar back into the cool, and cover with a fresh piece of silver foil when the lard has hardened again. Make absolutely sure that all the remaining pieces are still well covered with a thick layer of lard.

As the meat is cooked, you can eat it cold with a salad and new potatoes, or a potato salad. More frequently it is eaten hot (having been heated in a frying pan with some of its own fat), and accompanied by mashed potatoes. Odd pieces find their way into *cassoulet* (particularly goose confits) and *potée*, which is halfway between soup and stew (pages 168 to 169).

You can insert pieces of garlic into the pork, rabbit and goose before cooking them; and eventually serve them hot with a sprinkling of finely chopped garlic and parsley.

See also *Cou d'Oie* or *de Dinde* (page 122).

BELLY OF PORK
(*Poitrine de Porc*)

In France, belly of pork is either salted and smoked for bacon, salted and boiled to be eaten cold (*petit salé*, page 176); or else cooked slowly in lard and turned into *rillettes* and *rillons*. Both can be preserved for a long time under a deep layer of lard, but, in the *charcuterie*, *rillons* are usually sold soon after they are made, and *rillettes* as well. The difference between them is one of size (*rillons* being solid cubes of golden brown, and *rillettes* being a solid mass of pounded and succulent fibres); they can quite well be cooked together in the same pan:

BASIC METHOD

1 lb. belly of pork, cut into 2-inch cubes

1½ lb. belly of pork, cut into small strips about 1 inch long and ¼ inch wide (you can use shoulder of pork instead)

1 lb. flair fat cut into smallish pieces (use the hard fat from under the skin, if you can't get flair fat)

Salt, pepper, spices, thyme, bay leaf

Using a heavy pan, put in the pork pieces and 2 oz. of water, so that the meat doesn't stick. Cook over a gentle heat, or in a low oven, covered, for four hours.

Separate the cubes of pork (the *rillons*) from the rest, and leave them to brown in a hotter oven, uncovered, or in an open pan on top of the stove.

Whilst they are finishing off, deal with the *rillettes*.

Put a larger strainer over a strong earthenware bowl, and pour the meat and fat from the cooking-pot into it. Press the meat gently, so that as much fat as possible falls through the mesh of the sieve, and transfer it to a mortar so that it can be pounded. Finally put it back in the sieve, and tear it apart with two forks into an even mass of fibres.

I cannot pretend that this is quick or easy, but the success of *rillettes* depends on it. You can eliminate the pounding by dropping the meat onto the fast-whirling blades of an electric blender. This demands judgement, because you must not reduce the meat to a porridge-like slush.

But whatever you do, don't put rillettes through the mincer, either before or after cooking.

Now season with salt, pepper, *quatre-épices* or other spices, a little garlic and thyme. Flavour is needed. Return to the pan and give the *rillettes* a quarter of an hour more on a gentle heat, so that the seasonings are well distributed. Pack lightly into sterilized stoneware (or glass or porcelain) pots, and cover with the fat from the cooking melted to a pouring consistency. Be careful not to include the meaty juices when you take the fat out of the bowl. A depth of half an inch of lard will preserve the *rillettes* beneath for six months to a year.

Next day, cover the lard with a close covering of silver foil, and another piece of it over the top of each pot, tied on with string. If you intend to keep the *rillettes* for a day or two only, no lard covering is required.

During all this, keep and eye on the *rillons*; put them to drain when they are an appetizing brown all over. Eat them cold, like *rillettes*, as an hors d'œuvre.

Alternatively, you can pot *rillons* like *confits*. In that case they are best heated through in an open pan when you come to eat them, in a little of their preserving fat, and served with mashed potatoes and a tart apple purée, or baked apple rings.

Rillettes de Paris

    1 lb. belly of pork
    1 oz. good lard
    ½ oz. salt
    Pepper and spices according to taste

The point of this recipe is the very prolonged gentle cooking of the pork, so that it is in the most melting condition possible by the time you have finished – and not 'dry and sandy'.

Cut the meat into pieces about 1 inch or 1½ inches long. Put them on to cook with the lard in a heavy pan on a very low flame indeed. Keep stirring so that the meat colours evenly to a pale gold.

Pour off the fat, and leave the meat to go on cooking for a further five hours on the lowest possible heat. From time to time pour on a little water to prevent the meat sticking.

Let the meat get quite cold. Then drop it onto the blades of an electric blender, if you have one. Otherwise you are condemned to chopping and pounding. The final result is a smooth, 'unctous' pâté, which you season with salt, pepper and spices, and add according to your own discretion as much of the drained-off fat as you like. 'Too high a flame will fry the pieces of meat and harden them', so this is the point to watch.

Rillettes d'Angers

1 lb. fresh pork
2 lb. boned goose
½ lb. of best lard
1 oz. salt, pepper and spices to taste

Follow the Basic Method.

Rillettes du Mans

1 lb. fresh pork (shoulder)
1½ lb. speck fat from the back, skinned
1 lb. chicken or rabbit, boned when weighed
1 oz. salt, pepper, cloves, bay, thyme

Follow the Basic Method, but include the bay leaf and thyme from the start of the cooking, and the cloves too.

Rillettes de Lapin

2 lb. young rabbit, weighed with bone
¾ lb. belly of pork, not too lean
¼ lb. speck fat from the back, skinned
Pepper, spices, and salt as required

Follow the Basic Method. The meat is cooked when the rabbit falls from the bones easily.

You can use salt pork for this recipe – if you do, you probably won't need to add extra salt at the seasoning stage.

Rillettes d'Oie, de Dinde, or de Canard

2 lb. of goose, turkey or duck, jointed but not boned
2 lb. of flair fat (panne)
Salt and paprika

Mince the flair fat, put it in the cooking pot to melt slowly. When it runs add the meat and 3 oz. water. Cook for six to eight hours, so that the meat simmers in the fat and juices rather than fries. The bones should fall out. Drain off the fat, and pound the meat (or use the electric blender, see basic method) until it is smooth. Season with salt and paprika, and add a proportion of the drained-off fat to taste. Hot it through gently for 15 minutes and pot.

Rillettes d'Oie, or de Canard

Same ingredients as previous recipe, except that you have to bone the goose or duck before weighing, and have an equal quantity of flair fat.

Set the fat to melt, then pour off the liquid and add the goose or duck to the *grillons* left behind. Put in 4 oz. of water to every 2 lb. of poultry.

NOTE: For economy's sake, pork is often substituted for part of the poultry.

Keep this cooking at a simmer for five to six hours. Reduce by pounding and chopping, or by means of the electric blender, to a smooth mass. Season with salt and paprika pepper, add as much of the drained-off fat as you think the mixture requires. Heat through for 10 minutes; pot, and keep in the cool, in the usual way for *rillettes*.

NOTE: Poultry and rabbit *rillettes* can afford to be very smooth indeed – the texture almost of English potted meat. But I find that most people prefer pork *rillettes* to be a lighter, thready texture. All *rillettes* should be well-seasoned, and served with salt, butter and hunks of crusty bread or toast.

Quiche Tourangelle

SHORT-CRUST PASTRY, to line a shallow 8½ inch diameter tart tin (*tourtière*).

8 oz. plain flour, sifted with a tablespoon icing sugar, and a good pinch of salt

5 oz. butter and lard, rubbed into the flour, etc.
Enough very cold water to mix to a dough

Line the tin, brush with white of egg, to keep pastry crisp.

FILLING

4–6 oz. of *rillettes* (pork), spread about ¼ inch thick
6 oz. *rillons*, no bones, cut into small dice, and laid on the
rillettes
¼ pint boiling milk, poured on to 2 beaten eggs, and whisked
together
2–3 oz. thick cream added to the milk and eggs, with a seasoning
of salt, pepper and parsley

Pour this custard onto the *rillons* etc., and bake for 40
minutes in a gentle oven (Mark 4, 350°F.).

Serve warm, not hot from the oven, or cold.

Blood and Black Puddings or Boudins Noirs

BLACK PUDDINGS are the easiest things to recognize in the *charcuterie*. They may hang in a long string of black sausage-shapes, contrasting with the creamy whiteness of *boudins blancs* (page 144), and the mottled brownish-pink of the usual *saucissons* (page 133); or they may lie on a basket-work tray in a smooth unbroken spiral or coil, aubergine-black and gleaming. In either case they are about the cheapest thing you can buy there, and not the least delicious, whether fried or grilled, and served with a purée of apples or potatoes, or used to stuff a roasting chicken.

If you are accustomed to English black puddings, you will find the French ones a lot lighter in texture. This is because the blood is mixed with pork fat, onions and cream, rather than barley, flour and oatmeal. They are spiced, too, with considerably more finesse.

The rub comes when you get home, and want to make French-style black puddings yourself. Unless you know somebody who is killing a pig, it means a trip to the slaughter-house, or a particularly understanding butcher.

One friend of ours, a Vendômois farmer's daughter, always tried to persuade the visiting *charcutier* to cook some of the blood for her very gently over the fire, mixed with a little fat and cream; a *sanguette* she calls it. I suppose her success was the measure of her beauty. On pig killing day few people have time to stand and stir a small pan over a low fire. The moment blood boils, it curdles, so great care has to be taken. But apart from treats for small girls, the blood would be put aside until the intestines had been cleaned, scraped and cleaned again in the river. The mixture would be varied according to the resources of the farm – a tree of *reinette* apples, a good row of spinach, or a nearby chestnut wood, certainly cream, onions, spices and a locally-produced *eau-de-vie*.

If you don't want to risk filling skins – though this is not really difficult – any black pudding mixture can be baked slowly in shallow, greased dishes. When you want to use it, cut in slices and fry.

BASIC METHOD

You will need a funnel, in plastic so that the edge won't pierce the intestines; and either a ham kettle, a fish kettle, a chip-basket or metal lettuce-shaker, so that the *boudins noirs* can be lowered into hot water with the minimum chance of their bursting.

> Intestines or skins, in suitable lengths, knotted at one end, and
>   lying in a bowl of water
> 5 pints of blood
> 3 lb. onions, chopped
> 3 lb. pork fat, flair fat for preference
> 1¼ pints thick cream (you can use evaporated milk)
> 4 oz. breadcrumbs
> 3 oz. salt
> 1 teaspoon *quatre-épices* (or other spices)
> 1 teaspoon of sugar (brown, preferably)
> Chopped parsley, or chives, or sage – to taste
> 1 liqueur glass of rum – optional

Put the breadcrumbs to soak in the cream.

Add the seasonings to the blood.

Cut the fat into small dice, and try out about half a pound in a heavy frying pan. When the lard runs out, add the chopped onions and cook them slowly without allowing them to catch. They should melt rather than fry.

When they are ready mix in the rest of the fat, which has been diced, and the cream and the breadcrumb mixture. Stir it well together and pour in the blood, still stirring.

Take the first length of intestine and fit the unknotted end over the edge of the funnel, being careful not to split it. Then ladle your mixture into the funnel, which should be held firmly in the left hand so that the skin does not slip off. Don't fill the skins too full, as the mixture swells in the cooking; and let the *boudin* fall into a coil on your strainer-tray or into your wire chip-basket. The next coil can go on top, if there is room. Leave enough skin at the end to be knotted.

Bring the cooking pan, half-filled with water, to the boil. Remove it from the heat, and lay in the tray of *boudins*. Be absolutely sure that the water is off the boil when you do this, otherwise your labours will be lost in a blood and water mush.

Return the pan to a low heat for about 20 minutes, keeping the water at a bare shudder. After 15 minutes,

Making black puddings

prick the *boudins* very gently with a needle. If a brown liquid comes out, they are cooked; if blood comes out, they aren't, so try again in five minutes. They will be nicest if they are caught as soon as they are firm, and before they are overcooked. If they float to the surface whilst cooking, prick with the needle.

Remove the pan to the sink-board, and transfer the strainer-tray or basket *carefully* (they can also burst quite easily when they are hot) into a bowl of cold water. Leave it for one minute. Transfer the load to a flat surface, where the coils can be laid out separately to be brushed with some melted lard to form a glaze, and to finish cooling.

To serve the *boudins*, cut them into lengths, prick them all over as you would a sausage, and fry or grill them. Dish up on a bed of lightly sweetened apple purée, or mashed potatoes with fried apple rings. Spinach is an ideal accompaniment too, either outside the skin, creamed, or inside with the mixture:

Boudin de Poitou (aux Épinards)

    5 pints blood
    2½ lb. spinach, or spinach and the white part of salad endive
        (curly-leaved), mixed
    ¾ lb. flair fat, or good-quality lard
    ¼ pint of hard liquor; vodka or gin would be better than a fine
        cognac, in this instance
    ½ gill of Orange Flower Water (obtainable at chemist)
    Quatre-épices and crushed thyme to season, and salt

You can use more or less spinach according to taste. Frozen spinach will do – allow 1½ lb. With fresh spinach and endive, wash it well, then cook it covered in a large pan, in which you have first melted some of the flair fat or lard. Add no more water, enough will cling to the washed leaves. Drain it well when it has cooked down, chop or sieve or blend in an electric blender to a purée. Cook frozen spinach according to directions.

Melt the lard (or the flair fat), and cook the spinach purée gently in it for ten minutes. Mix into the rest of the ingredients, season it well with salt and spices, and fill the skins according to the Basic Method.

Boudin de Poitou (aux Épinards)

A very delicate, digestible recipe, adapted from *La Charcuterie à la Campagne*, by Henriette Babet-Charton.

    4 pints blood
    1½ pints thick cream
    1 pint milk
    1½ lb. spinach, or spinach and white endive
    3 medium eggs
    1½ oz. semolina
    1 oz. Boudoir biscuits
    4 oz. chopped onions
    Extra butter and lard for cooking vegetables, salt, pepper

Make as dry a spinach purée as possible (see above). Cook the chopped onion to a melting mass in some lard, and give the spinach purée ten minutes in some butter and lard.

Cook the semolina and milk to a thickish cream, stirring to prevent lumps. Add the cream and eggs off the heat.

Crush the Boudoir biscuits.

Stir everything well and thoroughly together, season to taste, and finish as described in the Basic Method, page 327.

Boudin de Lyon

    5 pints blood
    1½ lb. flair fat
    1½ lb. chopped onions
    ½ oz. pepper
    1 oz. *quatre-épices*
    4 oz. salt
    A dash of paprika
    Plenty of chopped chives, parsley and thyme
    ½ gill of good brandy

Melt a scant half pound of the fat, and cook the onions to a pulp in it without letting them brown. Meanwhile cut the rest of the fat into strips about the width of a little finger and 5 inches long, if you have plenty of time; otherwise cut them into much shorter pieces, and not quite so thick.

Add herbs, spices, salt and brandy to the onion pulp, stirring it well together. Take the pan off the fire and add the contents slowly to the blood turning it well all the time. If you have chopped the flair fat into small, rather than long, chunks, stir that in too. Fill the skins and cook according to the Basic Method.

If, however, you have cut the correct longer strips of fat, you have to introduce them skilfully in between ladles of the mixture so that they lie end to end of the *boudin noir* coil. Finish according to the Basic Method.

Boudin d'Auvergne

    5 pints blood
    ¾ lb. fat from the back (speck, or hard fat)
    ¼ lb. flair fat
    2 lb. onions
    Scant pint of milk
    3 oz. salt, and pepper and *quatre-épices* to taste

Cut the two sorts of fat into small dice, melt them gently and add the onions chopped. Cook to a mush. Add to the milk, blood and seasonings. Finish according to the Basic Method, but cook for half an hour.

Boudin du Languedoc

This is a meatier affair altogether, including lean pork as well as fat.

    5 pints blood
    3 lb. of pork taken from the neck
    ¾ lb. flair fat
    2 lb. onions, chopped
    1½ oz. salt approximately, and ground pepper, *quatre-épices*, and
        a good pinch of caraway seeds or aniseed

For the neck of pork, you could substitute 2 lb. of belly of pork and 1 pint of milk; and plenty of chopped green herbs, if you don't like the characteristic caraway and aniseed flavour.

Cook the neck of pork (or belly) the previous day, simmering it for about an hour and a half in salted water. It should get quite cold before you chop it into small dice.

Follow the Basic Method, page 327, adding the chopped lean meat with the onions and seasonings to the 5 pints of blood, and the milk, if you are following the second alternative.

Boudin aux Pommes

All over Northern France, apples are added to *boudins noirs*, in Normandy of course, but also in Brittany and Nancy. Usually it is the firm, yellow, keeping apple that one sees on every garden tree, vying with the quinces in golden pleasure. Returning to France in the following May, I've been handed great baskets of these *reinettes* by my next-door neighbour, a little more crinkled than they were in October, but sweet-smelling and delicious still. Bauchant put them into his tapestry, *La Fruitière*, and going into caves near Montoire where he died, one suddenly remembers him by the way they shine out of rocky shadows in unexpected order on their wooden racks.

Orléans *reinette* – 'the best apple grown in Western Europe' – has been grown in England fairly widely during this century.* If you don't have a tree of them, substitute Cox's Orange Pippins, Blenheims, or Ribstons. They will provide you with a much finer tasting apple-sauce too, than cooking apples and sugar.

5 pints blood
1¼ pints thick cream
4 lb. flair fat
2½ lb. apples, and 2 tablespoons butter
3 lb. onions, chopped
2 oz. white breadcrumbs

You can cook the apples the previous day, in which case peel, core and cut them up. Melt 2 tablespoons of butter

*Edward A. Bunyard, *The Anatomy of Dessert*, 2nd edition, 1933, Chatto and Windus.

in a heavy pan, and stew the apples slowly with the lid on. Add more butter if necessary – *never stew apples in water*.

Alternatively, you can cook them with the chopped onions when you intend to make the *boudins noirs*. In this case you won't need the butter. Melt some of the flair fat instead, and cook onions and cut-up apples in that. Keep stirring every so often to prevent them catching. This is a slow operation which should take about an hour; don't rush it.

Mix all the other ingredients, adding the apple and onion last of all. Finish according to the Basic Method.

Boudin à la Crème

An expensive version, not usually to be found on sale in the *charcuterie*. Having regard to the price of cream in England, the quantities are small.

    2 pints blood
    1 pint thick cream
    1 medium egg
    6 oz. butter
    1 lb. onions, chopped
    1½ oz. salt
    Quatre-épices and other spices

Melt two tablespoons of butter in a heavy pan and gently cook the onion almost to a purée. When this is done, take the pan off the fire and add the rest of the butter. Whilst it is melting combine the cream, egg, spices, salt and blood, and finally add the onions. Finish according to the Basic Method, but take great care not to fill the skins too tightly, and be very gentle when putting the *boudins* into the cooking water and taking them out.

Boudin aux Marrons

The most satisfactory *boudins noirs* I've ever bought came from a small *charcuterie* on the outskirts of Brive in the Corrèze. Our fingers were sore with picking up a boxful of chestnuts, after a picnic in the hills above Collonges, and we wondered what we were going to do with them all; then we saw the notice *Boudins aux Marrons*. They were so good that from that time on I've added roughly chopped, cooked chestnuts both to *boudins noirs* and sausage-meat *crépinettes* (page 115), always with great success. Most recipes tell you to purée the chestnuts, but I think that the *boudins* taste better if the chestnuts are chopped into small bits. The ones we bought were like that, and they could not have been nicer.

    5 pints blood
    3½ lb. flair fat
    2 lb. chestnuts
    1½ pints cream
    2 lb. onions, chopped
    1½ oz. salt; black pepper and *quatre-épices* to taste

Deal with the chestnuts the day before, unless you have helpers. Slash them on the rounded side, put them in a hot oven for 10 minutes, remove both skins, and simmer in salted water for 20 minutes. Chop them small, but not to a crush.

Follow the Basic Method, adding the chestnuts to the mixture last of all. Fill the skins and cook with great care.

Boudin Noir à l'Ail

In some parts of Périgord, they add a large egg and half a pound of chopped garlic to the basic mixture – no alcohol or spices either, to get between you and the garlic. Use half flair fat, half hard fat from the back.

Boudin de Saint-Quentin

Boudin de Saint-Quentin provides another, almost equally demanding test of family affections. Perhaps that is why one is recommended to eat it at midday, rather than in the evening. Good solid food against the cold winters of Aisne – and of Great Britain too, for that matter.

4 pints blood
4 lb. onions, chopped
3 lb. flair fat
½ lb. finest lard
3 oz. salt
1 oz. black pepper and *quatre-épices*, mixed
¼ teaspoon Cayenne pepper
1 tablespoon brown sugar

Mix according to the Basic Method, but cook the *boudins* for a little longer. Serve with a very light purée of potatoes, and apple sauce made with eating apples, stewed in a little butter, and finished with a squeeze of lemon juice.

English Black Pudding

6½ pints blood
4 lb. flair fat
¾ lb. pearl barley
¾ lb. fine oatmeal
¾ lb. flour
½ lb. onion
3½ oz. salt
2½ oz. black pepper, Cayenne and coriander

Cook the pearl barley in boiling water. Follow the Basic Method, adding the barley at the end. Because of the cereals, this takes 45 minutes simmering.

I cannot recommend this recipe. It makes too solid a black pudding for pleasant eating. But the comparison with French recipes is interesting.

Gogue

Black and white puddings are festive fare in France, for the *Reveillon* meal after Christmas Midnight Mass. In Anjou they make a very large black pudding, using the big intestine of the pig, for Easter as well. The springtime note is the use of chard or beet leaves, which have a nice combination of spinach-like green and seakale-tasting white ribs.

5 pints blood
2 pints thick cream
½ pint milk
2½ lb. beet leaves
3 large eggs
1 large onion
2 oz. white breacrumbs
4 oz. best lard
1 oz. salt
¼ teaspoon white pepper
A length of the pig's large intestine, cleaned and tied at one end

Melt a little of the lard in a heavy pan, add the washed beet leaves, and put on a well-fitting lid. Make into as dry a purée as you can, preferably in an electric blender as it halves the work.

Soak the breadcrumbs in the milk.

Cook the onion, chopped, in a little more of the lard, very slowly until it has melted almost to a purée too. Add the rest of the lard, and when it is in a liquid state, put in the beet leaf purée, and mix it all up well. Season, and leave on the heat for ten minutes. Take off the fire to cool down whilst you mix together thoroughly all the other ingredients, adding the vegetable mash last of all.

It is a good idea to have some help whilst you ladle the filling into the large intestine. It is more convenient to make two or three *boudins,* rather than one.

Poach them in water which barely simmers, for half an hour. Drain them, leave them to dry and hang them up in a cool, dry place for four days. To serve, cut in slices and fry quickly, or grill.

Index

Abu Smoking Box, 120, 144, 194
Acton, Eliza, 210
Albuféra sauce, 45–6
Allemande sauce, 45
Allspice, 39
Alsace Choucroute, 158
Alsace-Lorraine sausages, 127
Amiens duck pâté, 94, 96
Andouilles, 15, 269–73
   Basic Method, 271
   de Campagne, 273
   de Vire, 276–7
   to cook, 272–3
Andouillettes, 16, 269–76
   Basic Method, 271
   fines de porc, 273
   omelette, 275
   de Nancy, 274, 277
   de Troyes, 275, 277
   to cook, 272
Animelles de porc à la crème, 307
Animelles de porc frites, 307
Anise, 34
Apple chutney, 46
Apple purée or sauce, 46
Apples
   spiced, 46–7
   with petit salé, 179
   with sausages, 154
Apricot chutney, 47
Apricots, spiced, 47
Arles sausage, 138
Aspic jelly, 47–9, 265
   quick, 49

Babet-Charton, Henriette, 195, 290
Bacon, 18

Baguettes, 19
Bain-marie, 30
Baked beans, see Cassoulet
Baking dishes, 29
Basil, sweet, 34, 65
Bath chap, 245
Battendier of Paris, 74
Bay leaves, 34
Bayonne ham, 174, 198
   simplified version, 200
Beans, dried, 163
Beard, James, 80
Béchamel sauce, 49–50, 57, 66
Beef
   jarret de bœuf en daube, 230
   muzzle, sliced and dressed, 15
   roasting joints, 309
Belly of pork, 320–23 (see also
     Petit salé, Rillettes, Rillons)
Bercy butter, 50
Bercy sauce, 50, 57
Beurre
   Bercy, 51, 296
   ciboulette, 287
   Colbert, 51, 287
   d'échalote, 167
   de Gascogne, 167
   Maître d'Hôtel, 51
   manié, 51, 56
   moutarde, 51, 287
   noir, 52
   noisette, 52
   paprika, 51
   pimento, 51
   ravigote or chivry, 51
Bigarade sauce, 50
Black pudding, English, 335
Black puddings, see Boudins noirs

Bouchées à la reine, 251
Boudins blancs (white puddings),
    16, 144–8
  de lapin or lièvre, 147
  du Mans, 146
  de Paris, 145
  to cook, 28, 145
  to use up egg whites, 146
Boudins noirs (black puddings),
    17, 326–35
  Basic Method, 327
  à l'ail, 334
  d'Auvergne, 331
  à la crème, 333
  aux épinards, 329
  du Languedoc, 331
  de Lyon, 330
  aux marrons, 333
  aux pommes, 332
  de Saint-Quentin, 334
Boulettes, 118
  de Bretagne, 120–21
Bouquet garni
  definition, 34–5
  recipes, 53, 61–2, 72
Bourgogne sausage, 138
Bowls, 28–9
Brains, see Cervelles
Braising, 225–31
  pans for, 29, 254
  pig's ears, 248
  tongue, 254
Brawn, 14, 25 (see also Fromage de
    tête)
Bread, 19
Brine
  English, 185–6
  Italian, 141, 183
  Scottish, 194
  for pork and hams, 173–6, 184–7
  for sausages, 142–3
Brioches, 19
  dough for, 161–2
  saucisse en brioche, 160–61
Brochette, 286–7, 295, 301

Brown sauce, see Espagnole
Burgundy (Bourgogne), 38, 138,
    206, 257–8
Butters, compound, 51–2 (see also
    Beurre)

Cabbage, red, with Frankfurters
    157–8
Cabbage, stuffed, 148–51
Cabbage Soup, 168–9
Calf's foot, 47–8
Canard, see Duck
Capers, in sauces, 68, 71
Caraway, 35
Carême, Antoine, 292–3
Carré de porc au fenouil, 223
Carré de porc en gelée, 226
Carving, 205
Casseroles, 29, 163–4
Cassoulet, 124, 163–7
  au beurre de Gascogne, 167
Caul fat, 116–22, 268, 312
Cayenne pepper, 39
Celery, 35
Cervelles de porc (pig's brains)
  au beurre noir, 250
  en chausson, 56, 252
  en matelote, 250
  à la reine, 251
  à la sauce Béchamel, 250
  soufflé of, 252
  soufflé la chanoinesse, 252
Chair à saucisse, 17, 115
Champy, Madame, 223
Charcutière sauce, 52
Chartres game pâtés, 98
Chartres meat pâté, 82
Chaudfroid sauce, 48, 55
Chervil, 35, 51
Chicken
  galantine of, 43, 109–10
  pâtés, 87–9
  poulet à l'éstragon, 43
  sauces for, 54, 65
Chicken liver:
  in crépinettes, 117–18

in forcemeat, 81
pâtés, 88–9
Chitterlings, 277–8
Chives, 33
Chivry butter, 51
Chopping implements, 29
Chops, *see* Côtes de porc *under* Pork recipes
Chorizos, 15, 129–30
Choucroute, 36
with Frankfurters, 158–9
Choucroute soup, 159
Chou farci (Stuffed Cabbage)
Basic Method, 148–9
aux câpres, 150
au fromage, 150–51
à la provençale, 150
aux saucisses de Francfort, 151
Chutney, 46
Cider sauces, 53–4
Cinnamon, 35, 40
Civet de mou de porc, 302
Clarifying, 48
Claudius, Emperor, 171, 177
Cloves, 35
to grind, 40
Cobbett, William, 188
Cochon de lait, *see* Sucking pig
Cœur de porc à l'orange, 300
Cœur et rognons en brochette, 301
Colbert butter, 51
Confits (d'oie, etc.), 123, 309, 318–20
Consommé, jellied, 264–5
Coriander, 36
Cornichons, 55
Côtes de porc, *see* Pork recipes
Court-bouillon, 34–5, 41–2, 271
to make, 53–4
for pig's head, 243
Crab apples, Spiced, 46–7
Crawfish sauce, 89–90
Cream sauces, 54
Crépinettes, 17, 41, 115–18, 334
Basic Method, 116–17

au cumin, 117
de foie, 118
aux marrons, 117
aux pistaches, 117
to keep, 124
Croissants, 19
Croque-monsieur, 19, 212
Croquettes de jambon, 213
Cumin seeds, 34
Curing
alcohol cure, 183
brine cures, 173–6, 184–93, 198–201
dry salt cure, 175–6, 182–5, 190, 201
Curnonsky, 61, 189
Curry powder, 36

Daube à la Montigny-en-Vexin, 254
David, Elizabeth, 25–7, 59, 63, 88–9, 99, 106, 126, 150, 160, 226
Demi-glace sauce, 58
Diable sauce, 55–6
Dinde, *see* Turkey
Duck
pâté, 94–7
preserved, 318
rillettes, 323–4
terrine de, 94–5
Dumas, *Grand Dictionnaire de Cuisine*, 171
Duxelles, 56, 256

Electric blender, 24, 26
En croûte, meat, 56, 189
Endives au gratin, 214–15
Épaule roulée, 192
Equipment for charcuterie, 24–32
Espagnole sauce, 57–8

Faggots, 121
to keep, 121–3
Farmhouse Fare, 174
Fennel, 36, 223
Ficelles, 19

Fidget pies, 105
Filet de porc fumé, 199–200
Filets mignons de porc sautés, 231
Fines herbes, 36
Fines herbes sauce, 58
Fish, accompaniments for, 36, 68
Fish kettle, 28, 327
Foie de porc (pig's liver)
  à l'anglaise, 295
  au beurre Bercy, 296
  à la bourgeoise, 297
  braisé, 297
  en brochette, 295
  à l'espagnole, 296
  faggots, 121
  gayettes de Provence, 119
  à la lyonnaise, 296
  pâtés, 78–81, 90
  rôti aux truffes, 297
  saucisson au, 140
Foie gras pâtés, 73, 90–94
  en brioche, 92–3
  aux raisins, 93–4
  aux truffes, 92
Forcemeat
  for galantines, 109, 112
  for pâtés, 81–2
  mushroom, 56
Fraise, see Mesentery
France, Anatole, 164
Frankfurters, 15
  à la choucroute d'Alsace, 158
  au chou rouge, 157–8
  with stuffed cabbage, 149, 151
French dressing, see Vinaigrette
Fressure de porc à l'anglaise, 299
Friandises, 17, 153
Fromage de foie d'Italie, 80
Fromage de tête, 14, 40, 239
Frying, 231–5
Frying pans, 27–8

Galantines, 108–13, 239
  Basic Method, 109
  chicken, 43, 109
  pheasant, 112

pig's head, 243–4
pork, 14, 113
sucking pig, 113, 237
veal, 112
Game pâtés, 14, 74, 97–101
Game pies, 106
Garbure, 168, 169–70
Garlic, 33
Garlic crusher, 29
Garlic sausage, 15, 133, 136
Garnishes, 36
Gâteau berrichonne, 105–6
Gâteau de foie blond de poularde
  de bresse, 89–90
Gâteau de lièvre, 98
Gayettes, 115
  economical recipe, 119–20
  aux épinards, 120
  de Provence, 118
Gelée de cochon, 264
Gendarme sausage, 134
Gerrard, Frank, 175, 185
Gherkins, in sauces, 52, 61, 68, 71
Gien, thrush pâtés of, 98
Gigot, see under Pork, fresh
Ginger, 37
Glazes:
  for baked ham, 41
  for roast meat, 38, 58, 223–4
  for salt pork, 188
Gogue, 335
Goose
  neck sausage, 122–3
  pâté, 91–3
  rillettes, 323–4
  to preserve, 309, 318
Gratin dishes, 24–5
Grattons, 312, 316–18
Grilling, 231–5
Grillons, fines, 316

Hachoir, 29
Ham recipes (see also Jambon)
  cold cooked, 216–18
  hot, 210–16
  with fruit, 190, 216

Hams, 171–218
  picnic, 191
  shoulder, 192
  Smithfield, 190
  smoked, 194–201
  uncooked brands, 198
  unsmoked, 189–94
  York, 185, 191–2
  to carve, 205–6
  to cook, 202–8
  to cure, 171, 182–7, 189–201
  to finish, 204
  to glaze, 41
  to smoke, 194–7, 201
  to soak, 202
  to store, 197–8
  to treat with hay, 201, 210
Hare pâtés, 74, 99–100
Hare pies, 106
Heart, 299–301
Heptinstall, William, 129
Herbs, 29, 33–43
  to chop, 29
Hochepot, 180
Horseradish sauce, 69–70
Hure, 14, 239, 242
  à la pistache, 243

Intestines, to clean and prepare, 268, 277

Jambon (*see also* Hams)
  à l'américaine, 190
  à l'anglaise, 56, 205
  de Bayonne, 15, 198, 200
  de campagne, 184
  de campagne fumé, 198
  en cornets, 216
  à la crème, 208
  croquettes de, 213
  au foin, 210
  au gratin, 212, 214
  au Madère, 207
  mousse, 216
  with orange and chicory salad, 217

de Paris (jambon blanc), 15, 185
  189
  persillé de Bourgogne, 38, 206–7
  persillé au gratin, 215
  de Reims en croûte, 56, 189
  au sauce moutarde, 212
  with Swedish mayonnaise, 217
  timbales, 214
  vol-au-vent, 215
  de York, 15, 191
Jambonneau, 15, 18, 191
Jambons crus, 15
James, Henry, 227
Jarret de bœuf en daube, 230
Juniper berries, 37, 63, 106

Kebabs, 288, 301
  marinade for, 71
  sauce for, 45
Kidneys, 18, 286–94 (*for recipes see* Rognons)
  to roast, 286
  sauce for, 65
Knives, 27

Languedoc, 94, 164, 331
Langues de porc (pigs' tongues)
  braisées, 254
  à l'écarlate, 256
  fumées, 258
  garnies, 255
  à la mode de Troyes, 257
  pochées, 255
  en rillettes, 253
  sauce diable, 256
  sauce Duxelle, 256
Lapin, *see* Rabbit
Lard, 18, 314–15
  preparation of, 314
Larding, 310, 313
  larding needle, 28, 313
Larousse Gastronomique, 40, 232, 273, 317
La Varenne, 56
Leeks, 34
  purée of, 157

Leeks-contd.
with petit salé, 179
Leszczinska, Marie, 251
Lights (lungs – *mou*), 299, 302–5
Liver
pâtés, 79–81, 88–90
recipes for, *see* Foie de porc
sausage, 140
Loire district, 33, 97, 293
Longe de porc (loin), *see under* Pork
Lorraine quiche, 181
Lorraine sausage, 138
Lungs, *see* Lights
Lyons sausage, 136, 142

Mace, 37–8
Madeira sauce, 59, 60
Maître d'hôtel butter, 51
Marinades, 71–2
Marjoram, sweet, 42
Mayonnaise, 67–9
for coating, 68
green, 69
suédoise, 68
Measuring
comparative weights and measures, 22–3
equipment for, 31–2
Mesentery, 268
to prepare and cook, 278–9, 316
Mirepoix, 59
Mornay sauce, 59
Mortadelle, 141
Mou (lights)
en blanquette, 304
à la bonne femme, 303
à la bourgeoise, 303
civet de, 302
à la provençale, 304
Mousse, 216
Moutarde butter, 51
Moutarde sauce, 60
Museau de bœuf en salade, 15
Mushrooms, cultivated, 36
forcemeat of, 56

Mustard (*see also* Moutarde)
English, 37
French, 37–8
glaze, 41
Mutton, to marinade, 71; 72

Normande, sauce, 54, 221
Normandy, 94, 269, 276, 279, 280, 332
Nutmeg, 38, 40

Oeufs, en gelée, 265
Offal, 18, 286–308
Oie, *see* Goose
Omelettes
andouillette, 275
fines herbes, 36
ham, 210
kidney, 292
Onions, 33
onion sauce, 260
Orange and chicory salad, 207
Oreilles de porc (pig's ears), 16
braisées, 248
au diable, 247
grillées Sainte-Ménéhould, 64, 247
aux lentilles, 248
Ovenware, 25–6, 29

Paprika, 39–40
Paprika butter, 51
Parma ham, 198
Parsley, 38
sauce, 60
Parsmint, 29
Partridge, 98, 100, 112
Pastry
raised pie, 102
shortcrust, 156, 181, 205, 324
Pâtés, cold, 73–104
de campagne, 14, 75
de canard d'Amiens, 94, 96
cheap recipe (pig's head), 75
chicken, 87–9
chicken liver, 81, 88–9

chicken liver and crawfish, 89–90
foie gras, 73–4, 91–4
foie de porc (pig's liver), 14, 79–80, 90
game, 14
goose, 93
hare, 15
maison, 73
picnic, 80–81
pork and game, 100–101
pots for, 24–6
rabbit, 14, 82–6
to preserve, 78–9
turkey, 87–90
de Vendange, 83
de viande de Chartres, 82
Pâtés, hot, 104–8
game and poultry, 106
gâteau berrichonne, 105–6
de ris de veau (sweetbreads), 107
Peaches, pickled, 46–7, 60
Pears, pickled, 46–7, 60
Peppercorns, 39
Pepper mill, 30
Peppers, 39–41
Périgord, Périgueux, 73, 92, 226
Périgourdine sauce, 60
Périgueux sauce, 60, 297
Persillade de bœuf, 38
Petit salé, 14, 176
aux champignons, 179
aux choux, 177
aux marrons, 180
aux petits pois, 178
aux poireaux, 179
aux pois secs, 177
Petits pois au lard, 178
Pheasants, 98, 101
galantine of, 112
Picnic ham, 191
Picnics
gayettes (hot), 119
pâté for, 80
pie (hot), 106–7

ready-to-eat charcuterie, 14–15
sausages for, 114, 133
stoves, 22
Pieds de porc (see also pig's trotters)
farcis, 262
panés, 261
à la Sainte-Ménéhould, 261
truffes, 262
vinaigrette, 260
Pigeons, 100, 112
Pies
hot, 17, 73, 104–8
raised, 101–4
Pie mould, 103
Pig's brains, see Cervelles
Pig's ears, 16, 246–9, 264
Pig's head, 75, 239–45
Pig's kidneys, 286–94
Pig's liver, see Foie de porc
Pigs' tails, 16, 263–5
Pig's tongue, 253–8
Pig's trotters, 16, 259–63
to prepare, 259
recipes for, 259–64
sauces for, 60, 64, 68, 71
Pimento butter, 51
Piquante sauce, 61
Pistachio nuts, 40
Pithiviers cake, 293
Pithiviers lark pâté, 73, 85, 98
Pithiviers aux rognons, 292
Pliny, Natural History, 33, 38, 39
Poitrine, see Belly of pork
Poivrade sauce, 61–2
Pork, fresh, 219–38
chops, 219, 229, 232–6
cuts of, 18, 219
extremities, to use, 239–66
fat of, 309–25
leg, 220, 227
loin, leg end (longe), 220–21
loin, small end (carré), 223, 226
marinade for, 71–2
pie, 102
tenderloin of, 231

Pork-contd.
terrines and pâtés, 75–82, 100–101
to braise, 225–31
to fry, 231–5
to glaze, 223
to grill, 231–5
to pot-roast, 225–30
to preserve, 173–4
to roast, 15, 41, 220–24
to stew, 229–30
(*See also* Pork recipes *below*)
Pork recipes
carré de porc au fenouil, 223
carré de porc en gelée à la vendômoise, 226
côtes de porc ambassadrice, 234
côtes de porc avesnoise, 234
côtes de porc à la bayonnaise, 232
côtes de porc à la charcutière, 233
côtes de porc sautées à la gasconne, 232
côtes de porc Vallée d'Auge, 234
côtes de porc au vin blanc, 233
côtes de porc à la vosgienne, 229
enchaud de porc à la périgourdine, 226
filets mignons sautés, 231
galantine of, 14
gigot de porc en sanglier, 227
gigot de porc truffé, 220
longe de porc à la bourgeoise, 222
longe de porc Clamart, 221
longe de porc à la normande, 221
longe de porc aux pistaches, 221
longe de porc Rôtie, 221
longe de porc truffée, 220
porc aux pruneaux de Tours, 227, 231
porc rôti à la berrichonne, 222

porc rôti à la bourgeoise, 222
porc rôti aux choux rouges, 223
porc rôti aux herbes, 222
porc rôti à l'orange, 224
porc rôti aux pommes, 224
ragoût de porc, 229
raised pork pie, 102
Pork, salt, 171–89
accompaniments for, 46–7, 52–3, 56, 60, 61, 69
to cook, 202–3
to cure, 185–8
to preserve, 318–20
Port-wine sauce, 62
Potatoes
with bacon, 179
fried with fennel, 36
salad, hot, 69, 155–6
Potée, 168
economy recipe, 169
Pot-roasting, 225–31
Pots
for braising, 29
for fat, 309, 311
for pâtés, etc., 24–5
for storage, 310
Poulet à l'estragon, 43
Provence, 33, 119, 139, 150, 304

Quatre-épices, 38, 39, 40–41
Queues de porc, 16
Basic Method, 263
braisées, 264
grillées, 264
aux lentilles, 264
Quiches
au jambon, 212
Lorraine, 15, 181
aux saucisses et poireaux, 156
tourangelle, 310, 311, 324

Rabbit (*lapin*)
Boudins, 147
Pâtés, 14, 82–5
Pies, 106
Preserved, 318
Rillettes, 323

Terrine (hot), 86
Ragoûts, 165, 225, 229–30
Raifort sauce, 69–70
Raised pies, 101–4
Ravigote butter, 51
Ravigote sauce, 71
Red cabbage recipes, 157
Relishes, 45–72
Rémoulade sauce, 69
Rillettes, 14, 309–12
  d'Angers, 323
  de canard (duck), 324
  de dinde (turkey), 323
  de langue (tongue), 253
  de lapin (rabbit), 323
  du Mans, 323
  d'oie (goose), 324
  de Paris, 322
  in quiches, 325
Rillons, 14, 28, 305–6, 309–12,
  320–25
Ris de veau pâté, 107
Roasting, 220–24
Robert sauce, 62–3
Rognons (kidneys)
  en brochette (kebabs), 286–8
  en casserole, 291
  Clementine, 292
  à la liégeoise, 291
  omelette, 292
  pilaff, 289
  pithiviers, 292
  sautés, 289–90
  au vin blanc, 290
Rousseau, Jean-Jacques, 254
Roux, 63

Saffron, 41
Sage, 41
Sainte-Ménéhould sauce, 64
Salad, orange and chicory, 217
Salad dressings, 70–71, 156
Salaison
  à sec, 176–88
  par saumure, 185–8
salami, 15

Salpicon, 109, 113
Salt, 41–2, 171–3
  to salt meat, see Curing
Salt mill, 30, 42
Saltpetre, 42
Sauces, 45–72
  basic three, 49–50, 66
  cooked, 45–66
  oil-based uncooked, 67–72
  Recipes
  Albuféra, 45
  allemande, 45
  apple, 46
  Béchamel, 49–50
  Bercy, 50
  bigarade, 50
  charcutière, 52
  chaudfroid, 55
  au cidre, 53
  à la crème, 54
  diable, 55
  à l'échalote, 57
  espagnole, 57
  fines herbes, 58
  Madère, 58–9
  mayonnaise, 67–9
  mornay, 59
  moutarde, 60
  normande, 54
  Périgueux, 60
  au persil, 60
  piquante, 61
  poivrade, 61
  au porto, 62
  raifort, 69
  rémoulade, 69
  Robert, 62
  Sainte-Ménéhould, 63
  saupiquet, 63
  soubise, 64
  suprême, 65
  tartare, 68
  tomate, 65
  velouté, 66
  verte, 69
  vinaigrette, 70

Saucisses
  allemande (d'Augsbourg), 131
  d'Alsace-Lorraine, 127
  en brioche, 17, 114, 124, 142
  en brioche à la lyonnaise, 160
  de campagne, 125
  au champagne, 128
  à la charcutière, 155
  à la choucroute d'Alsace, 158
  au chou rouge, 157
  au cumin (croquantes), 131
  d'Espagne, 15
  espagnoles, 130
  au foie de porc, 126
  de Francfort, 17, 132, 157–8
  aux lentilles, 160
  aux œufs, 148
  de Périgord, 127
  aux pois chiches, 159
  aux pommes, 154
  de Strasbourg, 15, 132
  aux tomates, 152
  de Toulouse, 126
  viennoise, 130
  au vin blanc, 153
  en vin rouge, 155
Saucissons
  à l'ail, 15, 133, 136
  d'Arles, 138
  de Bourgogne, 138
  de campagne, 135
  cervelas, 17, 143–4
  au foie de porc, 140
  gendarme, 134
  d'Italie, 140
  de Lorraine, 138
  de Lyon, 136, 142
  au Madère, 134
  de ménage, 135
  de Provence, 139
  secs, 135–9
  smoked, 139–43
  à trancher, 138
Saumure
  anglaise, 185–8
  écossaise, 194

  italienne, 193
Saupiquet de jambon, 209
Saupiquet des Amognes, 210
Saupiquet sauce, 63
Sausage casings, to prepare, 271–2
Sausage-meat, 17
  to make, 115–16
  to use, 148–52
Sausage rolls, 153
Sausages
  for boiling, 143
  drying of, 135–9
  equipment for making, 24
  large, 133–44
  recipes for making, 125–44
  recipes with, 152–70
  for slicing, 138
  small fresh, 123–5
  smoked, to make, 129–33, 139–43
  of tripe, 269–77
  without skins, 116–23
Saveloys, 17, 143–4
  Scotch eggs, 148
  Seasonings, 33–44
Shallots, 33
Shallot sauce, 57, 63
Simon, André, 242
Smithfield ham, 190
Smoking, methods of, 129, 173–4, 194–7, 201, 258
Sorrel, 69
Soubise sauce, 64
Souffles
  de cervelles, 252
  de cervelles à la chanoinesse, 252
  au jambon, 211
Soup, clear, 264–5
Soyer, Alexis, 242
Spice-blend, 35–6, 38
Spleen, 299, 305–6
Spoons, 30, 31
Stock
  for espagnole sauce, 57

for galantines, 110–13
to clarify, 48
Storage jars, 310, 311
Strabo, *Geographia*, 171–2
Stuffings
herb and vegetable, 236
for pig's head, 244
with sage, for pork, 41
Sucking pig
galantine of, 113, 237
roast and stuffed, 236
Suprême sauce, 65
Sweetbreads, hot pie, 107

Tarragon, 43, 54
Tartare sauce, 68
Tenderloins, 231
Tendret, Lucien, 89
Terrines, 73–101
Basic Method, 75–9
de canard (duck), 94
de gibier (game), 98
de lapin (rabbit), hot, 86
de lièvre (hare), 99
de porcet de gibier (pork and game), 100
Testicles, 306–8
Tête, de porc, 239–45
fromage de, 239
galantine de, 244
hure, 242
stuffed, 243–4
Thrush pâtés, 98
Thyme, 43
Timbales, 214
Toad-in-the-hole, 154
Tomato sauce, 65
Tongue, 253–9 (*see also* Langue de porc)
braised, 254
brine for, 257
potted, 253
smoked, 258
Toulouse sausage, 163
Touraine, 146, 227

Tripe, 18, 279–85
à l'espagnole, 285
fried, 284
à l'italienne, 283
à la lyonnaise, 282
à la mode de Caen, 280
cooking pot for, 279
Tripe sausages
large (*see* Andouilles), 15, 133–4, 269–73, 276–7
small (*see* Andouillettes), 16, 270–76
Truffles, 43, 60–61, 220–21
Turkey
galantine, 112
neck sausage, 122–3
pâtés, 87–90
preserved, 318
rillettes, 323–4

Veal galantine, 112

Velouté sauce, 55, 65, 66
Verte sauce, 69
Vinaigrette sauce, 70
variations of, 70–71
Vinegars, 41, 43–4
Vol-au-vents, au jambon, 215
(*see also* Bouchées à la reine)

Watercress, 36
Weights and measures, 22–3, 31–2
Westphalia ham, 198
White puddings, *see* Boudins blancs
White sauce, *see* Béchamel
Wienerbeuscherl, 305
Wild duck, 100, 101
Wine, 22
Woodcock, 98

York ham, 185, 191
Yorkshire pudding, 154

Zeuner, Professor, 91

MORE ABOUT PENGUINS
AND PELICANS

Penguinews, which appears every month, contains details of all the new books issued by Penguins as they are published. From time to time it is supplemented by *Penguins in Print*, which is a complete list of all titles available. (There are some five thousand of these.)

A specimen copy of *Penguinews* will be sent to you free on request. For a year's issues (including the complete lists) please send 50p if you live in the British Isles, or 75p if you live elsewhere. Just write to Dept EP, Penguin Books Ltd, Harmondsworth, Middlesex, enclosing a cheque or postal order, and your name will be added to the mailing list.

In the U.S.A.: For a complete list of books available from Penguin in the United States write to Dept CS, Penguin Books Inc., 7110 Ambassador Road, Baltimore, Maryland 21207.

In Canada: For a complete list of books available from Penguin in Canada write to Penguin Books Canada Ltd, 41 Steelcase Road West, Markham, Ontario.

SPICES, SALT AND AROMATICS IN THE ENGLISH KITCHEN:

English Cooking, Ancient and Modern, Volume 1

Elizabeth David

With this volume Elizabeth David (so famous for her books on French and Mediterranean cooking) opens the full-scale study of English cooking which she is writing for Penguins. Her known expertise, her literary flair, and her unique library of English cookery books together qualify her perfectly for the task.

Here she sets the table of English recipes which are notable for their employment of spices, salt, aromatics, and herbs. As usual, in her notes and introductory essays, Elizabeth David seasons instruction with information, explaining the names and origins of such ingredients as nutmeg, cardamom, and fenugreek, and stressing the influence of imperial connexions on the English kitchen, where oriental spices and Indian curry, kedgeree, and tea are now perfectly at home.

Elizabeth David is no culinary chauvinist and she includes here a number of immigrant dishes (*risottos* and *paellas,* for instance): nevertheless this book, with its brawns (or pig's head cheese), briskets, and bloaters, its salt beef, sprats, and horse-radish sauce, its junkets and catsups, sounds a welcome, if uncommon, English note in the kitchen.

THE PHILOSOPHER IN THE KITCHEN

TRANSLATED BY ANNE DRAYTON

Anthelme Brillat-Savarin

'Whoever says "truffles" utters a great word which arouses erotic and gastronomic memories among the skirted sex, and memories gastronomic and erotic among the bearded sex.

This dual distinction is due to the fact that the noble tuber is not only considered delicious to the taste, but is also believed to foster powers the exercise of which is extremely pleasurable.'

'"Rejoice, my dear!' I said one day to Madame de V–; "a loom has just been shown to the Society for Encouragement on which it will be possible to manufacture superb lace for practically nothing."

'"Why," the lady replied, with an air of supreme indifference, "if lace were cheap, do you think anybody would want to wear such rubbish?"'

Jean-Anthelme Brillat-Savarin (1755–1826), Mayor of Belley, cousin of Madame Récamier, Chevalier de l'Empire, author of a history of duelling and of a number of racy stories (unfortunately lost), whose sister died in her hundredth year having just finished a good meal and shouting loudly for her dessert, is now best known for his *Physiologie du Goût*, here brilliantly translated as *The Philosopher in the Kitchen*, which was first published in December 1825. The work has a timeless appeal – being wise, witty, and anecdotal, containing some of the best recipes for food and some of the most satisfactory observations on life.